DELIVER US FROM EVIL

ALSO BY SEAN HANNITY

Let Freedom Ring

DELIVER US
FROM EVIL

DEFEATING TERRORISM, DESPOTISM, AND LIBERALISM

SEAN HANNITY

1☻ ReganBooks
Celebrating Ten Bestselling Years
An Imprint of HarperCollins*Publishers*

A hardcover edition of this book was published in 2004 by ReganBooks, an imprint of HarperCollins Publishers.

First paperback edition published 2005.

Designed by Kris Tobiassen

Printed on acid-free paper

The Library of Congress has cataloged the hardcover edition as follows:

Hannity, Sean, 1961–
    Deliver us from evil : defeating terrorism, despotism, and liberalism / Sean Hannity.—1st ed.
      xiii, 338 p. ; 24 cm.
    ISBN 0-06-058251-0 (alk. paper)
    Includes bibliographical references and index.
    1. War on Terrorism, 2001– 2. Terrorism—Government policy—United States.
3. United States—Foreign relations—2001–

E903.H36 2004
327.73'009'0511—dc22   2004041786

ISBN 0-06-075039-1 (pbk.)

05 06 07 08 09 WBC/QW 10 9 8 7 6 5 4 3 2 1

Once again:
to my wife, Jill, the love of my life,
and the greatest gift God ever gave me—
our two children, Patrick and Merri Kelly

Our father who art in heaven,
hallowed be thy name.
Thy kingdom come,
Thy will be done, on earth, as it is in heaven.
Give us this day our daily bread.
And forgive us our trespasses,
as we forgive those who trespass against us;
and lead us not into temptation,
but **deliver us from evil:**
For thine is the kingdom,
and the power, and the glory,
for ever, and ever.
Amen.

CONTENTS

In the Spider Hole

He was found cowering in a hole in the ground, near a farmhouse in a desolate country town. Bewildered and disoriented, he had only the clothes on his back, a pistol, two AK-47 rifles, and $750,000 in uncirculated U.S. currency. This man, who had terrorized and plundered his own people while living in immeasurable luxury, spent his final hours before capture in a hiding place so base that it could only be described in terms befitting an animal: He was cornered like a rat, caught in a lizard's den, in a spider hole.

Within hours, the sight of his face was being broadcast around the world. Haggard and disheveled, hidden behind a graying beard, this apostle of evil closed his eyes while a doctor probed under his tongue for hidden cyanide capsules.

Saddam Hussein's lifelong flight from justice had finally come to an end.

In Baghdad, the Iraqi people celebrated the event with jubilation. Radio stations played celebratory music and young men drove through the streets shouting their excitement. *Al-Zaman,* Iraq's leading daily independent newspaper, described the news with unmistakable joy and relief:

The capture of Saddam is another window of hope for a clean Iraq, swimming in sunshine and far away from a dark past crowded by the dungeons of the secret services in which hundreds of thousands of Iraqis have disappeared because of a word or a whisper or an opposing view.[1]

With the capture of this brutal despot, the world was granted a rare opportunity to look evil in the face. What we saw was a fugitive from righteous justice; a killer, broken but without remorse; a man who had dispatched his own sons to die for his perverted cause, yet surrendered himself without a struggle.

This pivotal moment, this reckoning, occurred because of the stern determination of an American president with the clear moral vision and courage to commit this country and its braved armed services to the cause of defeating international terrorism.

A future once undreamed of by Iraqis is now within reach. Saddam, a man who only months ago was beyond the reaches of his own law, will be held accountable for his actions by the very people he mercilessly oppressed. His atrocities will be aired before the world, and judged by a legitimate system of justice.

In the end, God willing, Saddam Hussein will die for his crimes. And when our soldiers finally suppress the last loyalist insurgency, the Iraqi people, for the first time in a generation, will reclaim a measure of peace.

In America, this event took place in the early days of a presidential campaign. At the time, it seemed to stop the president's already-fragmented opposition in its tracks. For months, most of his Democratic opponents had been pretending to support the war while undermining the president at every turn. Now they paused at the edge of the precipice to regroup and reconsider: how to capture even a small part of this spotlight? How to find a dark cloud in this silver lining?

None of them succeeded. John Kerry called Saddam's capture "an important step toward stabilizing Iraq for the Iraqis," but soon reverted to form, calling upon the administration to "share the burden, bring in other countries and make it clear to the world that Iraq belongs to the Iraqi people."[2] Wesley Clark said he hoped it would lead to "a diminishing in the violence against American soldiers in Iraq."[3] Carol Moseley Braun called the capture "good news," but claimed that it "does not change the fact that our troops remain in harm's way and we are no closer to bringing them home."[4]

Governor Howard Dean made the most improbable claim of all: "The capture of Saddam," he ventured, "has not made America safer."[5] His contention was met with mingled scorn and silence.

Over all their heads hung the inevitable thought: *If America had followed your path, Saddam Hussein would still be in power today.*

President Bush, in contrast, kept his focus on the task at hand: prosecuting the War on Terror to its conclusion.

"Now, the former dictator of Iraq will face the justice he denied to millions," President Bush told America. "For the vast majority of Iraqi citizens, the torture chambers and the secret police are gone forever. . . .

"We've come to this moment through patience, and resolve and focused action. . . . Our security is preserved by our perseverance."

And he capped his remarks with this renewed pledge: "The USA will not relent until the war is won."[6]

Justice, patience, resolve and focused action: the principles that drove this evil actor from the world stage.

As America casts its eye to the future, let us not forget them. We will need them again.

ONE

ONE

Terrorism, Despotism, and Liberalism

Three years ago, evil surfaced in the Western world in a way it had not in six decades, since the day of infamy at Pearl Harbor. Americans were forced to confront pure human wickedness in a way we had not in generations. And in that moment we rose as one nation to the challenge—led, fortunately, by a leader who had the clarity of vision to recognize that evil for what it was, and to rally America and the world against it. Even many of the most committed liberals seemed to have their compasses reoriented in the face of that unmistakable act of war and crime against humanity.

But nearly three years have passed. And in the intervening time our wounds have healed, our senses and memories dulled. The nation rallied behind its leader long enough to expel the state sponsors of evil in Afghanistan. Yet by the time the confrontation with Iraq presented itself, our courage and moral certainty seemed to fade in the face of partisan bickering and posturing. We toppled a murderous dictator in Iraq—and yet now the political left and the Democratic Party are trying to use the demanding aftermath of the war to exploit our national cause for their own political advantage. How could we allow ourselves to forget so soon?

I decided to write this book because I believe it is our responsibility to recognize and confront evil in the world—and because I'm convinced that if we fail in that mission it will lead us to disaster.

Evil exists. It is real, and it means to harm us. I believe this strongly, and not just because of my Catholic faith, although that's the root of it. When you work in the news business, you deal with the ugly side of life. Every day across your desk comes story after story about man's inhumanity to man, from mass murderers to child molesters to mothers who drown their children to husbands who murder their pregnant wives. These stories push the limits of our ability to imagine man's potential for depravity, and yet they are horrifically true.

Still, isolated events like these pale beside the pure evil of September 11. How could anyone witness the horrors of that day, or the mass graves discovered in Iraq after the fall of Saddam Hussein, and dismiss the idea of evil? And yet many people do—most of them political liberals. Even when they can bring themselves to acknowledge the brutality of a venal tyrant such as Saddam Hussein, they qualify it. "We are not denying that Saddam is a repressive dictator," they say, "but we don't believe we should have attacked Iraq without giving him more time to comply with the U.N. resolutions." For the appeasement-minded liberals of our country, there's always a "but."

It's difficult for liberals to see such moral questions clearly, because most of them are moral relativists. They reject absolute standards of right and wrong. In their worldview, man is perfectible, human nature is on a linear path toward enlightenment, and the concept of sin is primitively biblical. In their view, society's unfairness compels people to break the law. To them people like Saddam and Osama bin Laden are not morally depraved murderers, but men driven to their bad acts by the injustices of Western society.

The emphasis is always on giving bad actors—domestic and foreign—the benefit of the doubt, never on personal accountability. After all, if we can blame external circumstances or internal imbalance, then we can avoid the messy business of calling the evildoers to account. This kind of thinking is all too familiar from our courtrooms at home. The justice system today is crawling with "experts" eager to exonerate the most heinous criminals on the grounds that they're "genetically predisposed" to murder, rape, take drugs, or otherwise endanger the welfare of others; the media fills its airwaves with liberal advocates eager to sympathize with murderers on death row, instead of the families of the innocent victims.

The trouble with tolerating evil, of course, is that while we're averting our eyes, the evil itself only grows and festers around the world. This has been true throughout history. Neville Chamberlain assured a wary England that an appeasement pact with Adolf Hitler would lead to "peace in our time." Cold War liberal elitists ignored or downplayed the atrocities of communism, from the gulag of "Uncle Joe" Stalin to the killing fields of Cambodia. Bill Clinton stood idly by while Islamic terrorists attacked American targets throughout the 1990s, in a long prelude that should have alerted us to their burgeoning war on America.

The primary evil we face today is terrorism. But we will never triumph over the terrorists until we realize that groups like al

Qaeda are not working alone. Without the deep pockets of terrorist-friendly dictatorships like Saddam Hussein's Iraq to support them, the loose networks of Islamic terrorism would pose only a fraction of the danger to civilization they currently do. And those dictatorships, we must realize, are the same brutal regimes that have oppressed their own people for generations.

As President Bush has declared, we can no longer wait around for terrorists to attack us. We must take the war to them, rooting them out of their swamps and destroying the despotic regimes that furnish their lifeblood.

But the president also warned that this would be a war like no other. It would be fought on a variety of levels, against a largely invisible and unconventional enemy. Sometimes our efforts would be conducted out in the open, for all to see; at other times, though, they would be as invisible to the public as the terrorists themselves. And they would be ongoing, because new terrorists are being born and trained every day, raised to hate us with every fiber of their beings.

One challenge of a long and drawn-out war is that public commitment to the war effort can flag—especially in an unpredictable situation like the War on Terror, where a few weeks of dramatic battle can be followed by months of difficult activity behind the scenes. And if the public should lose its resolve to win, if its attention should wander from the evil that confronts us and the necessity of defeating it, victory will only stray further from our reach.

Under such circumstances, some of the most dangerous attacks our nation faces can come from those on the home front.

America has faced evil before, from Nazi Germany to Soviet Russia in the twentieth century alone. Each time, we (and our allies) have had to overcome opposition from within as part of our battle against these enemies. For when it comes to confronting evil, the fact is that there are essentially two types of people: those who are willing to fight it, and those who try to excuse it—or, worse, deny it even exists. Throughout history, the appeasers have refused to recognize evil, let alone confront it. They make excuses for it, ignore and coddle it. And by refusing to fight, they nourish and encourage it. Every great champion of freedom in the modern era has had to overcome a prominent voice of appeasement. For Winston Churchill there was Chamberlain, for Ronald Reagan there was Jimmy Carter. Today, George W. Bush faces the modern Democratic Party.

Indeed, the greatest threat to our resolve today in the War on Terror is the political liberalism—and selfish opportunism—of the Democrats. From its leaders on down, America's left-wing party is ideologically inclined toward appeasement, toward dismissing or understating the terrorist threat, and toward containing, rather than confronting, the despotic regimes that aid and abet the terrorists. Whatever momentary interest its members may show in the war is inevitably swamped by the party's unquenchable thirst for political power.

Terrorism, despotism, and liberalism: these are the forces America must be concerned about in the War on Terror today. The terrorists themselves, of course, carry on their war against America in covert fashion—but they, at least, are the enemy we know. The totalitarian regimes that support them are more difficult to trace, using every devious means available to hide their role in funding and training the terrorists. And at home the professional apologists of the Democratic Party are eager to turn any setback in the war into a referendum on the Bush administration, sapping our commitment to the war even as they ignore the damage they may be causing to our long-term national security.

The lessons of history are clear: You cannot negotiate with evil. You can't sweet-talk it. You can't compromise with it. You can't give ground to it. You can only defeat it, or it will defeat you.

Ever since September 11, the voices of the left have been treating the terrorists as though they were merely another player in the same old political game. They have tried to play both ends against the middle, aligning themselves with the war effort when it suited their political needs, but shifting their allegiances as soon as an election loomed on the horizon.

But the terrorists are no mere political sideshow. Though it manifests itself differently, the threat they represent is every bit as grave as the one we experienced during World War II or the Cold War. There is no appeasing this enemy; they will stop at nothing in their quest to destroy the United States, and they will lay waste to every human life they can in the process.

As you read these words, the evildoers are plotting the disruption of our lives, the destruction of our property, the murder of our families. Today or tomorrow, fanatical extremists could come into possession of suitcase nuclear weapons or other weapons of mass destruction, whether through rogue nations or via black-market thugs from the former Soviet Union. We face the possibility of our civilization being destroyed, as surely as we did during the Cuban Missile Crisis; indeed, with recent advances in technology and the ongoing instability in the Middle East and around the world, the danger may be worse than ever.

We rose to the challenge then; we cannot afford to fall short now.

★   ★   ★

Despite the irrefutable evil of terrorism, there are those who still have doubts about whether absolute evil truly exists—who persist in believing that every bad act can be blamed on social or psychological circumstances, on economic or cultural differences.

To those moral relativists, let me start with a direct challenge. The following three news stories are all drawn from our own shores, from the ranks of middle-class Americans. None of those involved was ever subjected to institutional torture, or raised in a culture that devalued human life. Read these stories—and try to explain them without invoking the idea of evil.

- A suicidal twenty-six-year-old woman is about to jump to her death from a bridge in Seattle. Distraught about a broken relationship, she teeters on the edge of a 160-foot fall to the river below. She's afraid to die, but equally afraid to stay alive. Hours pass, and as police cordon off the area, traffic nearby grinds to a halt. Frustrated with the delay, rubbernecking travelers start calling out to her. "Jump, bitch! Jump!" they scream. The woman jumps, only narrowly escaping death.[1]

- To make some extra money, a pharmacist in Kansas City, Missouri, starts watering down the cancer drugs prescribed for his customers. Thirty-four people are affected after being given inadequate doses over a period of time. One woman dies of ovarian cancer after her chemotherapy fails. "How in the world could someone do something like this?" her husband asks a *Washington Post* reporter. "When the love of money comes in, people will do anything[,] I guess."[2]

■ In his younger days as a priest, Robert Burkholder molested more than twenty boys. Now retired in Honolulu, eighty-two-year-old Burkholder reflects back on the experience as he faces prosecution, calling it consensual. "The boys work in the rectory with the priest and you just get friendly," says Burkholder, most of whose victims were between ages eleven and thirteen. "You sit down in the rectory and have a Coke. It's a mutual deal . . . an affectionate thing and a friendly thing." The ex-priest tells the *Detroit News* that on occasion he and the boys had oral sex. "But not often," he says. "It's a friendship between two people that has been made into something horrible, rotten. People are trying by hook or by crook to make me look bad. Some of the accusations are true, but so what? I was a priest—a good priest—who had a weakness."[3]

These examples of evil behavior may seem vastly different in scale from the stories of wholesale slaughter we hear from Iraq or Rwanda, but the behavior in each case is repugnant: when facing a choice between good and evil, each of these figures took the path of evil. The onlookers in Seattle valued their own convenience, and the temptation of a sick joke, over the life of a fragile individual in distress. The pharmacist in Kansas City chose his bank book over the lives of his customers. And the molesting priest indulged his own urges at the expense of his young parishioners.

But two of these stories also highlight our tendency to dismiss evil casually, to look for impersonal "causes" for deplorable behavior. A pedophile priest pleads "weakness," claiming he was helpless in the face of irresistible temptation. Even a grieving husband, reaching for some explanation for his wife's cruelly hastened death, concludes that human nature is powerless when it comes to money. But our so-called weaknesses, whether lust or greed, do not excuse our evil actions. As human beings, we're confronted with moral choices every day. And if we choose to concoct excuses instead of making moral judgments, before long our sense of good and evil will disappear altogether.

I believe that's just what has happened to the leaders of the modern Democratic Party. Unlike President Bush, who has personified moral clarity and vision in the War on Terror, America's liberal elite sneers at the "simplistic" notion that good and evil are legitimate concepts in our society. They mock the president for seeing the world in such starkly black and white terms, and impugn his Christian faith for inspiring the thought. They've even convinced themselves that Bush's moral compass is a dangerous instrument—as threatening, some have hinted, as Islamic fundamentalism itself.

This kind of moral relativism is disturbing to me as an American. It discounts the very idea of accountability, devalues our right to fight for our principles. And without an unwavering grasp of what is right and what is wrong, how can we ever expect to stand in judgment of our terrorist enemies? Even after 9/11, some voices have charged that one man's terrorist may be another man's freedom fighter. To that I ask: How many noble freedom fighters target innocent women and children? How many build torture chambers in the basements of their official buildings?

By blurring the lines between good and evil, liberals have rendered our society more vulnerable to evil's influence. With secular liberals largely in charge of our cultural institutions—not to mention their influence on the courts and even our churches—

America is increasingly ill-equipped to recognize, much less respond to, the evil that threatens our nation.

Today's moral relativism is clearly out of step with the traditions of our nation, as the Framers' own words reveal. The founders of our country recognized the presence of evil in the world and in human nature, and arranged the structure of the government under the Constitution to protect against its ill effects. As James Madison, the father of our Constitution, reveals in Federalist Paper No. 51, the matter of evil was very much on the Framers' minds as they debated the form and nature of the new government.

"If men were angels," Madison wrote, "no government would be necessary. If angels were to govern men, neither external nor internal controls on government would be necessary. In framing a government which is to be administered by men over men, the great difficulty lies in this: you must first enable the government to control the governed; and in the next place oblige it to control itself."

Madison's point is especially trenchant today, though the voices of the left might well deny it. Unlike our Framers, modern liberals tend to see government as the grantor of our rights. Uncomfortable with the idea of God-given natural rights, they seek to substitute their own concepts of liberty and justice—whatever they may happen to be in the moment. They prefer the idea of a "living and breathing" Constitution, one that can "change with the times." Yet what they fail to see is exactly what Madison warned against: that a government with unchecked power—whose authority is not grounded in a more fundamental source of morality—leaves its people unprotected from evil.

This blind spot has also left liberals far less suspicious than they should be of totalitarian regimes. Monarchism, National Socialism, fascism, communism—all these forms of authoritarianism are illegitimate and inherently unjust. They enable a relative hand-ful of people to hold the state's levers of power, and use them to impose their will on an entire population. And inevitably they lead to abuse, oppression, even mass murder.

Indeed, the Framers recognized that even the Constitution they crafted was not a fail-safe guarantee against governmental abuses of power. Why? Because, as John Adams warned, "Our Constitution was made only for a moral and religious people. It is wholly inadequate to the government of any other."[4] That's an-other reason that conservatives are dedicated to opposing the ero-sion of our traditional moral values—we recognize them as the foundation of our constitutional liberties.

But conservatives don't object to every energetic exercise of governmental power. We heartily endorse the government taking a proactive role in those areas the Framers intended, such as foreign policy and national security. By and large—unless they happen to be in power at the time—liberals tend to take a dim view of gov-ernmental action in these areas. And all too often their reluctance to use force leads them to excuse the evil behavior of foreign regimes, to offer appeasement to tyrants, and to blame U.S. policy for planting the seeds of evil.

Conservatives see things much differently. We believe that America is a superior society *not* because Americans are superior human beings, but because our culture was founded on a recogni-tion of our God-given natural rights—the "unalienable rights" re-ferred to in the Declaration of Independence. From that awareness flows a basic, shared respect for humanity, individual liberty, limited government, and the rule of law.

More than 225 years after that Declaration, America has become, without rival, the world's most beneficent nation. As

Ronald Reagan was fond of reminding his Soviet counterparts, we have the power to conquer any nation, but we don't. We have the power to enslave any people, but we don't. We have the power to loot any nation of its natural resources, but we don't. Instead, America sends her young men and women to war to defend the weak. She sends her resources to help feed the poor. And she offers a hand to any nation that seeks friendship and peace.

Liberals have shown a constant reluctance to confront the enemies of freedom around the world. They preach the absolute value of peace, accuse every Republican leader of "warmongering," and act to cut defense spending whenever possible. Yet many of America's greatest moments have come when its people have taken up arms to defend liberty. Was it "warmongering" when the Greatest Generation defeated the Axis powers of Hitler's Germany, Mussolini's Italy, and Tojo's Japan, and liberated untold millions in World War II? When Reagan's courageous stand against communism—and renewed commitment to military strength—led to the fall of the Berlin Wall and the end of Soviet repression? When today's brave soldiers rescued 26 million people in Afghanistan, and 24 million in Iraq, from brutal regimes?

Just as any police officer has the right to fire upon an attacker who has raised his weapon to shoot the officer or another, America has the moral right—no, obligation—to fight for its own security, and that of any oppressed nation. Conservatives take pride in our tradition of standing up to tyranny and dictatorship; indeed, this may be one reason they appear to be prouder of America overall than their liberal counterparts. According to a poll released on July 3, 2003, by the Gallup News Service, 80 percent of conservatives are extremely proud of their country—compared with only 56 percent of liberals![5] And I'd hazard a guess that the liberal leaders of the Democratic Party may be even less proud of America than the average Democratic voter.

George W. Bush makes liberals very nervous, not just because he won the presidency back for the Republicans after eight years of Bill Clinton, but because he truly understands—and articulates—the bigger picture. Like most of America's great leaders, he grasps the nature of evil. And he has risen to the occasion, exercising decisive leadership, all the while firmly and openly relying on God—a fact that disturbs liberals even more.

In his State of the Union address after September 11, in that moment of deep grief and national consensus, President Bush focused our attention on the character of our enemy, contrasting it with that of the American people.

"The last time I spoke here," he said,

> I expressed the hope that life would return to normal. In some ways it has. In others it never will. Those of us who have lived through these challenging times have been changed by them. We've come to know truths that we will never question: Evil is real, and it must be opposed.
>
> Beyond all differences of race or creed, we are one country, mourning together and facing danger together. Deep in the American character there is honor, and it is stronger than cynicism. And many have discovered again that even in tragedy—especially in tragedy—God is near.
>
> In a single instant, we realized that this will be a decisive decade in the history of liberty; that we have been called to a unique role in human events. Rarely has the world faced a choice more clear or consequential.

Our enemies send other people's children on missions of suicide and murder. They embrace tyranny and death as a cause and a creed. We stand for a different choice, made long ago, on the day of our founding. We affirm it again today. We choose freedom and the dignity of every life.

Steadfast in our purpose, we now press on. We have known freedom's price. We have shown freedom's power. And in this great conflict, my fellow Americans, we will see freedom's victory.

Thank you all and may God bless.[6]

In that stirring speech and his other public statements during those first frightening days, when the nation looked for direction and confidence, the president spoke of first principles—our founding principles, which were and remain the target of our enemies. As the president knew, it's from those very principles that we draw our strength—not from liberal notions of "diversity" and "tolerance," but from our Judeo-Christian roots. Those themes are normally anathema to liberals, but during that brief post-9/11 honeymoon, the secular liberals held their tongues. And I have no doubt that some of them were sincere in their momentary cease-fire, caught up in the emotion of the moment.

But it didn't take long for the left to get back on message. Soon they were publicly mocking Bush for invoking the concepts of good and evil and the spiritual implications of this struggle. Editorial writers gasped at the horror of America's commander in chief harboring such a "simplistic" and "dangerous" worldview. As liberals eventually shook the mantle of patriotism from their shoulders, their attacks became more pointed and mean-spirited. Assaults on the president's faith and worldview returned with a vengeance. Not only did they question his propriety and judgment in openly acknowledging God, they complained that such statements were *offensive to Muslims.*

On February 10, 2002, the *Baltimore Sun*—quoting unnamed sources—published an article claiming that Bush's Christian references had upset Muslim listeners. "Some foreign policy analysts say Bush also is taking a sizable risk in solidifying his image as a Christian believer when he is on the verge of launching a war against Iraq," the article claimed. "Since America's war on terrorism began, radical Islamic leaders and terrorist groups have vilified the anti-terror drive as a holy war against people of Islamic faith."

The *Sun* went on to suggest that Bush's frequent affirmations of faith risked leaving the impression that the war on extremist Islamic terrorists was actually a war against all Muslims—though Bush had taken pains to express his respect and goodwill toward the Muslim faith. The article quoted Edward S. Walker Jr., president of the Middle East Institute and a former State Department specialist, on the subject. "If the war is put too much in the context of, 'The Christian faith is somehow burdened, so we have to assume the role of good Christians,' it sends a very negative signal," said Walker. "The president has been very careful that no one misinterprets this as a fight between religions, but he has to be careful about quoting evangelical hymns."[7]

The irony of this warning would be laughable, if it weren't so infuriating. A group of Islamic extremists attacks us because we're a largely Judeo-Christian nation that supports Israel, and *we're* supposed to keep silent about our religious faith? I've heard of political correctness, but this is taking it to absurd extremes. To tell you the truth, I think we should give moderate Muslims more credit than that. Why should we assume they'll object if American Christians look to their Bible for support and guidance in times of need? America has nothing to apologize for in its spiritual heritage—certainly no more than honorable Muslims have in theirs.

The left, of course, has never missed an opportunity to chastise conservative leaders for their religious faith. But to do so in this moment of crisis, when even the most confident leader might look to a higher power for guidance, only shows how far liberals have strayed from the American mainstream. The day a president cannot invoke God as his guiding light, and the source from whom he *and our nation* derive strength and direction, is the day America ceases to be great.

Today, with the Taliban deposed in Afghanistan and Saddam toppled in Iraq, liberal voices are grasping at every straw they can, trying to prove their relevance in the post-9/11 world. After the Bush administration and its allies scored a decisive victory in Iraq—overthrowing a brutal dictator who had gassed his own people, and thumbed his nose at world opinion for years—all the Democrats can do is fume about the "missing" weapons of mass destruction in Iraq. Certain they've located the president's Achilles' heel, they claim baldly that he "lied" about the existence of nuclear weapons in Iraq.

The Democrats on the Hill, and those who are running for president in 2004, can't see past their myopic hatred of George Bush; they can't get beyond their partisan pettiness to understand the sobering reality of what we've discovered in Iraq. If there's any reason to be disturbed, it's not because the weapons programs were never there: voices from all sides, from Bill Clinton to the former Iraqi scientists who have described such programs in detail, have confirmed that Saddam's regime was intent on building an arsenal of WMDs. The real question is whether Saddam was able to hide the evidence before the allied invasion—or if he managed to smuggle it out to like-minded nations.

The Iraqi regime was unimaginably evil, as the evidence has now proven beyond any doubt. We know that he ordered the mass extermination of Shi'ite Muslims, Kurds, and other political enemies on an unthinkable scale. We have found botulinum toxins, mobile weapons labs, and more than a hundred general munitions storage facilities in his country. We know that he supported terrorism against Israel, among other nations; that he was capable of using weapons of mass destruction against America; that he had used weapons of mass destruction against the Iranians and Kurds. And we have seen tapes of his medieval torture chambers, of rooms where unknown hundreds of citizens were raped, of mass graves filled with murdered Iraqi citizens.[8]

Yet liberals still refuse to acknowledge that our invasion was a beneficial thing. They're more tolerant of Saddam Hussein than they are of George W. Bush. They refuse to consider any evidence that Saddam and his bloodthirsty regime were tied to international terrorist networks, or that Iraq harbored, sponsored, comforted, and abetted terrorists. They pretend that Saddam's willful violations of the Gulf War Treaty were no justification for war, and that twelve years of dodging, deception, obstructionism and defiance were not long enough to "let the inspections run their course."

This kind of rhetoric may surprise some, but honestly I don't know why. After all, George W. Bush is a much greater threat to the Democrats' purely political agenda than Saddam Hussein could ever be.

Back in 1998, on the other hand, when their own president, Bill Clinton, turned his attention briefly to Saddam, the Democrats hardly wasted a breath criticizing him. In fact, during the Clinton years the Democrats seemed to have no problem with the idea of military intervention overseas. They supported Clinton's endless deployments, regardless of cost—and regardless of whether American interests were truly at stake. Yet now that we are really at war, now that we've been deliberately attacked, they demand the strictest burden of proof before consenting to military action. (And even when they do consent, they later try to wriggle out of it, as Senator John Kerry has done.)

Now that the public has learned this much about the evils of Saddam Hussein's regime, though, it's chilling to realize that Bill Clinton knew about it all during his eight years in office—and yet took no effective action to stop it. Hamstrung by the liberal unwillingness to oppose evil in the strongest terms, Clinton tolerated the human-rights violations and growing military threat Iraq posed to the world. He appeased the blustering dictator. On the few occasions when Clinton did respond to Saddam's chicanery, he did so in feckless half-measures, lobbing over a handful of cruise missiles that did little damage and provided no deterrent. And in doing so Bill Clinton made Saddam bolder and Iraq stronger. There, in a nutshell, is the difference between a powerful leader and an ineffectual failure: Where Bush has shown courage and strength in the face of challenge, Clinton was simply shortsighted and reckless. And America paid dearly for his neglect.

From the very start of the War on Terror, George Bush signaled a dramatic shift in American policy. Calling for a National Day of Prayer and Remembrance on the Friday following the attacks, he issued a one-page proclamation in which he referred to the terrorists as "evildoers" who had committed an "act of war." And he promised that they, along with those who "helped or harbored" them, would be "punished—and punished severely."[9]

I thanked God at that moment that our new president had the courage to see the events of September 11 for the declaration of war they were. Unlike Bill Clinton, who had treated the 1993 World Trade Center bombing as a mere criminal act—another half measure that only invited more trouble—President Bush wasn't looking for a legal remedy. The attacks violated all principles of civilized behavior, and they demanded an unqualified response.

The president took his stand despite some tough odds. As we learned in the days and weeks to come, al Qaeda had been nurturing terror cells all over the world. It also had a secure base in Afghanistan, long considered the "graveyard of empires" by worrying scholars. Yet with every succeeding address to the American public, President Bush made it clear that America would go after every sponsor of terrorism, whether independent actor or rogue nation. "From this day forward," he told the American people in a joint session of Congress on September 20, "any nation that continues to harbor or support terrorism will be regarded by the United States as a hostile regime."[10]

But the president's resolve would not be shared by everyone. As the administration prepared to respond militarily to the attacks, a number of world leaders headed to Washington in an effort to dissuade President Bush from taking unilateral military action. A broad-based coalition and U.N. support was essential, they would argue. Egyptian President Hosni Mubarak warned the United States against taking "military action that might kill innocent civilians, divide Christians against Muslims and further inflame attitudes against American foreign policy in the region."[11]

These leaders immediately put us on the defensive—as if we were the aggressors and not the victims of a murderous attack. It was astonishing. Imagine someone punching you in the face, and as you prepare to punch back a supposedly objective onlooker warns you not to strike back because you might "inflame" the attacker and his friends. Bush was able to build a serious international coalition to topple the tyrannical Taliban regime in Afghanistan, but by the time the conflict with Iraq came to a head early in 2003, the liberal nations of Europe and much of the Arab world had withdrawn their support.

It was alarming, and frustrating, to see just how many world leaders had fallen back in love with appeasement. Their refusal to support our reasonable response had nothing to do with any supposed failure of diplomacy on the Bush administration's part. Rather, it reflected these nations' political antipathy toward America, and their general cowardice when it comes to confronting evil actors on the world stage.

It was as if Bill Clinton's appeasement virus had suddenly infected the rest of the world. If Clinton had been president in 2001, it's easy to imagine how different things would have been after 9/11. Even if Clinton himself had been inclined to take decisive action (which is highly doubtful), he would surely have been paralyzed by world resistance. There would have been months of high-level diplomatic meetings, full of talk about how everyone wants the same thing—peace. But any such talk overlooks the sad reality: that *not everyone wants peace.* The terrorists and their dishonorable sponsors have no intention of peaceful coexistence with America. They are defined only by their violent goals. And when confronted with such aggressors, we have limited choices. We can either ignore them, inviting further attack as we bury our heads in the sand, or we can resist them—with force.

To liberals, the pacifist approach may appear more civilized. But human nature, and the lessons of history, tell us that such naive efforts to avoid bloodshed generally lead to even greater bloodshed. Pacifism, in short, rarely leads to peace, and never to freedom or security.

Ronald Reagan, the twentieth century's greatest president, intimately understood the importance of confronting evil. "Trust but verify," he famously warned, describing the perils of dealing with the Soviet Union. But the full text of Reagan's advice may be even more important: "Trust but verify," he said, "and don't be afraid to see what you see."[12] As a member of the World War II generation, Reagan well remembered the dangers of trying to negotiate with brutal and unscrupulous regimes. Those who refuse to see evil for what it is are doomed to relive history's most tragic lessons.

When President Bush drew his line in the sand, the voices of evil abroad, and appeasement at home, erupted as one in mockery and protest. Apparently emboldened by Bill Clinton's lackluster cruise missile response to previous terror attacks, Osama bin Laden responded immediately with a defiant and taunting video message to the Arab world and to the American public (especially to the appeasers among us). Until the terrorists' goals were met, bin Laden declared, "America will not live in peace."[13]

And despite their seeming support in the first few weeks after 9/11, American liberals began to show their true colors as soon as Bush's tough talk graduated into military action. The liberal media revealed its essential lack of confidence in our military's strength and resolve, clucking that if the formidable Soviet army couldn't defeat Afghanistan, we might not be able to do it either. Under the headline "On the Home Front, Nagging Uncertainty About Consequences," the *New York Times* ran a skeptical essay by R. W. Apple Jr. in October 2001. "[I]t was not easy to grasp all the implications" of attacking the Taliban, Apple wrote, "even as the generals and the politicians talked of precision munitions and the suppression of enemy air defenses in Afghanistan, a little-known country 7,000 miles away. . . . Never before has the United States launched a military campaign against such an elusive and hydra-headed foe, with so little clarity about precisely how it will prevail."[14]

A few weeks later, after our forces went into action, the *Times* editorial page followed Apple's piece with a naysaying statement of its own, complete with the liberals' customary allusions to Vietnam. "The recent era of nearly casualty-free American military operations abroad—including the air strikes against Afghanistan—seems to have ended yesterday as combat operations commenced on the ground. That is just one of the grim realities that come with this new and more dangerous phase of the war against terrorism. The nation should brace itself—emotionally and politically—for the kind of close combat it has not seen over an extended period since the Vietnam War."[15]

The implication of these statements was clear: America, the *Times* believed, was not strong enough to conquer these foes, so we might as well compromise before we suffer too much. It was only the latest evidence of how little faith the *Times*—traditionally considered the newspaper of record—truly has in the resolve of the American military.

A month later, as the battle of Afghanistan drew to a close, even the media was forced to concede our victory. Tom Raum of the Associated Press, a journalist who has covered five presidencies, said it all with his opening paragraph on November 25. "Afghan Taliban rulers have been routed, the al-Qaida terror network breached and Osama bin Laden put on the run, a fugitive with a $25 million bounty on his head. Suddenly, some important goals in President Bush's war on terrorism seem within grasp."[16]

But the appeasement lobby has a short memory for the lessons of war. Toward the end of 2002, the media went through the very same cycle during the buildup to the invasion of Iraq. Even before European nations like France and Germany withdrew their support, the press went digging for dissent anywhere they could find it. One longtime Democratic aide, quoted in the *Washington Post,* argued that no action was necessary: "We have Iraq pretty much right where we want them—under constant observation. Under those circumstances, Saddam won't move against us or move to aid Osama bin Laden or anything else that constitutes a clear and present danger to us."[17] And the editors of New York *Newsday* declared that "it would be irresponsible, arrogant, and politically obtuse for Bush to rush into war without laying out a detailed case for why Saddam Hussein today poses an imminent threat. . . . If he is ready to go into battle, then he must explain why the costs of going to war—in treasure and lives—are less than those of continuing the inspection regime with a credible threat of military force."[18]

Clearly the lessons of appeasement must be learned over and over again.

This is a book about the reality of evil in the world, about the importance of acting against it, and about the urgency of confronting and opposing those who won't. In essence, it is a book about dramatically different worldviews, and about the role of mature leadership in recognizing and defeating our enemies. Only with this kind of leadership will we remain a free people.

America in 2004 is confronted with a special challenge. In November we will go to the polls to vote for president. But this year—and quite possibly for many years to come—this race is about more than just the niceties of tax policy or the size of government. It is about choosing a leader who possesses the moral vision to recognize evil, and the will to confront it.

And regardless of which candidate stands for the Democratic Party in November, America must realize that the candidate who opposes George Bush will be the candidate of appeasement. He will be standing for the party of Jimmy Carter, of Bill Clinton—for the party of moral relativism, of toleration and hesitation in the face of threats at home and abroad. Our nation cannot afford another Carter, another Clinton.

As Edmund Burke once said, "The only necessary thing for the triumph of evil is for good men to do nothing." The Democratic candidates in 2004 may or may not be good men, but make no mistake: if confronted with terrorism, they will do nothing. We cannot afford this crime of apathy, this failure of courage or commitment. We cannot afford for evil to triumph. Our nation's liberty—our nation's safety—is too hard-won, too dear.

As we confront this critical moment, let us turn first to the lessons of history, starting with the disgraceful record of appeasement during the Second World War.

TWO

Evil on the Record: The Holocaust

As an American who feels strongly about the reality of evil in the world—a reality recognized by our greatest modern presidents, Ronald Reagan and George W. Bush—I often wonder why we as a nation have grown so resistant to the very idea of absolute evil.

Perhaps it's because those my age and younger have always known freedom. For our entire lives, we've enjoyed a level of peace and liberty unknown to earlier generations of Americans, not to mention the rest of the world. Can it be that, since so few of us have had to sacrifice anything to preserve our freedom, we tend to undervalue this gift our predecessors bestowed upon us? Can it be that we've been so secure in our freedom that it's hard for us to imagine the alternative? After all, even the threat posed by our greatest enemy—the Soviet Union—was abstract, rarely darkening our shores in any tangible way.

Or perhaps we have such a hard time recognizing evil abroad

because of our own popular culture's disdain for American values here at home. There's long been a prevailing attitude in the culture that the United States doesn't deserve its prosperity, that we're unfairly exploiting a disproportionate share of the world's resources. How, then, can we rightly condemn any foreign nation, regardless of its record of crimes against its own people? The left-wing elites in this country have pushed their obsessive anti-Americanism so far that they've lost all perspective on the real evils being perpetrated around the world.

And yet there was a time, within our parents' lifetimes, when Americans banded together to fight a power universally recognized as evil—when petty political opposition evaporated in the face of a common enemy. To many younger Americans today, World War II may feel like ancient history. But I find that very troubling. To me it's desperately important that every American look back and understand the role that totalitarian Nazi Germany played in the twentieth century. Not only was America unified in opposition to this great threat: we also awakened to our larger responsibilities as a global power, to protect both ourselves and our allies. We learned that we could no longer ignore the rise of political evil in the world.

This was not a wisdom earned cheaply. It began with the Japanese attack on Pearl Harbor, in which thousands were killed or wounded. The "greatest generation" instantly learned one of the great lessons in American history: The age of isolationism was over. The technology of warfare had changed, and with it the world. After a century of safety, protected by two great oceans, America was no longer secure from foreign powers.

Through the 1930s, we had watched as the Nazis unleashed their brand of "Blitzkrieg warfare" on Europe, leaving massive death and destruction in their wake. We watched as the Empire of Japan built its military machine, wreaking havoc in the East. "The latest refinements of science," said Winston Churchill, "are linked with the cruelties of the Stone Age."[1] A deeper understanding of those cruelties was yet to come, but America's age of innocence had already reached its end.

With the unconscionable horror that had overtaken the world by 1941, it's surprising now to realize that America still had to be dragged into the war. Gallup polls indicated that 70 percent of Americans regretted our involvement in World War I, and the political scene of the 1930s was dominated by isolationists who wanted nothing to do with "foreign wars." In 1935, as the fascist storm brewed in Europe, fifty thousand veterans demonstrated for peace in Washington, D.C.; that same year 175,000 students held an antiwar strike. Congress was forced to pass a Neutrality Act—the first of four to be enacted between 1935 and 1939, binding government from taking sides in any conflict, even to help Europe's embattled democracies.[2]

Yet America changed overnight after December 7, 1941.

To me, the most important lesson of World War II is that evil is a reality—and that confronting it is the *only* course of action. We ignore foreign affairs at our peril: technology has rendered the world too small and dangerous for us to isolate ourselves from the world. The evil of Nazi Germany first reared its head less than a hundred years ago, in a part of the world many Americans counted as their homeland. It spread primarily from one man—Hitler himself—to a small circle of fanatics, and through them it infected the entire German culture. And within a few years it transformed a Western democracy, first into a tyranny, and then into a massive, horrifying death machine. The flame of evil lit by one man became a Holocaust.

Nazism was the purest form of evil modern man has known. It was rooted in virulent anti–Semitism, hatred of biblical Judeo-Christianity, and the firm belief that *the state,* not any higher power, is the ultimate source of truth. Even today it remains astonishing that the depths of depravity witnessed in the Nazi Holocaust occurred within a historically Christian nation, but Winston Churchill recognized that the evils of the Third Reich were rooted in its "barbarous paganism" and rejection of "Christian ethics." For much of the German population in the 1930s and 1940s, the führer became God; only with his death in a Berlin bunker did the Nazi nightmare finally come to an end.[3]

But evil did not disappear from this world when the Allies defeated Nazism in 1945, or when the Cold War ended. Today, in the early twenty-first century, we are once again facing an absolute and aggressive evil. Its scope has not yet reached that of Nazi Germany, thank God. But its nature is the same. Somehow, though, liberals in our culture refuse to even recognize dictators like Saddam Hussein as evil; instead they dismiss them as madmen. Instead of judging a terrorist like Osama bin Laden in absolute terms, they grope for excuses and reasons to lay the blame on America. It must have been something we did, they say; the crime lies with us, with our successful system, our thriving culture or booming economy.

Japan made one miscalculation: after Pearl Harbor, it had expected America to become demoralized into paralysis.[4] But ask yourself what would have happened if the appeasers had won the day. *Better not to risk American soldiers in a war,* we might have told ourselves. *After all, what happens in the Far East isn't really our business. Are American interests really at stake? Do we really want to go to war with the Empire of Japan? We need to understand their point of view.*

Shouldn't we be reserving our resources for our domestic problems? War is always the wrong answer!

But that's not what happened. Instead of trying to negotiate a peace, begging to avoid war on two fronts, President Roosevelt asked Congress to declare war on Japan—and on Germany after Hitler rushed to declare war only a few days later.[5] Though we had lost 2,403 lives, eighteen warships, and nearly two hundred planes at Pearl Harbor,[6] America took on the challenge of an all-out war against two major world powers. And before the war was over, we had not only prevailed, but exposed the full horror of the Holocaust—and brought two diabolical totalitarian states to a righteous and final end.

Japan and Germany had misjudged the American character.

It's important that we remember our role at that crucial point in history, even as we confront a new species of evil today. When President Bush visited Auschwitz in 2003, he inscribed a simple message in the guest book: "Never Forget." With his leadership in the War on Terror, he reminds us that we must do more than remember the horrors of the Holocaust. We must take a page from our own history, and rise to confront evil once again.[7]

I know how hard it can be to comprehend a phenomenon as thoroughly evil as the Holocaust. Growing up in an Irish family in Long Island in the 1960s, my own experience was worlds apart from that of the persecuted families of midcentury Europe. Today we have institutions like the Simon Weisenthal Institute and the National Holocaust Memorial Museum in Washington, D.C., to help educate future generations of Americans about what happened. But nothing has affected me as much as the time I've spent talking to Hannah, a Holocaust survivor who has been a longtime caller and friend of my ABC radio show. Every time we talk, I know it's *my* opportunity, not hers, to learn. Soon we will be losing the last of these survivors—the firsthand witnesses to Adolf Hitler's inhumanity. If we are to remain alert to humanity's tragic capacity for evil, we must make every effort to understand testimony like Hannah's.

In the story of Nazi Germany, we see what happens when man forsakes faith, morality, and conscience in favor of unquestioned loyalty to the state. In contemporary America, the instances of evil we witness tend to be isolated: the tragedy of one little girl kidnapped from her home, never to be found again; a series of fatal shootings around Washington, D.C., leaving ten dead and six more wounded. And yet millions of people were killed in such fashion during the Holocaust, many of them children grabbed by Nazi SS officers from Jewish orphanages and tossed into the backs of trucks like stray dogs. With the passage of time, the horror of state-sponsored evil tends to fade, to be reduced to statistics. Yet the numbers hide millions of individual stories, each of them as heartrending as the worst of today's headlines.

One fact that's increasingly lost to history is the way Hitler and his evil agenda slithered into power in what was then a democratic Germany. Disguising himself as a statesman, this demon was first appointed by the democratically elected leader of Germany, his nature largely unnoticed by an unsuspecting electorate and an apathetic world community despite the publication of the violently anti-Semitic *Mein Kampf* years before. He then proceeded to charm and intimidate world leaders, as if he were merely a canny diplomat and not a murderous tyrant. At first his own people and most of the world were fooled by his wiles. Though many dismiss him today as a deranged megalomaniac, Hitler possessed the personal skills, charisma, and mental capacity to fulfill his evil intentions by devising, executing—and almost winning—a war against the greatest powers of the world.

Though in retrospect Adolf Hitler seems unquestionably evil, in his time he managed to cast his spell over some influential political figures. The Duke and Duchess of Windsor were photographed with him, and may have been in line to return to power in a Nazified Great Britain.[8] Even America's ambassador to the Court of St. James—Joseph P. Kennedy Sr.—was at least initially sympathetic. As Edward Renehan Jr. has written, Kennedy and his friend Viscountess Astor saw Hitler as "a welcome solution to [the] 'world problems' " of Communism and Judaism in Europe. As Renehan points out, Kennedy told his Nazi counterpart at the Court of St. James that Franklin Roosevelt was "the victim of 'Jewish influence' "—and the German reported back to Berlin that Kennedy was "Germany's best friend" in London.[9]

But Hitler's record in influencing individuals pales in comparison to his success in creating the Nazi death machine. As the gruesome history of the Holocaust demonstrates, the mastermind of such systematic and thorough devastation cannot be dismissed as "mentally disturbed." He must be recognized, studied, and understood as an architect of profound evil, who held the world at bay long enough to enlist an entire people in a decade of genocide.

A MACHINE OF DECEPTION AND EXECUTION

It was Hitler's Axis partner Benito Mussolini who became famous for "making the trains run on time" in Fascist Italy. Yet Hitler's death machine, organized around his infamous system of concentration camps, was perhaps the most cruelly efficient governmental system in human history.

The Jews of Europe reached the camps mostly by rail. The trains—sometimes fifty cattle cars long—were packed tight with exhausted men, women, and children, who had been traveling many days with nothing to eat or drink. Some died from the trip; many more were killed immediately upon arrival. Not all the "pieces," as the SS called the victims, could be killed at once, so families in the rear cars waited in ignorance on the tracks outside the train station for the front cars to be "unloaded." The whole murderous process—from getting off the train to being turned into ashes and dumped in a nearby river—often took no more than a few hours.

The fiendishly efficient system was described by the commandant of Auschwitz, Rudolf Hess, not long before he was hanged for his crimes. The Jewish prisoners, he said, were "made to undress near the bunker, after they had been told that they had to go into the room in order to be deloused. All the rooms—there were five of them—were filled at the same time, the gasproof doors were then screwed tight, and the contents of the gas containers discharged into the rooms through special vents. After half an hour the doors were reopened (there were two doors in each room). The dead bodies were then taken out and brought to pits in small trolleys, which ran on rails. Those too ill to be brought to gas chambers were shot in the back of the neck."[10]

One key to the death-camp system was sheer speed. The moment the Jews got off the train they were surrounded by armed guards yelling at them to hurry, and beating them to keep them moving. The faster the process, the less chance there was for panic or rioting. The Nazis were brutally calculating: any revolt would force a bloody massacre right there on the train platform—costing precious time in cleanup.

Perhaps even more important than speed, though, was deception. The camp administrators went to elaborate lengths to deceive the prisoners until the very last moment, sure in the knowledge that few could foresee what lay in store. The Nazis knew how to prey on the psychology of their vulnerable prisoners. In Claude Lanzmann's remarkable Holocaust documentary *Shoah,* survivor Filip Muller describes how the Nazis inspired false hope among the Jews in the camp, even as they were being led to their death. "It was obvious that hope flared in those people," he remembered. "You could feel it clearly."[11]

Muller recalled the horrific moment when the German executioners gathered a group of prisoners in the crematorium courtyard.

> Grabner spoke up: "We need masons, electricians, all the trades." Next, Hossler took over. He pointed to a short man in the crowd. I can still see him. "What's your trade?" The man said: "Mr. Officer, I'm a tailor." "A tailor? What kind of a tailor?" "A man's . . . no, for both men and women." "Wonderful: We need people like you in our workshops." Then he questioned a woman: "What's your trade?" "Nurse," she replied. "Splendid! We need nurses in our hospitals, for our soldiers. We need all of you! But first, undress. You must be disinfected. We want you healthy."
>
> I could see the people were calmer, reassured by what they'd heard, and began to undress. Even if they still had their doubts, if you want to live, you must hope. Their clothing remained in the courtyard, scattered everywhere. Aumeyer was beaming, very proud of how he'd handled things. He turned to some of the SS men and told them: "You see? That's the way to do it!"[12]

As Muller describes in the film, the deception extended even to the gassing process:

As people reached the crematorium, they saw everything— this horribly violent scene. The whole area was ringed with SS. Dogs barked. Machine guns. They all, mainly the Polish Jews, had misgivings. They knew something was seriously amiss, but none of them had the faintest of notions that in three or four hours they'd be reduced to ashes.

When they reached the "undressing room," they saw that it looked like an International Information Center! On the walls were hooks, and each hook had a number. Beneath the hooks were wooden benches. So people could undress "more comfortably," it was said. And on the numerous pillars that held up this underground "undressing room," there were signs with slogans in several languages: "Clean is good!" "Lice can kill!" "Wash yourself!" "To the disinfection area." All those signs were only there to lure people into the gas chambers already undressed. And to the left, at a right angle, was the gas chamber with its massive door.

In Crematoriums 2 and 3, Zyklon gas crystals were poured in by a so-called SS disinfection squad through the ceiling, and in Crematoriums 4 and 5 through side openings. With five or six canisters of gas they could kill around two thousand people. This so-called disinfection squad arrived in a truck marked with a red cross and escorted people along to make them believe they were being led to take a bath.[13]

As Franz Suchomel, a Nazi SS officer at the Treblinka camp, says in the film:

You must remember, it had to go fast. And the Blue Squad
also had the task of leading the sick and the aged to the "infirmary," so as to not delay the flow of people to the gas
chambers. Old people would have slowed it down. Assignment to the "infirmary" was decided by Germans. . . . Old
women, sick children, children whose mother was sick, or
whose grandmother was very old, were sent along with the
grandma, because she didn't know about the "infirmary." It
had a white flag with a red cross. A passage led to it. Until
they reached the end, they saw nothing. Then they'd see the
dead in the pit. They were forced to strip, to sit on a sand-
bank, and were killed with a shot in the neck. They fell into
the pit. There was always a fire in the pit. With rubbish, paper
and gasoline, people burn very well.[14]

I know this is painful to read, but the only way to come to
terms with such absolute evil is to confront it directly. Rather than
treating the Holocaust as dry history, I believe we must pull something deeper from it, *something real*—that can make us understand
evil more intimately. It's not just the mass killing we need to ex-
plore, it's also the Nazi philosophy that gave rise to it, and the cold-
hearted bureaucracy that carried it out.

The Nazi bureaucrats, for example, were responsible for seizing
the wealth of the victims—from their real estate and bank accounts
right down to their jewelry and luggage. Since the concentration-
camp system had no formal budget to pay expenses (which would
have left too much of a paper trail), monies "earned" from the de-
portation and mass killing were placed in a Nazi SS bank account to
"defray costs." Even railroad cargo costs for the human "shipments"
had to be paid for by the SS, to draw as little attention as possible to

their horrific system. Nothing "useful" was wasted, from the hair on their heads to the gold in their teeth. It all went into Nazi coffers, counted and allotted *day after day* by untold numbers of Nazi loyalists who went home at night to their families.

One especially chilling detail involves the Nazis' use of portable gas chambers, or "gas vans," to kill their occupants with carbon monoxide. After noticing that the victims rushed en masse to the rear door trying to escape the gas, Nazi officials reacted by shortening the trucks by three feet, in order to avoid damaging their rear axles. In letters of the time, the victims are described as "merchandise": for the Nazis, evidently, thinking of their victims as dry goods rather than human beings only helped make the process more efficient.[15]

Nearly 70 percent of European Jews were slaughtered in these camps during the war, and millions of other human beings with them—men, women, children, and babies. But it didn't happen with a snap of the fingers. To kill millions of people in the midst of their functioning society the Nazis needed a system, a plan devised by bureaucrats and executed by efficient men who had analyzed all the difficulties of managing the "task," and who worked constantly to refine the "process."

A CULTURE OF BLOODLUST, COMPLICITY, AND DENIAL

As documents from the Nazi era reveal, the efficiency of the genocide was also abetted by virulent anti-Semitic propaganda, which demonized the victims and glorified their Nazi murderers. The Jews were depicted as members of "an international conspiracy against National Socialist Germany, who operated as parasites on society, extracting society's resources for their covetous benefit.

They were lesser beings, whose extermination would benefit society as a whole. Reich Minister Dr. [Joseph] Goebbels, one of the most influential members of the Nazi Regime, wrote that 'there were good and bad humans. . . . The fact that the Jew still lives among us is not proof that he is one of us, no more than the flea's domestic residence makes him a domestic animal.' "[16]

The Nazi focus on Jewish extermination was clear from the regime's beginning. In 1935, the Reichstag unanimously passed the Law for the Protection of German Blood and German Honor, which was intended to dehumanize the Jewish people in the minds and hearts of the German people. The "purity of the German blood," it proclaimed, was "the prerequisite for the continued existence of the German people." The law prohibited "marriages between Jews and citizens of German or kindred blood," and marriages performed abroad to circumvent the law were declared void. The law also prohibited "extramarital intercourse between Jews and citizens of German or kindred blood." Jews were forbidden from employing German females under age forty-five, and from displaying the German flag. Punishments for violating the law included hard labor and, in some cases, prison.[17]

Even while waging war in 1941, Goebbels kept up his public excoriation of the Jewish people. In an article for the Nazi weekly *Das Reich,* he claimed that the Jews had "provoked" the war, because they intended to "destroy the German state and nation." "Every Jew," wrote Goebbels, "is a sworn enemy of the German people. . . . Every German soldier's death . . . in this war is the Jew's responsibility." And the Jews, he concluded, "must pay for it." He charged Germany's enemy nations with protecting the Jews, proving "their destructive role among our people." He told his German readers that Jews had no claim to equal rights, and that they should be silenced "wherever they want to open their mouths." Even if a Jew should perform an act of kindness toward them, he warned his readers not to be fooled—and to punish him in return with contempt.[18]

Some might categorize such thought as the ravings of a psychopath. In my opinion, though, to dismiss Goebbels's attitude as the by-product of mental disability is to miss the point. Whatever his psychological makeup, it's clear that this "madman" was pursuing a conscious and deliberate campaign to spread anti-Semitic hatred throughout the German people. His motives, his words and actions, and their consequences were all unthinkably cruel, and undeniably evil.

Goebbels, of course, wasn't alone. In 1943, SS leader Heinrich Himmler addressed his high-level lieutenants, the supervisors of the genocide. His words reveal a man bent on emboldening his foot soldiers, on instilling pride in them for their vicious acts against the Jews. Moreover, they demonstrate how anxious the Nazi leaders were to insulate themselves from the moral depravity of their actions—in both the eyes of history and whatever shreds of personal conscience they might have retained.

Though they would never "speak a word of it in public," Himmler told the SS, they were succeeding in their goal of exterminating the Jews. He congratulated them, and himself, for presiding over the thousands of deaths while remaining "a decent person throughout. . . . That is a page of glory in our history that never has been and never will be written," he boasted. Further, he reminded them that they "had the moral right, and the duty . . . to kill this people." Himmler concluded: "But in all, we can say that we fulfilled this heaviest of tasks in love to our people. And we suffered no harm in our essence, in our soul, in our character."[19]

Whatever Himmler and his ilk may have claimed about their "moral right and duty" to implement Hitler's Final Solution, their guilt is revealed in their words. Why would their page in history "never be written"? Why would Himmler feel compelled to insist that the Nazis remained "decent throughout," with "no damage . . . in our character," unless he knew otherwise?

From Hitler on down, Nazi Party records reveal that the regime was intent on maintaining "plausible denial" about the Holocaust. Yet even as the dangers of Nazism were being debated in Britain and elsewhere, Nazi policy on "the Jewish problem" was a public matter. From the laws on its books to the brutal oppression on its streets, the "character" of Nazi Germany was clear long before war broke out.

Only through the courageous leadership of Winston Churchill and Franklin Roosevelt was the Third Reich finally held accountable for its actions. In taking on the German military—a war machine every bit as fierce as the Nazi death machine—the Allies were compelled by three basic principles: that totalitarian government is the enemy of freedom; that the systematic oppression and cruelty it fosters is not merely senseless, but utterly evil; and that appeasement can never defeat that evil—it can only embolden it.

As the War on Terror progresses, these three lessons are equally important today.

LESSON ONE: TOTALITARIANISM AND EVIL

I'll say it again: The most profound political lesson of the Holocaust is that totalitarian states are a breeding ground for evil. The voracious evil of a Nazi Germany, or a Soviet Russia, can survive only under a totalitarian regime and a closed society, where dissent is outlawed and the tenets of traditional morality are replaced by the dictates of the state.

This idea of subordinating the individual to the state wasn't born in 1930s Germany. It was firmly rooted in the irreligious philosophies that spread throughout Europe in the nineteenth century, giving rise to Marxist communism, socialism, and eventually their fascist cousin national socialism or Nazism. These essentially atheistic belief systems replaced God with the state, often imbuing their leaders with quasi-religious powers, as the Bolsheviks did with Lenin and the Nazis with their führer.

The Nazi movement is well-recognized for its anti-Semitism, but it was also virulently opposed to the tenets of Christianity. It was in thrall to the philosopher Friedrich Nietzsche's vision of a "superman," which was built on the belief that Aryans were superhumans and Jews non-humans. Nietzsche had famously declared that "God is dead"—and the leaders of the Third Reich saw that without God, the state and its leaders were free to shape morality for themselves. In the Nazis' "German Christianity," Hitler stood in place of God; he decided who lived and who died.

Nietzsche, whom the Nazis could practically quote on demand, had written that for the average citizen "there is no such thing as the right to live, the right to work, or the right to be happy: in this respect man is no different from the meanest worm." The superman, on the other hand, Nietzsche exalted as a "beast of prey," a "magnificent blond brute, avidly rampant for spoil and victory."[20]

For a government to perpetrate such ideas on a whole people—innocent of any wrongdoing—it has to have absolute power. It must see itself as superior to any "limiting" concept of God, or truth or justice. "The notion of a 'higher moral order,' to be determined by the state's convenience," writes the historian Paul Johnson, "was to find expression, in the twentieth century, in what Lenin called 'the Revolutionary Conscience' and Hitler 'the Higher Law of the Party.' "[21] Two systems with the same root, totally alien to the founding principle of the United States of America, which recognized that its right to freedom came from the Creator.

Today, most liberals and many academic historians place Nazism and communism as two extreme ends of the ideological spectrum—far right and far left. But in truth these two totalitarian models are actually very similar. Both were avowedly socialistic, and both established the state as God (just as liberalism increasingly does today). Ronald Reagan recognized the fallacy of describing Nazism as a "far right" philosophy, and he challenged his liberal opponents on the issue. In his eyes, it was not a matter of left or right, but of "up or down": up toward individual freedom, or down toward the tyranny of statism.[22]

Just as totalitarian states have historically been seedbeds for evil, in today's world they are also ripe for collusion with terrorists. Having no higher moral compass, the totalitarian regime forms its alliances on the basis of power and expedience. Thus it should come as no surprise that terrorists get their nourishment from these regimes. In this symbiotic relationship these totalitarian states have forged with their terrorist henchmen, they are the direct descendants of the tyrannical regimes of the last century, including Nazi Germany. They are united by a bond of evil that transcends the generations.

In the wake of the 2003 Iraq war, Saddam's legacy of terror toward his own people was laid bare before the world. Soon after his overthrow, American troops discovered horrific torture chambers in places like Iraq's Military Intelligence Directorate, where a grim paper trail documented decades of atrocities. "Pictures of dead Iraqis, with their necks slashed, their eyes gouged out and their genitals blackened, fill a bookshelf," Jack Kelley wrote in *USA Today*. "Jail cells, with dried blood on the floor and rusted shackles bolted to the walls, line the corridors. And the screams of what could be imprisoned men in an underground detention center echo through air shafts and sewer pipes."[23] By November, human rights officials in Iraq reported the discovery of 250 mass graves dating to Saddam's regime, estimating that they might hold the bodies of hundreds of thousands of executed Iraqis.[24]

In the aftermath of the war in Iraq, still evidence is mounting that Saddam Hussein's regime was also in collusion with Osama bin Laden's al Qaeda network. In a detailed article based on top-secret U.S. intelligence documents, Stephen F. Hayes in the *Weekly Standard* has revealed that Saddam's lieutenants held regular meetings with bin Laden and his emissaries from 1990 through the period immediately before the American invasion in 2003. CIA reports from 1993 reveal that "bin Laden wanted to expand his organization's capabilities through ties with Iraq," and that Saddam's vice president and other intelligence officials met with al Qaeda leaders in Baghdad, Sudan, and Afghanistan in 1998 and 1999.[25]

Even today, the antiwar lobby still dismisses the evidence that Saddam was in league with the terrorists. Yet here is a man who had tortured and killed thousands of innocent Iraqis for the merest infractions, who gassed his own people, who ruled by fear and fiat. How can anyone believe he would hesitate to join forces with bin Laden?

As President Bush has said, the nations who support terrorism are also our enemies. Those who deny that connection—between the terrorists and their state sponsors—do so at our peril.

LESSON TWO: INSANITY OR EVIL?

In the media, Adolf Hitler is commonly described as a "madman"; in conversation I've often heard him referred to as "crazy." And the subject of Hitler's sanity has long been a source of fascination for both academics and the media. A recent spate of books and movies has tried to find answers by imagining Hitler's early years, and the Swiss psychoanalyst Alice Miller (whose book *The Drama of the Gifted Child* is a favorite of Al Gore) is one of several academics who have linked Hitler's behavior to his abuse by his father.[26]

But I'm suspicious of any attempt to go hunting for root causes in Adolf Hitler's childhood. To me, looking for some psychological explanation for his campaign to decimate the Jewish population of Europe is a dangerous distraction. The behavior of a cold and vicious mass murderer like Adolf Hitler—or Saddam Hussein—is the result of conscious choice. And if we fail to evaluate it in moral terms, looking for excuses from the past instead of lessons for the future, we risk losing our own moral compass.

Recently, even the "experts" have begun to seem embarrassed at this kind of oversimplification. After the fall of Iraq, when the revelations about Saddam's brutal regime began emerging in the news, an article on the subject appeared in the Sunday *New York Times*. This is about as close to a full retraction as liberals ever come:

> Like Stalin and Hitler, Mr. Hussein has sometimes been referred to as a madman, in part because people are reluctant to accept such ruthlessness and cruelty as the product of anything but insanity. But bad does not equal mad. Most histor-

ical analysts have rejected the notion that mental illness could explain the actions of either Stalin or Hitler.[27]

I don't believe "most historical analysts have rejected" mental illness as an explanation for Stalin and Hitler. In fact, this concession from the *Times* was a rare acknowledgment by a major voice of the liberal elite that such a shallow characterization of Hitler, Stalin, and the likes of Saddam Hussein, is insufficient.

Still, the *Times* couldn't maintain its newfound discipline for very long. The real focus of the article was the work of two researchers who have labeled Saddam, along with Hitler and Stalin, as "malignant narcissists." To them, a dictator who slaughters millions of people, and tortures hundreds of thousands more, is just a victim of a *personality disorder.* The researchers focused on the "traumatizing experiences" of Saddam's youth—but surely most Iraqi citizens would have far less sympathy for their oppressor's childhood trauma than for their own family members who had been raped, beaten, or killed at the hands of his regime.

Which raises another question: if "malignant narcissism" is supposed to excuse the behavior of a Hitler or a Saddam, then how did his "disorder" permeate the minds of millions of Germans? After all, hundreds of thousands of Germans directly cooperated with Hitler, and Saddam didn't manage his decades of oppression without the participation of thousands of loyalists. Certainly fear must have played a part: it's true that the Nazis tortured and killed resisters. But the painful truth is that multitudes of German citizens were willing participants in the Holocaust, not out of fear or the desire for self-preservation, but because *they believed in it.* Many became aggressive collaborators, and passionate exterminators.

The explanation, to my mind, is simple: the evil intentions of a charismatic leader have often incited groups of followers to band together in evil and immoral behavior. On a smaller scale, we've even seen glimpses of this kind of "group evil" in our own culture. And they seem to be occurring with more frequency.

The Associated Press reported one example, from June 2003. Sixteen-year-old Jason Sweeney lived in a working-class neighborhood in Philadelphia. Rather than going home after work one evening, his "first girlfriend," Justina Morley, led him to a path by the Delaware River, where three teenage boys lay in wait for him. According to news reports, the four attacked Jason with a hammer and a hatchet, breaking all but one of his facial bones and eventually sinking the hatchet in his skull. The four teens shared a "group hug," then stole the $500 he was carrying and used it to buy drugs.

"We took Sweeney's wallet and split up the money, and we partied beyond redemption," said Dominic Coia, one of the assailants.[28] Coia told police that the boys had listened over and over to the Beatles song "Helter Skelter," one of serial killer Charles Manson's anthems of inspiration, to prime themselves for the mayhem they were about to commit. Authorities charged the three attackers and their fifteen-year-old accomplice, Justina Morley, with first degree murder, though Morley is too young to face the death penalty.[29]

As Judge Seamus P. McCaffery declared from the bench: "This is something out of the Dark Ages. I'm not so sure we can call ourselves a civilized society when stuff like this happens."[30] What clearly horrified the judge is that at least two of these alleged killers knew this boy as a "friend," but plotted his death together, and slaughtered him without a care, as the boys' confessions made clear. Sweeney apparently remained conscious for some time after the attack began, begging for his life. Whatever the case, one thing is evident: by their own admission, these sadistic killers were enjoying themselves.

Must we diminish this shared evil act by calling it "malignant narcissism"? Let's face it, even if intoxicating drugs were involved—and authorities suspect the killers were using antidepressants—it's hard to grasp the true significance of that final "group hug" without reference to the concept of evil. Whether these four were looking for a thrill, trying to satisfy a sadistic urge, or indulging a twisted power trip, by their own account they *conspired together* to accomplish it. At any point during the planning and execution of Jason's assassination, any one of them could have stopped to dissuade the others, reported them to the authorities, or merely chosen not to participate. What they committed was pure, conscious evil—not the result of individual mental illnesses. And they did so in the heart of Philadelphia, not in the Nazi death camps. Cases like theirs demonstrate that evil is everywhere; it is part of the human condition.

Even in the face of such evidence, though, the liberal elites still avoid using the very word "evil." For them, the term is too judgmental; it smacks of religion—of "fundamentalism." Reflecting on George Bush's reference to Iraq, Iran, and North Korea as an "axis of evil," the University of Chicago professor Mark Lilla wrote, "How, one wonders, did the president and his speech writers blunder into this mess?" Susan Sontag, one of the most strident voices of moral relativism since September 11, has referred to Bush's use of the word as "jihad language."[31]

But if we can't face such acts of evil on a relatively small scale and identify them for what they are, our modern culture will certainly forget the true horror of the Holocaust, and ignore the evidence of torture from Iraq. By dismissing evil as a social construct, relabeling it as the product of hard times or childhood abuse, we gradually become desensitized to death, losing our appreciation for the individual worth and dignity of human life. And in the end we forfeit our ability to make moral judgments.

Ironically, that may be just what the Nazis had in mind. After all, when we renounce our moral authority in favor of moral relativism, behavior that once was clearly evil gets redefined as a "social problem" with a "sociological solution." The individual's right to judge, in other words, is subordinated to the secular "wisdom" of the group or the collective. And that is how the Nazis intended their society to work. "The difference between National Socialism and all previous systems," said Goebbels, "is that its starting point is the community, not the individual. This gives a very different character to all our social ideas."[32] Indeed it did: It convinced a shocking number of Germans to torture and murder their fellow human beings—as a service to the state.

LESSON THREE: APPEASEMENT OR CONFRONTATION?

Those who fail to recognize evil, finally, are doomed to fall into the trap of appeasement. And no story in the last century has thrown the danger of appeasement into greater relief than the sorry tale of Neville Chamberlain, the British prime minister who tried to beg peace with Adolf Hitler—and returned having lost everything at the bargaining table. The contrast between Chamberlain and his successor, Winston Churchill, is an object lesson for anyone who still believes a murderer like Saddam Hussein or Osama bin Laden can be tamed by half-measures.

Like all appeasers, Chamberlain should have seen it coming. The Nazis' rise to power in the years before Munich was swift and merciless. In January 1933, Hitler was appointed chancellor of Germany, head of the cabinet. In February a suspicious fire burned down the Reichstag, leading to mass arrests by the Gestapo; enemies and perceived enemies of the Nazi Party were murdered in the streets. By April of that year, the Nazi-controlled Reichstag had passed a series of laws that gave Hitler unlimited power over Germany, rendering its constitution meaningless. In a few short years, the Nazi Party had remade itself as a state within a state, banning newspapers that didn't support its dogma, dissolving non-Nazi labor unions, outlawing other political parties, summarily suspending civil rights for political opponents. And it demanded that all members of the German military swear a personal loyalty oath to Adolf Hitler.

By 1938, after nearly five years of oppression at home, Nazi Germany had annexed Austria and was spoiling to invade the Sudetenland region of Czechoslovakia. First under Stanley Baldwin and then under Neville Chamberlain, Great Britain had looked on in fear as Hitler's appetites grew. When the Sudetenland crisis erupted, Chamberlain went to Munich to meet with Hitler—and returned to announce that he had agreed not to oppose Germany's annexation of the region, in deference to "the desire of our two peoples never to go to war with one another again." At 10 Downing Street, the prime minister's residence, Chamberlain told his anxious nation: "My good friends, for the second time in our history, a British Prime Minister has returned from Germany bringing peace with honor. I believe it is peace for our time. . . . Go home and get a nice quiet sleep."

When the House of Commons was presented with the Munich Agreement, however, Chamberlain's hollow triumph was greeted by many as the sellout that it was. One of his cabinet members, Duff Cooper, left the government in protest. "The Prime Minster," he said in his resignation speech, "has believed in addressing Herr Hitler through the language of sweet reasonableness. I have believed that he was more given to the language of the mailed fist."[33] Chamberlain's response was telling:

> Ever since I assumed my present office my main purpose has been to work for the pacification of Europe, for the removal of those suspicions and those animosities which have so long poisoned the air. The path which leads to appeasement is long and bristles with obstacles. The question of Czechoslovakia is the latest and perhaps the most dangerous. Now that we have got past it, I feel that it may be possible to make further progress along the road to sanity.[34]

But it took the moral vision of Winston Churchill, one of Chamberlain's chief critics, to recognize the dangerous folly of the prime minister's position. "We have sustained a defeat without a war," he said, ". . . and do not suppose that this is the end. This is only the beginning of the reckoning. This is only the first sip, the first foretaste of a bitter cup."[35]

In his comments on Munich, Churchill showed that he understood the danger of attempting to negotiate with a totalitarian power with no accountability to its own people:

> The Prime Minister [Chamberlain] desires to see cordial relations between this country and Germany. There is no difficulty at all in having cordial relations with the German people. Our hearts go out to them. But they have no power. You must have diplomatic and correct relations, but there can never be friendship between the British democracy and the Nazi Power, that Power which spurns Christian ethics, which

cheers its onward course by a barbarous paganism, which vaunts the spirit of aggression and conquest, which derives strength and perverted pleasure from persecution, and uses, as we have seen, with pitiless brutality the threat of murderous force. That Power cannot ever be the trusted friend of the British Democracy. What I find unendurable is the sense of our country falling into the power, into the orbit and influence of Nazi Germany and of our existence becoming dependent upon their good will or pleasure.[36]

No equivocation, no spin, no false hope, just blunt, powerful words from a great man.

In the end, of course, Churchill was right. The Munich Agreement forced Czechoslovakia to surrender 11,000 square miles of territory to Germany. This area, home to 800,000 Czechs and 2.8 million Sudeten Germans, constituted one of the most important lines of strategic defense in Europe. Further, Czechoslovakia lost large percentages of its natural resources, including coal, lignite, and timber, and its chemical, cement, textile, iron, steel, and electrical power plants. As William Shirer wrote in *The Rise and Fall of the Third Reich,* "A prosperous industrial nation was split up and bankrupted overnight."[37]

How did Churchill see what Chamberlain had missed? Each man had access to the same information about Hitler and Nazi Germany; each had many years of political experience. When Chamberlain returned from his meeting with Hitler, he felt certain that he had secured victory for his people. Yet Churchill knew at once—as history has confirmed—that the Munich Agreement was one of the most grievous acts of self-delusion in history. (Though neither Chamberlain nor Churchill would know it at the time, after the prime minister's return to London, Hitler referred privately to the British prime minister and his ilk as "little worms.")[38]

Ultimately, Chamberlain and Churchill had entirely different views of human nature. Churchill knew evil when he saw it. He knew the Nazis were the opposite of everything Britain stood for, and that they needed to be stopped. He was wise enough to know that the British people would greet the news from Munich with relief, at least at first, because war had been averted. But he also knew the other shoe had yet to drop, and that Britain and the world would pay a horrible price for their denial. He wanted his countrymen to know the truth, and he was forthright about the challenges they faced: Britain, he warned, would suffer further calamities unless they experienced a "supreme recovery of moral health and martial vigor" to "arise again and take our stand for freedom."[39]

Churchill understood the gravity of that moment in history. He knew that Chamberlain's agreement with Hitler would weaken the European democracies' ability to resist Nazi aggression. Yet he also recognized that the underlying conflict was more than just a border dispute. Czechoslovakia had been betrayed, dooming millions of people to "be engulfed in the Nazi regime." He grieved for the Sudeten people: "All is over," he said after Chamberlain's return. "Silent, mournful, abandoned, broken, Czechoslovakia recedes into the darkness."[40]

Churchill was a moral force against that darkness—not only because he warned Britain of Nazi Germany's evil designs (though he was mocked by appeasers for doing so), but also because he called attention to the basic spiritual enmity between the two countries. He knew that nations needed not only "martial vigor" but "moral health" to fight. As Czechoslovakia and then Poland fell in the final months of Chamberlain's tenure, Churchill would call on Britons to summon their inner strength, to find both the courage and the "understanding" to see evil for what it was. And in the end, of course, he would lead his country to victory.

What would happen if we in America were faced with the same challenges today?

I'd say we already are. And, while George W. Bush has honored Winston Churchill's example in confronting evil, the voices of appeasement have been even stronger than they were in London in the 1930s.

I'm convinced that the growth of international terrorism could pose as dire a threat to our national security as Hitler posed to Britain in the 1930s. And if Churchill were among us today, I'm afraid his warnings would be met with squabbling and derision by the mainstream media, and by leading Democrats and liberals who are eager to exploit the war for their own partisan advantage.

When President Bush focused attention on Saddam Hussein's growing defiance of world opinion in 2002, he encountered nothing but opposition from the left. As Saddam thwarted international weapons inspectors, shredded the Gulf War Treaty, and ignored one U.N. resolution after another, antiwar activists at home and abroad pressed for more time, more negotiation, more accommodation. Even today, as American troops work to maintain peace and build a stable government in Iraq, the appeasers protest our presence there, hoping that their attacks will buy them a few votes in November.

Like Neville Chamberlain, today's appeasers are fooling themselves about the realities of war. They insist that the avenue to "peace in our time" is through accommodating and pacifying the enemy. They refuse to understand the inherent moral corruption of totalitarian regimes like Saddam's, of terrorist networks like bin Laden's. They reject the very notion of evil, grasping instead at sociological explanations and psychological excuses.

But just as it is a grave error to mistake evil for insanity, it is suicidal to approach evil from a position of weakness. Both errors are a result of misapprehending the nature of evil. Like the mouse that freezes at the sight of a snake, hoping it will go away, the appeaser just doesn't understand the nature of his foe.

As I've often said on my radio show, liberals define peace as an absence of conflict, or an absence of war. As a conservative, on the other hand, I believe that true peace can only be maintained when a nation has the ability, and the courage, to defend itself. There is no question in my mind that if the terrorists keep pursuing their murderous agenda, the Democratic Party may one day nominate an "appeasement candidate" for president. (In fact, that day may come very soon.) But to elect such a candidate would be to put ourselves in the hands of another Neville Chamberlain.

The appeasers may prefer to ignore history. But the horrors of the Holocaust demand that we never forget. We must never again be ambushed by a ruthless enemy, as Britain was before World War II, and as we were before September 11, 2001. We owe it to those who died, and to our own children, to remain vigilant in the battle against evil.

And in doing so, let us turn forward a few decades, to take a lesson from America's great crusader for freedom: Ronald Reagan.

THREE

Fighting Communism: The Reagan Way

A decline in courage may be the most striking feature that an outside observer notices in the West today. The Western world has lost its civic courage, both as a whole and separately, in each country, in each government, in each political party, and, of course, in the United Nations. Such a decline in courage is particularly noticeable among the ruling and intellectual elites, causing an impression of a loss of courage by the entire society.

—ALEXANDER SOLZHENITSYN,
Harvard graduation ceremony, 1978

If there's ever been a nation that embodied the principle that totalitarianism and evil go hand in hand, it's the Soviet Union. Yet even today, with the U.S.S.R. fully dismantled, repudiated, gone from the face of the earth, and an entire generation of survivors bearing witness to its evils, much of the American public has failed to register the enormity of the evil its murderous leaders perpetrated. Why? At least in part because America's liberal establishment was committed to apologizing for this bloodthirsty regime. They minimized, concealed, denied, and discredited factual reports of the atrocities and oppression, and demonized those who tried to bring them to the public's attention.

Thankfully, in the end, there is a positive message for us in the saga of the Cold War: that once again the American commitment to freedom, and willingness to confront evil, prevailed over a vicious foe—despite the fervent opposition, obstruction, hostility, and appeasing mind-set of sympathetic liberalism.

None of this would have been possible without the determination of one man: President Ronald Reagan, who was driven to take his place in American history by a basic faith in the American experiment in freedom, and an equally passionate contempt for the evil of the Soviet empire and the communist system that enslaved it.

Before Reagan came onto the scene, however, the outlook for America in its historic struggle against Soviet communism looked anything but promising. By the late 1970s the nation had slipped into a state of military decline and had degenerated into a spirit of pessimism and defeatism, with long gas lines, stagflation, double-digit interest rates, mushrooming unemployment, and no prospect for better times. President Carter's proposed solution was austerity and sacrifice, doom and gloom, and ultimately, surrender—to the idea that America's better days were behind us.

We were in such a state of despair that it demanded a person with Reagan's extraordinary optimism about America to lead us back onto the path to greatness—from rebuilding the military and the economy, to restoring a sense of hope and national pride. Reagan believed in America's greatness because of his innate faith that any people would flourish when unshackled by the burdens of government.

Today, the primary threat to our security and freedom is from terrorists and their state sponsors. They have made evil in the world increasingly difficult to ignore. But once again the left-wing establishment in this country is back to doing what it does best: blaming America. They are attempting to shift the focus away from the malfeasance of foreign leaders, and toward America's own supposed moral lapses, Jimmy Carter style.

Here again, though, the best lessons for dealing with the terrorist threat are in our own past: if we're to conquer liberal defeatism at home and win the war on terror, we must first look back and take inspiration from Reagan's example. He proved that the vision of one strong leader could topple a totalitarian regime half a world away. And as we'll see, he didn't do it by reacting and playing defense. He seized the moment, taking the offense, crushing the Soviet Union primarily by unleashing the American spirit that since Vietnam had been mired in paralyzing self-doubt and melancholy.

One of the hardest things to explain to someone who didn't live through the Cold War is just how perilous it really was—not just because of our foreign enemies, but also because so many Americans appeared to lose their commitment to liberty. They were unable, or unwilling, to acknowledge the evil nature of our enemy. From antiwar protestors to liberal government leaders, Americans sought to accommodate Soviet communism, ignoring its history of conquest, oppression, and murder, and according it moral equivalence with the greatest, freest system of government ever devised by man. Like other historical confrontations between good and evil, there were those who sought to confront and those who were all too willing to appease.

By the late 1970s, it seemed as if America, dragged down by its top-down malaise, was no longer equipped to stand up to a totalitarian system that did not have to answer to its subjugated people. The godless Soviet regime continued to offer itself as the model of a benevolent governmental system that could deliver people worldwide from the excesses and inequities of capitalism. Shamelessly ignoring the poverty of its own citizens, it focused its full energy against the West.

At the same time, America was hardly in a position to be making official moral arguments against the secular Soviet system, when it had begun consciously to divorce God from its own public square through a series of Supreme Court decisions mandating a "wall of separation between church and state." No longer was it fashionable, in our culture or in our court system, to assert that our rights had derived from God. The conventional wisdom of the day—persisting into the present—was that government was the creator of our liberties. Our growing secularism thus reduced the great debate between the two countries to the question of which system could best provide for its people.

Having undermined our own moral vision, we seemed to be losing our ability to make official moral arguments against secular socialism. But at the same time, Americans were beginning to awaken to the idea that something had gone terribly wrong, that the radical cultural rebellion of the 1960s and 1970s was leading to America's demise.

In the late spring of 1978, the world's most prominent Soviet dissident, Alexander Solzhenitsyn, spoke at Harvard's graduation ceremony. His message was in keeping with his reputation: confrontational. It was a speech that would make the liberal elite very uncomfortable, but it wasn't intended for the left alone. Solzhenitsyn knew that much of the world looked to America as an inspiration and source of hope, and thus his words were directed to all Americans. Solzhenitsyn knew what Ronald Reagan and other conservatives also knew—that America had lost her way, and that fact put the whole world in danger.

In his speech, "A World Split Apart," Solzhenitsyn eloquently indicted the "political and intellectual functionaries" of the West for basing their state policies "on weakness and cowardice" and offering "self-serving rationales" to justify them. He noted that while they engage in "occasional outbursts" in dealing with "weak governments" they become "paralyzed" when dealing with foreign powers and international terrorists.

Historically, observed Solzhenitsyn, a "decline in courage" has been the "first symptom of the end." He characterized the current conflict "for our planet" as a physical and spiritual war that had already begun. And he identified the Soviet aggressors as "the forces of Evil."

Solzhenitsyn's speech also redirected the attention of the audience of Harvard students—and the world—to the realities of the Soviet system, as embodied in the gulag where he was sentenced to serve eight years. Millions of people had been killed in the gulag prison-camp system,[1] and Solzhenitsyn had seen it all firsthand. He and his wife had memorized fellow prisoners' names so they would not be forgotten.[2] He had seen the torture and mass murder. He knew well what a choking lack of freedom did to the human soul.

But Solzhenitsyn also knew something that must have taken his intellectual audience aback: he knew the power of prayer.

There he stood before a body of young Americans who had

grown up during the massive domestic upheaval of the 1960s—
not just Vietnam and Watergate, but the era of sex, drugs, rock 'n'
roll, and social "liberation."

Solzhenitsyn knew what *real* liberation was. And in his
speech, he asked questions—and gave answers—that must have
perplexed the Harvard elite. "How has this unfavorable relation of
forces come about?" he asked.

> How did the West decline from its triumphal march to its pres-
> ent debility? Have there been fatal turns and losses of direction
> in its development? It does not seem so. The West kept advanc-
> ing steadily in accordance with its proclaimed social intentions,
> hand in hand with a dazzling progress in technology. And all of
> a sudden it found itself in its present state of weakness.
>
> The mistake must be at the root, at the very foundation
> of thought in modern times. I refer to the prevailing Western
> view of the world, which was born in the Renaissance and
> has found political expression since the Age of Enlighten-
> ment. It became the basis for political and social doctrine and
> could be called rationalistic humanism or humanistic auton-
> omy: the proclaimed and practiced autonomy of man from
> any higher force above him. . . . The humanistic way of
> thinking, which had proclaimed itself our guide, did not ad-
> mit the existence of intrinsic evil in man, nor did it see any
> task higher than the attainment of happiness on earth. It
> started modern Western civilization on the dangerous trend
> of worshiping man and his material needs.[3]

And with those few words, Alexander Solzhenitsyn suddenly
found himself a pariah. Once lionized by the media, now this great

man was treated as if he didn't exist—all because, within the rule book of the intellectual elite, no one who believes in God is to be taken seriously. What's more, the late 1970s were supposed to be an era of détente, a time of lessening tensions; to issue moral judgments about communism was seen as destructive to all chances for world peace. But Solzhenitsyn was never interested in lessening tensions. He knew that standing for the truth meant confronting the lie—confronting evil.

Not everyone in this country shared the left's lack of moral vision. Like Solzhenitsyn, whom he greatly admired, Ronald Reagan also saw the free world's conflict with communism in moral terms. When most of those around him wanted to believe that Soviet communism and the Western democracies could coexist in peace, Reagan saw confrontation as inevitable, morally as well as historically.

As he would later confirm in his autobiography, Reagan felt that our policy of détente toward the U.S.S.R. was a license for the Soviets, under the cover of apparent peace and goodwill, to pursue "policies of subversion, aggression and expansionism . . . anywhere in the world."[4] The consistent purpose of the Soviet communist regime, according to Reagan, was to destroy democracy and impose communism throughout the world.

As history has proven, Reagan's view of the Soviets was realistic. But at the time it was dismissed with contempt by his liberal detractors, who saw Reagan and his brand of anticommunism as "extremist" at best, McCarthyite or even fascist at worst.

Jimmy Carter had a very different view of America, the Soviet Union, and their relative places in the world. He paid lip service to the notion that the president of the United States had a duty to restore "moral authority" to America's international policies, without recognizing that moral authority might involve any attempt to curb the brutality and repression of the Soviet system. He expressly rejected the notion that "the world is a jungle of competing national antagonisms," and that military and economic prowess should be the determining factors in world affairs.[5] His naïve approach, apparently, was to ignore the hostile nature of aggressor nations, and to attempt to tame them with loving kindness.

The world "will always be complex and confused," Carter told an audience at Notre Dame shortly before the 1980 election. "I understand fully the limits of moral suasion," he continued, "but I also believe that it is a mistake to undervalue the power of words and of the ideas that words embody."[6]

The critical difference between Carter and his successor, Ronald Reagan, was that Reagan knew that "words" must be backed up by wisdom, by a sure knowledge of when it is time to act. Even the liberal *Washington Post* acknowledged during the 1980 election that Carter's inability to turn his beliefs into consistent policy had become a campaign issue.[7] Carter's failure to act with conviction, coupled with his liberal view of the world, helped create a geopolitical mess that Ronald Reagan would spend much of the 1980s trying to correct.

THE MASK COMES OFF

In 1979, a year of many spectacular setbacks for America, the most shocking and frightening among them was the December 25 Soviet invasion of Afghanistan.[8] Since the end of World War II, the Soviet communists had rarely attempted such direct military action; when they invaded a country, it was to put down "rebellion" in places already under their control—Hungary in 1956, Czechoslovakia in 1968. More often, the Soviets or their surrogates planned and supported revolution in Third World countries, then used those countries as bases of operations to carry the "revolution" forward to neighboring countries.[9]

Reagan recognized that communism had an insidious power to use its "egalitarian" message as a seductive trap. But once the trap was shut, swallowing some new communist satellite, the Soviets saw to it that it never opened again. From the Warsaw Pact forward, once they achieved control over a country, they had no intention of letting go—even if it meant crushing popular uprisings. The Soviets' commitment to preserving their stranglehold over countries they had absorbed came to be called the Brezhnev Doctrine, after the U.S.S.R.'s then-premier.[10] "One man, one vote, *once,*" the saying went: once a nation had fallen into communist hands, it gave up all chance of reversing its fortunes. The sovereignty of each country within the Soviet orbit was subordinate to the "interests of the world of socialism, the world revolutionary movement."[11] It was not until the advent of Ronald Reagan that the world saw a convincing reversal of this process.

Reagan was a man of faith. He believed in the ideal of a free nation, full of industrious people who with their own hands and hearts could create a full life for themselves and their families. And he believed that the hard work and creativity of the people could only flourish within a free and open society. In his vision, government was necessary, but when allowed to wield its power unchecked—as in the Soviet system—it could also be very dangerous. By its very nature, communism represented everything that Reagan hated: tyranny, brutality, aggression, and a godless view of the world that allowed it to justify virtually any act, no matter how ruthless and inhumane, to achieve its ends.

Reagan's vision went beyond simple anticommunism: it was antistatist. He put his faith in the free individual, whose natural duty is to a higher truth than government bureaucracy. And in the realm of foreign policy, during his presidency he would meet Brezhnev's aggression with what columnist Charles Krauthammer called the Reagan Doctrine. Whenever possible, Reagan resolved, America would support counterrevolutions and insurgencies to undermine and defeat communist expansionism. It would work to support the cause of freedom for oppressed peoples around the world. And it would take as its goal not the simple containment of the Soviet Union, but what Reagan saw as its inevitable defeat.

In 1979, as Reagan prepared for the Republican presidential primaries, the Cold War balance of power was shifting in the Soviet Union's favor. Nicaragua fell to the communist Sandinistas that year (with Cuba's help); Iran, once America's staunch ally, had fallen under the power of the Ayatollah Khomeini, and had taken scores of Americans hostage at the U.S. Embassy in Teheran. As Americans and their president watched helplessly, nightly images of Iranian crowds cursing America and burning our flag darkened our TV screens and seemed to shame us before the whole world.

But the Soviet invasion of Afghanistan that December took tensions to a new level. Using more aggressive tactics than usual, the Red Army entered the country with two airborne divisions, seizing Kabul, and following up with a massive influx of regular troops. In the 1960s, the Soviets had "helped" Afghanistan by building modern roads down through the country. Now those same roads were being used by 80,000 Russian troops.[12]

Jimmy Carter was in shock. "This action of the Soviets," he told ABC News, "has made a more dramatic change in my own opinion of what the Soviets' ultimate goals are than anything they've done in the previous time I've been in office."[13]

A comment like this, coming from an American leader three years into his presidency, was almost as shocking as the invasion itself. During Carter's own time in office the horror of the communist genocide in Cambodia unfolded. Before that, the world had witnessed the slaughters in Vietnam, Korea, and Red China. Certainly he would have known of Stalin's mass murders, of Solzhenitsyn's personal account of Soviet concentration camps. Carter knew that the Soviet army had moved into Hungary and Czechoslovakia to crush citizen freedom fighters. And he knew that desperate East Germans were regularly shot on sight simply for trying to escape communist tyranny over the Berlin Wall. The evil of communism was no secret.

Jimmy Carter is not a stupid man. The only conclusion we can draw is that he was willfully blind to the Soviet leadership's horrific history of violence. The communists' record for mass murder was well-known long before Carter's presidency. Given all that, how could a man like Jimmy Carter attain the highest office in the world's most powerful nation—and still be surprised at the Soviet Union's capacity for evil?

Former Texas Governor John Connally called President Carter's statement "absolutely frightening,"[14] and he wasn't alone in his assessment. Carter's comment wasn't just naïve, it was dangerously disconnected from reality. Let's look at the cold statistics. A recent accounting of the death toll under communist tyranny is sobering:

Region	Death toll	Region	Death toll
U.S.S.R.	20 million	Eastern Europe	1 million
China	65 million	Africa	1.7 million
Vietnam	1 million	Afghanistan	1.5 million
North Korea	2 million	Latin America	150,000
Cambodia	2 million	**Total:**	**More than 94 million**[15]

These figures are conservative; others have suggested a total closer to 150 million. To put this in perspective, the Nazis' death toll has been estimated at 25 million.[16] As Jimmy Carter well knew, communism had cut a bloody scar through the twentieth century.

By the end of his presidency, aided by an increasingly liberal Congress, Carter had left America in a geopolitical mess, weakening her as an opponent of communism and international terrorism. In 1982, Jeane Kirkpatrick, Ronald Reagan's ambassador to the United Nations, summed up the situation. "While Carter was President there occurred a dramatic Soviet military buildup, matched by the stagnation of American armed forces, and a dramatic extension of Soviet influence in the Horn of Africa, Afghanistan, southern Africa, and the Caribbean, matched by a declining American position in all these areas. The United States never tried so hard and failed so utterly to make and keep friends in the Third World. As if this were not bad enough, in one year, 1979, the United States suffered two other major blows—in Iran and Nicaragua—of large and strategic significance. In each country, the Carter administration not only failed to prevent the undesired outcome, but actively collaborated in the replacement of moderate autocrats friendly to American interests with less friendly autocrats of extremist persuasion."[17]

A few weeks before the 1980 election, the liberal *Washington*

Post characterized the upcoming election as a contest between two men on opposite sides of the ongoing nuclear arms race, including the SALT II treaty negotiations with the Soviets. As usual, the *Post* was on the wrong side of history: as blind as Carter to the unrelenting evil intentions of the Soviets, they described Reagan's proposal to withdraw from SALT II—because it was not directed clearly enough at actual arms reductions—as an "invitation to a renewed arms race."[18] Their preferred approach? Appeasement.

The *Post* also defended a 1977 speech at Notre Dame in which Carter had proclaimed that, in dealing with Third World nations, "we are now free of that inordinate fear of communism which once led us to embrace any dictator who joined us in that fear." According to the *Post,* Carter wasn't arguing that communism was no longer to be feared, but that our fear of it shouldn't keep us from working with "communists or Marxists" in some countries against anticommunist leaders.

Reagan's speech at the 1980 Republican convention presented a very different image. It was a defining moment, not unlike the one George W. Bush faced after 9/11.[19] After lambasting Carter's economic policies, Reagan denounced his rival's "equally sorry" foreign policy: "There may be a sailor at the helm of the ship of state, but the ship has no rudder." He listed the growing number of concerns on the international horizon: the Soviet army training in Cuba, and occupying Afghanistan; the pathetic contrast between American defense and the Soviets' growing military and nuclear might; our European allies' inability to rely on us for leadership; the Iranian hostage crisis. Carter's policies proceeded from weakness rather than strength, Reagan charged; his administration "lives in the world of make-believe."

Reagan argued that his rival's aimless administration was

governing its foreign affairs on a day-to-day basis, with no grasp of the long-term implications of the U.S.-Soviet standoff. "We know only too well that war comes not when the forces of freedom are strong," he reminded his listeners, "but when they are weak. It is then that tyrants are tempted." And while we should work in "good faith" with other nations to reduce international tensions, he said, America has an obligation not to "let those who would destroy freedom dictate the future course of human life on this planet." Reagan said he would interpret his victory in the election to mean that America had renewed its resolve to "preserve world peace and freedom." He pledged to commit America to regaining its position of strength toward fulfilling the goal of world peace.

In November 1980, Ronald Reagan was elected America's fortieth president in a forty-four-state landslide. The new president immediately set to work establishing a new tone of renewed pride in America and optimism for our future. In his inaugural address he made clear that he didn't believe America was on an inevitable path of decline—that we would decline only if we chose to do nothing. Although peace was our highest aspiration, he said, we would never surrender to achieve it. And, he added, our inclination against conflict should not be interpreted as a failure of will, for we would always act to protect our national security. Reagan believed that no weapons could compete with "the will and moral courage" of a free people; terrorists, he warned somewhat prophetically, should take that as a warning.

PSYCHOLOGICAL WARFARE: A TEST OF WILLS

As early as the 1950s, Reagan had recognized that the Cold War was a "battle of ideas" and "a test of wills."[20] He understood what too few people really comprehend today—that the Cold War was a psychological struggle as much as anything else. By the time he reached the White House, though, the problem was clear: the Soviets were playing offense, America defense. We were responding to their moves. As any chess player knows, of course—and Russia was a nation of chess players—an offensive game always beats a defensive one. You cannot merely react, as Carter did. You must confront, and press forward where you can. The accepted status quo of "containment" and "détente" had to end.

It is important to remember, as did Ronald Reagan, that throughout history the world's greatest powers have rarely been conquered from outside without first collapsing from within. After the Vietnam/Watergate era, and with a calamitous economy on its hands, America was facing a similar fate—of losing faith in the future, and losing the will to resist. But Reagan believed in American freedom, and in the strength of the American people. He believed not only that we could turn things around, but that we might also have a unique chance to turn the tables on Soviet aggression.

Speaking to the Heritage Foundation in 1997, Reagan's staunchest ally, former British prime minister Margaret Thatcher, recalled the situation America faced with the Soviets during those tumultuous years.[21]

"The doctrine of 'containment'," she recalled, "was envisaged as a way of conducting a strategic resistance to communist incursion. Similarly, the doctrine of 'détente' also had its honourable

Western advocates." But the problem with détente, she noted, was that it meant one thing to the West and another to the Soviets. "For the West, détente signified—as the word itself literally means— an easing in tension between the two superpowers and two blocs. This made a certain sense at the time, because it reduced the risk of a nuclear confrontation which Western unpreparedness had brought closer because we had allowed our conventional defences to run down."

But Thatcher realized that détente "also threatened to lead us into a fatal trap." To the Soviets, she pointed out, détente looked like a license for further expansion while our guard was down. The communists lulled us into a false sense of security through the rhetoric of peace, while redoubling their military strength and nu- clear arms capabilities. As long as Western leaders were falling for these lies, we were on a headlong path toward defeat. As Thatcher noted, the more savvy Soviet leaders could see the writing on the wall; they knew their economic and social systems were collapsing. But they resolved to prevail by terrifying the West, just as they had terrified their own citizens, to ensure their continued hold on power.

But Reagan didn't intend to let that happen. He took the battle to the Soviets on two main fronts: by attacking their ideas, and by demonstrating that the United States had the will to push back—and hard. He accomplished this last goal by building up the military; by pressing for the mutual elimination of nuclear arsenals; by confronting Soviet aggression in Afghanistan, Nicaragua, and elsewhere around the world; and by promoting innovative new technology to protect the nation from nuclear ballistic missiles.

At this remove, however, it's almost impossible to grasp just how challenging it was for Americans even to *imagine* taking on the

Soviets all at once, in so many areas. After all, the nation was still gripped by what Solzhenitsyn had called a "decline in courage" when it came to disturbing the "Soviet bear." With anticommunism no longer considered intellectually credible, the left was free to disparage anyone who aired a moral objection to communism; in many circles, even to suggest that there was a worldwide communist movement could get you dismissed as a kook.

Only with the arrival of Ronald Reagan was this tide turned.

MILITARY BUILDUP

In his first year in office, Reagan pushed hard for a huge increase in military spending. On entering office, he had been told by Pentagon officials that the Soviets had been outspending the U.S. by 50 percent each year in what Reagan later called "the largest and costliest military buildup in the history of man."[22] Though he knew he was faced with a considerable national debt—and inevitable resistance from liberals in Congress—the president was determined to reverse the tide of the Cold War.

To regain military and nuclear parity with the Soviets, Reagan set out to rebuild the military at a pace unparalleled in our peacetime history. He added army divisions and thousands of fighter aircraft for the air force, and restored the navy to nearly six hundred ships strong. He resurrected B-1 bomber plans Jimmy Carter had canceled, and went forward with the production of Trident submarines and Stealth bombers.[23]

Reagan's campaign to rebuild our defenses couldn't have come at a bleaker moment for the military. Perhaps even more than the American people, the armed forces had been substantially demoralized after Vietnam—a disgraceful period in American history, when liberal opposition to the war had a lasting and damaging effect on our long-term preparedness. (Some might argue that this was also the first time the United States had lost a war, but if by "losing a war" we mean that the American military failed in its mission, I would reject that claim. Simply put, I think the American people—particularly our politicians—failed the military, undermining the war effort by fanning the flames of protest.)

The benefits of Reagan's new emphasis on defense went beyond the arms race alone. As Dinesh D'Souza[24] has pointed out, much of the $1.5 trillion spent on defense in the succeeding years also helped to raise the standard of living of the American military through pay raises, the construction of modern communication centers, and child care and other amenities. At the time, though, the voices of liberal opposition greeted Reagan's spending initiatives as economic suicide. Recalling the economic costs of Vietnam, they argued that America couldn't afford both "guns and butter" at the same time. As usual, the *New York Times* was among the first to pounce, attempting to taint the proposed buildup by suggesting that there was something sordid about the "lucrative arms contracts" the defense industry would garner as a result. The *Times* also warned of "inflationary pressures" that "could rival" those of the Vietnam period.[25]

Both criticisms were unwarranted: There was nothing sinister about defense industry contracts, and the dire predictions about inflation never materialized. Still, the same old complaints have been dusted off by today's left with regard to President Bush's military buildup and action against Iraq. Some things never change.

CONFRONTATION: THE REAGAN DOCTRINE

Reagan was as determined to push back Soviet gains in other nations as he was to rebuild the military—both strategies part of his larger goal of defeating Soviet communism. Reagan was especially focused on reversing communism's gains in the Western Hemisphere. In the early years of his presidency, Reagan joined conservatives in Congress in pressing for free elections in El Salvador and Nicaragua, and their eventual success would have a profound effect on the credibility of the Soviet Union—and on communism in general.

Reagan's support for the Nicaraguan Contras would be among the most controversial aspects of his presidency, but it also revealed the stark contrast between his principles and the appeasement-minded tactics of the left. Liberals refused to accept Reagan's contention that a totalitarian socialist state was by definition evil and oppressive. A typical liberal argument in favor of the Marxist-Leninist Sandinistas—and I heard them all during the 1980s—was that the Nicaraguan people were so poor and exploited that simply having food, a roof over their heads, and a regular job was all they could ask. It was the same liberal mentality that praised Cuban dictator Fidel Castro for his great strides in Cuban literacy, without wondering what these literate communist children were being forced to read, and how few opportunities they would have to exercise their knowledge—assuming we could even believe the propaganda about the literacy itself.

Reagan's principles were clear and simple. Communism was unjust, wherever and whenever it appeared in the world. Its official mandate was always to spread and infect nations around the world—like a parasite that must seek a new host or die. And in Reagan's eyes it must be stopped, by any legitimate means.

To that end, the Reagan Doctrine took on many forms, not all of them military in nature—including quiet work with the pope to support the Solidarity movement in Poland. But where the Soviets were flexing their own military muscle, as in Afghanistan, Reagan was vigilant about aiding the opposition. Support for the mujahideen had been ongoing since the Carter era, but Reagan expanded U.S. covert assistance, supplying Afghan freedom fighters with Stinger missiles to defend against the firepower of the Soviet Hind attack helicopters. The Soviets would withdraw from Afghanistan just as Reagan was leaving office.

NUCLEAR ARMS OFFENSIVE

In the battle of wills against Communism, Reagan knew he'd have to contend with hostile forces other than the Soviets. But there was no more serious opposition to Reagan's plan to confront the Soviets than the Nuclear Freeze movement, which developed to stop the Western democracies in Europe from fortifying their nuclear arsenals to counteract the Soviet missiles aimed at them.

Reagan supported an existing plan to place intermediate-range nuclear missiles in Europe. The Nuclear Freeze movement emerged to oppose the plan, and gained substantial size and momentum as the democracies headed for their election cycles in 1982–1983. The Soviets were hoping to split the NATO alliance over this issue, and before long battle lines were being drawn in what became one of the most dramatic standoffs in Cold War history—a fight for the hearts and minds of the people of the free world.

The allies' plan was simple enough: a "two-track" approach that would introduce these missiles while negotiating with the

Soviets on an overall mutual reduction. But leftists in Europe were already characterizing America as "a bloodthirsty, militaristic nation,"[26] as Reagan later put it, and their propaganda was having an effect. With the fate of Europe hanging in the balance, Europe was faced with a choice: Do we believe the nation that saved us from Nazi totalitarianism, and then rebuilt Europe with the Marshall plan—a free nation whose governing principles rest on a respect for individual rights? Or do we put our faith in Soviet communism, which controls half of Europe against its will, tyrannizes the individual, and impoverishes its people?

A growing chorus of voices on the left—in Europe and at home—sympathized with the forces of tyranny over those of Western freedom. Partially to mollify European leaders who were dealing with vigorous antinuclear protests, in November 1981 Reagan proposed an alternative approach called "zero option," challenging the Soviets to withdraw all intermediate-range nuclear missiles from Europe and Asia; in exchange, the United States and NATO would agree not to deploy cruise and Pershing missiles.[27] Instead of arms *reduction,* for the first time an entire class of weapons would be eliminated.

"It was an offer Moscow could refuse, and promptly did, at least unofficially," reported the *New York Times.*[28] The Soviets had a substantial advantage with these medium-range weapons, and they weren't about to forfeit it, especially when they knew that leftist protests might convince the Western nations to drop the cruise and Pershing deployment anyway. The Soviet leaders were in the catbird seat: They could ignore the opinions of their own oppressed people, while counting on the appeasing left in the West to do their negotiating for them.

What Reagan later called the "Iron Triangle"—the liberal special interest groups, mainstream media, and Democratic politicians—were all working in concert to thwart the progress of liberty.[29] The Soviets played our left like a fiddle, accusing us of propaganda while distributing a seventy-four-page paper to substantiate their claim that parity already existed. Soviet premier Leonid Brezhnev made clear that the zero option would not even be on the table at the upcoming START negotiations in Geneva.

By 1983 there were six key European elections coming up,[30] with conservative leaders facing opposition from parties controlled by the "peace movement." The freeze campaign was reaching near-hysterical levels in Europe, culminating in demonstrations millions of people strong. Bleeding-heart leaders of the movement did their best to ramp up the emotional, irrational appeal of the debate. "We're thinking of our babies," cried one such leader, Dr. Helen Caldicott. "There are no Communist babies; there are no capitalist babies. A baby is a baby is a baby."[31]

Institutional forces across America jumped on the liberal bandwagon, from the American Catholic Bishops to the leftist voices in Hollywood. The ABC television network jumped on the bandwagon by showing *The Day After*—a made-for-TV movie depicting the horrors of a nuclear attack on America's heartland—just days after a new supply of cruise missiles arrived in Britain.

And opposition found plenty of takers among the Washington appeasement lobby. Democratic House speaker Thomas "Tip" O'Neill would call the freeze movement "one of the most remarkable political movements I have ever seen during my years in public service."[32] Senator Ted Kennedy charged that "the arms race rushes ahead toward nuclear confrontation that could well mean the annihilation of the human race."[33] As I've pointed out before, other freeze supporters included Al Gore, Dick Gephardt, Chris Dodd, Joe Biden, Fritz Hollings, Madeleine Albright; yesterday's freeze supporters are still today's Democratic Party. And Brezhnev capitalized on their "useful" opposition, accusing the United States of pushing "the world into the flames of nuclear war."[34]

Thankfully, the nuclear freeze movement would fail. In November 1983 conservatives Margaret Thatcher in Britain and Helmut Kohl in West Germany were reelected, and Europe began missile deployment soon thereafter. The Soviets walked away from the nuclear bargaining table, terrifying the "freezeniks." But Ronald Reagan told his aides they'd be back. And he knew why—largely because of an announcement he had made a few months earlier.

In March 1983 President Reagan delivered a speech that would change the course of history. In it he asked, "What if free people could live secure in the knowledge that their security did not rest upon the threat of instant U.S. retaliation to deter a Soviet attack, that we could intercept and destroy strategic ballistic missiles before they reached our own soil or that of our allies?"[35] It was the opening salvo in Reagan's drive to launch the Strategic Defense Initiative. The idea sent the Kremlin into a frenzy, afraid it would render their entire nuclear arsenal impotent and virtually neutralize their frantic military buildup of the preceding decade, with all its crippling economic costs. As *Policy Review* noted a decade later, this marked the transition from the containment movement to "the promise of propelling the world beyond communism and Cold War."[36]

Many who witnessed these events at close range, including Margaret Thatcher, feel that Reagan's promotion of SDI was the beginning of the end of the Cold War, and of the Soviet Union itself. Once again Reagan had seized the moral high ground, rejecting the long-held logic of Mutually Assured Destruction (MAD) in favor of a new approach that promised to neutralize the nuclear threat.

"The battle over SDI was another important example of Reagan's strategy," the longtime Reagan confidant and counselor Edwin Meese wrote years later. "Reagan thought we should exploit our technological advantages here, not unilaterally restrain them as most liberals were recommending. He favored SDI on its own merits because he wanted to move away from a deterrence strategy that relied on nuclear weapons. He also was convinced that U.S. missile defenses would bankrupt the Soviet Union, and force it to abandon the struggle."[37]

The Strategic Defense Initiative was a brilliant stroke on a number of levels. It was imaginative. It was daring. It was aggressive. And it scared the hell out of the Soviets, who hadn't forgotten that America had fulfilled President Kennedy's promise of a moon landing in less than a decade.

Liberals at home mocked SDI, derisively dubbing it "Star Wars." *Time* magazine and most other elements of the liberal media adopted the moniker, and scoffed at the idea that Reagan's plan was technologically feasible—a tack liberals have taken ever since. To them, SDI was nothing more than "a hostile escalation of the arms race."[38] More than one writer portrayed SDI as the "biggest problem" in the arms race, not a solution.[39] And ABC's Sam Donaldson warned that if we proceeded with SDI, "at some point in the future, and it's not infinity, then we're going to have a clash. And a clash with nuclear weapons means the end of us all."[40]

But Reagan stuck to his hope for a better future, created by a new technology that would deliver the world from its long-held fear of nuclear weapons. And before long Reagan's vision for SDI would bring the Soviets back to the negotiating table.[41]

"One of the president's real strengths is his inner compass," James Baker III once said of Reagan. "He not only believes certain things strongly but has believed them for a long time."[42] Reagan believed in America. He shared the can-do spirit of the greatest generation, and believed unquestioningly in what America could do. If the Soviets had one thing in common with Reagan, it was that they both had more faith in America's ability than the American left did.

The Soviets immediately recognized what a problem SDI posed for their negotiating posture. In November 1985, Reagan and the new Soviet premier, Mikhail Gorbachev, held a three-day summit in Geneva. They announced an agreement in principle to a 50 percent reduction in nuclear warheads,[43] but talks broke off when Reagan refused to bargain away SDI, and left Gorbachev fuming about his intransigence.

But Gorbachev faced even bigger problems at home. The U.S.S.R. was in a state of internal and financial near-collapse; the *Washington Post* had reported that Soviet officials were in despair over their nation's economy, convinced that America was trying to destroy the U.S.S.R. through the arms buildup and Reagan's strategic defense program. The Russians knew they could no longer maintain their military spending at the competitive levels they had managed throughout the 1970s. This communist system, whose leaders had once promised to "bury" American capitalism, suddenly found itself complaining that America was threatening to bring it down.[44]

It was against that backdrop that Gorbachev and Reagan returned to the bargaining table at Reykjavik, Iceland, in 1986.

By this time the Soviets were approaching full panic mode. At the Twenty-Seventh Party Congress of the Soviet Comunist Party in March of that year, party leaders had announced that "without an acceleration of the country's economic and social development, it will be impossible to maintain our position on the international scene."[45]

The Soviets understood that SDI would be the final nail in their coffin, which is why they were so desperate to stop Reagan from proceeding with it—and why they had paid such obsessive attention to it at Geneva. As Gorbachev adviser Aleksandr Yakovlev admitted, "We understood that it was a new stage, a new turn in the armaments race." If Reagan's SDI program remained in place, he said, "we would have to start our own program, which would be tremendously expensive and unnecessary. And this [would bring] further exhaustion of the country."[46]

At Reykjavik, Gorbachev attempted to sandbag Reagan, offering to reduce the Soviet nuclear missile arsenal drastically, only to reveal at the final hour that his offer was conditional on the United States scrapping SDI. Like the American left, however, Gorbachev had greatly underestimated President Reagan. Upon hearing the demand, the president announced, "The meeting is over. Let's go. We're leaving."[47] Many would describe this as Reagan's finest hour.

Predictably, though, Reagan's steadfastness and vision were met with skepticism in the media. Writing in the *Washington Post,* Lou Cannon was among his critics. "As in Afghanistan, Soviet purposes were indeed revealed at Reykjavik. So, too, were the limitations of a presidency [Reagan's] that lacks in negotiating skills and preparation what it tries to make up for with steadfastness of purpose," sneered Cannon. "Rarely do the ringside seats of history provide as many valid clues to reality as they did at Reykjavik. And rarely have journalists in a democracy been so blatantly advised by their government to reject the evidence of their eyes and ears in favor of an official instant revision portraying failure as success. Still, the reality of what we saw will linger long after the fantasies of the White House spin merchants have faded away."[48]

As Margaret Thatcher later observed, however, it was Reagan whose vision carried the day. "Three years later," she recalled in 1997, "when Mr. Gorbachev peacefully allowed Eastern Europe to slide out of Soviet control, Ronald Reagan's earlier decision to stand firm was vindicated" with Gorbachev's decision to release the Eastern bloc satellites from Soviet control. "And, of course, as soon as [the Soviets] embarked upon serious reform the artificial construct of the USSR, sustained by lies and violence for more than half a century, imploded with a whimper."[49]

THE BATTLE OF IDEAS

It's important to understand that Reagan's war of wills with the Soviet Union wasn't just a matter of political gamesmanship. As early as his first press conference, a few days after his inauguration, Reagan shocked the establishment by condemning the Soviet Union in purely ideological terms. He charged the Soviet leadership with having no moral core, with believing they had "the right to commit any crime, to lie, to cheat,"[50] to achieve their goals. This kind of language may seem familiar now, but at the time it was unheard of, and it immediately changed the tone of the Cold War, putting the Soviets on the defensive.

It also agitated the "containment and détente" crowd in America—particularly one of its primary architects, George F. Kennan, who had been America's ambassador to Moscow. In a speech at Dartmouth College, Kennan described Reagan's "rhetoric" in almost hysterical terms. He chided Reagan for conjuring an image of the Soviet Union "so far removed from what any sober scrutiny of external reality would reveal, that it is not only ineffective but dangerous as a guide to political action." He admonished America not to carry an air of "superior virtue" toward the Soviets.[51]

Undaunted by such critiques, Reagan stayed on message. Two months later, at a Washington conference of conservatives, he fired another salvo.

"At our last official function, I told [Margaret Thatcher] that everywhere we look in the world the cult of the state is dying. And I held out hope that it wouldn't be long before those of our adversaries who preach the supremacy of the state were remembered only for their role in a sad, rather bizarre chapter in human history. The largest planned economy in the world has to buy food elsewhere or its people will starve."[52]

Reagan went on to celebrate the "triumph of the human spirit over the mystique of state power," describing how certain "prisoners" of totalitarian states, through their spiritual values, became "rulers of their guards." He decried the "Marxist vision of man without God" as "an empty and a false faith."[53] The presidential bully pulpit hadn't seen such straight talk about communism in decades.

In 1982, as all of Europe listened, Reagan addressed the British Parliament in what he would later call one of his most important speeches.[54] Describing totalitarianism as a "terrible political invention," he said that not one such regime established in the last thirty-plus years had "yet been able to risk free elections." He complimented his British audience by praising their ideas of individual liberty, representative government, and the rule of law under God, as great contributions to mankind.[55]

Even this was met with more naysaying by the liberal media. They took particular exception to Reagan's insistence that

Marxism would be left "on the ash heap of history." The incorrigible *New York Times* called the speech's anticommunist rhetoric a "dark spot" in Reagan's trip.[56] "The stark, democracy-versus-Communism language of Mr. Reagan's speech to members of both houses of Parliament in the Royal Gallery stunned many Britons, including a number of leading Conservatives. 'To be invited to defend ourselves against Communism is one thing,' wrote Andrew Alexander, a columnist for the *Daily Mail*. 'To be asked to join a crusade for the overthrow of Communism is quite another,' contended Mr. Alexander, who derided Reagan's speech as an 'oversimplified view of the world.' "[57]

But the most resounding blow Reagan dealt in the battle of ideas was the now-famous Evil Empire address, which he delivered in 1983 to the National Association of Evangelicals in Orlando, Florida. In that one speech he articulated a set of priorities that still define conservatism today: denouncing the brutality of totalitarianism, embracing the role of God and faith in American life, and admonishing the liberal elite who had excused and coddled Soviet tyranny for decades. Perhaps most important, he stated flatly that his administration was guided by a basic recognition that America's greatness lay in her people, her families, her churches, her neighborhoods and communities—the institutions that promote traditional, not secular, values.[58]

Reagan went on to defend his contention that Soviet leaders were bent on world domination, subordinating everything else to that goal. "During my first press conference as President, in answer to a direct question, I pointed out that, as good Marxist-Leninists, the Soviet leaders have openly and publicly declared that the only morality they recognize is that which will further their cause, which is world revolution," Reagan said. "I think I should point out I was only quoting Lenin, their guiding spirit, who said in 1920 that they repudiate all morality that proceeds from supernatural ideas—that's their name for religion—or ideas that are outside class conceptions. Morality is entirely subordinate to the interests of class war. And everything is moral that is necessary for the annihilation of the old, exploiting social order and for uniting the proletariat."

As Reagan noted, "the refusal of many influential people to accept this elementary fact of Soviet doctrine illustrates an historical reluctance to see totalitarian powers for what they are. We saw this phenomenon in the 1930's. We see it too often today."[59] And, with no apologies, Reagan went on to describe the struggle as spiritual in nature, demonstrating why he was the right man to lead America at that critical moment in history. "While America's military strength is important, let me add here that I've always maintained that the struggle now going on for the world will never be decided by bombs or rockets, by armies or military might. The real crisis we face today is a spiritual one; at root, it is a test of moral will and faith."[60]

Reagan's words had a profound impact around the world. Lech Walesa, the leader of the Solidarity movement in Poland, has said that the speech inspired him and undoubtedly millions of others.[61] Even in the remote Soviet gulag, the Jewish dissident Natan Sharansky remembers fellow prisoners tapping on walls to communicate the American president's words.[62] No longer could the Soviets claim moral equivalence with the United States and other free nations: unlike the left at home and abroad, Reagan had exposed the Soviet emperors' new clothes.

But leftist passions die hard, even in the face of such an inevitable spectacle as the financial and geopolitical collapse of the Soviet Union. After the Evil Empire speech, the *New York Times* columnist Anthony Lewis penned a typical liberal response, denouncing Reagan for invoking the ideas of sin and evil, and "claiming" that "God favors his programs." Lewis was particularly exercised that Reagan had used "sectarian religiosity" to sell his political programs. "Primitive," he called the speech, with sneering elitist arrogance; "that is the only word for it."[63]

Lewis was hardly one of the most extreme voices on the left. And his snide attitude toward conservative ideals still permeates American media culture today. Repelled by the moral absolutism of religion, contemporary pundits still reject basic notions of good and evil as "primitive"—which renders them ill-equipped to understand the real forces at work in the world. Religion, to them, is a mysterious ritual best confined to church premises, or in the privacy of one's own home—and certainly one that should have no bearing on politics or government.

The talk show host and columnist Dennis Prager has aptly described this aspect of the liberal mind-set. "At the heart of liberalism," he has written, "is the naive belief that people are basically good. As a result of this belief, liberals rarely blame people for the evil they do. Instead, they blame economics, parents, capitalism, racism, and anything else that can let the individual off the hook. A second naive liberal belief is that because people are basically good, talking with people who do evil is always better than fighting, let alone killing, them. 'Negotiate with Saddam,' 'Negotiate with the Soviets,' 'War never solves anything,' 'Think peace,' 'Visualize peace'—the liberal mind is filled with naive clichés about how to deal with evil. Indeed, the very use of the word 'evil' greatly disturbs liberals. It shakes up their child-like views of the world, that everybody is at heart a decent person who is either misunderstood or led to do unfortunate things by outside forces."[64]

In the end, the Soviet Union fell not just because Ronald

Reagan was a canny negotiator, but because he had the courage to stand on his convictions. Reagan was not afraid to see the Soviet Union for what it was—in his phrase, *to see what he saw.* Equally important, he recognized the essential goodness of America, including its capacity for strength in the face of danger. It was his understanding of these two sides of the same coin that prepared him to lead America against the Soviet in the war of the wills. And in the end Reagan and his message prevailed: shortly after he left office the Berlin Wall came down, and not long thereafter the Soviet Union collapsed.

And yet somehow, despite the evidence of history, American liberals have clung stubbornly to their warped view of international politics. They have never issued any mea culpas about their misreading of the Cold War—neither during Reagan's presidency nor in the fifteen years since he left office. At the end of the 1980s, when *Time* magazine selected its Man of the Decade, it selected not Ronald Reagan but Mikhail Gorbachev for the honor.[65] To liberals, it wasn't Reagan whose heroic call brought down that wall in Berlin—it was Gorbachev, the former KGB official, who resigned himself to change only after he was backed against a wall by Reagan's principled defiance.

Despite its pretenses to open-mindedness and tolerance, liberalism was on the wrong side of the Cold War—the side of the oppressors, not the side of freedom. In the Soviet Union's last, desperate hours, it found a momentary ally in the Nuclear Freeze movement, and ample support among the American media. But the real lesson for contemporary America can be found in the courageous example of President Reagan, who challenged the will of the aggressor—and prevailed.

FOUR

Iraq I:
War and Appeasement

The crimes of the vanquished find their background and their
explanation, though not, of course, their pardon, in the follies
of the victors.

—WINSTON S. CHURCHILL,
The Gathering Storm[1]

The human capacity for evil is a frightening thing, whether it's
Nazism, communism, or Saddam Hussein's personality cult. But
appeasement of evil in its own way is equally frightening. Winston Churchill called World War II "the unnecessary war"[2]
because he witnessed the appeasement that caused it. He recognized that the largest and most destructive war in history
could have been prevented if Britain's leaders had awakened
sooner from what Churchill called their "pacifist dream."[3] Al-

though the Western allies were eventually able to achieve victory, it came only after tremendous loss. Millions of lives could have been saved had Britain's weak leaders been strong from the start.

Tragically, history repeated itself in the Middle East. The two wars America has fought with Iraq—not to mention Iraq's wars with Iran and Kuwait—all might have been avoided if Iran had remained what it was for over three decades: a powerful American ally. That's right, Iran was *an ally*—right next door to Iraq.

I realize this may come as a surprise for some of my younger readers. For the last quarter century, of course, Iran and Iraq have been vicious anti-American tyrannies. The two nations spent much of the 1980s at war with each other, and as liberal Democrats can't stop reminding us today, during that period America supplied Iraq with arms. What you won't hear from liberals, though, is that what paved the way for Saddam's rise to power, and the Iran-Iraq war itself, was the loss of Iran as an important American partner, due to the disastrous miscalculation of a liberal president.

By the 1970s, Iraq was already a well-armed client state of the Soviet empire. Iran, on the other hand, was our eight hundred-pound gorilla, an oil-rich, pro-Western state with a large military and a modern air force. Along with Turkey, another American ally in the region, it was perfectly positioned as a buffer between the Soviets and the rest of the Middle East. But our alliance with Iran ended abruptly in January 1979, and not because the Shah of Iran rejected us. It ended because America rejected him—despite the Shah's consistent loyalty and friendship to America. It was a loss that could probably have been avoided, but for the weakness and dangerous naïveté of a single American president—one celebrated today, ironically, as a peacemaker.

THE CARTER WAY

Admittedly, as even conservative historians concede,[4] the Shah wasn't a perfect ruler. In his attempts to rush his ancient Persian society into the modern world, he led an often oppressive regime. But our alliance with the Shah was strategically crucial, and his demise, facilitated by the reckless policies of Jimmy Carter, cleared the path for an extremely anti-American, authoritarian regime whose crimes far outstripped anything the Shah had done, and ignited decades of renewed turmoil in the Persian Gulf.

Looking back, I'm continually astonished at just how much damage Jimmy Carter managed to do in his single four-year term. Tolerating the Soviet arms buildup, endorsing Senator Frank Church's gutting of the CIA, giving away the Panama Canal—his administration undermined American interests at every turn. But it's hard to think of a blunder that had longer and more disastrous repercussions than his betrayal of Iran. Consider how an entire sweater can unravel when you pull just one thread, and you'll have an idea of what happened to American interests when Carter broke faith with the Shah. Today, as Iran is on the brink of acquiring the technology to build nuclear weapons, it's sobering to realize how American national interests were compromised by Carter's shortsightedness.

Within the context of the Persian Gulf, the Shah had actually been a moderate influence. But early in his administration, in his sanctimonious way, Jimmy Carter began pressuring the Iranian leader to stop holding military tribunals,[5] and to release certain political prisoners—some of whom were known terrorists—and try them in civilian courts. The ensuing civilian trials became spectacles of anti-Shah propaganda; though he was nowhere near as radical as Islamic fundamentalist leaders generally were, Marxists and Islamists painted the Shah as an extremist ogre.[6] Carter also strongly urged the Shah to permit "free assembly"[7]—though under the circumstances that meant declaring open season for potential insurgents to meet and plot revolution. With Carter threatening to cut off military aid and training unless he did so, the Shah had little choice but to comply.[8] His change in policy was interpreted as a weakness in his authority; supported by Moscow, local dissidents exploited the situation to stir up further unrest.[9]

In the meantime, the streets of Teheran were filled with demonstrations, as angry college crowds and a Shiite clergy who resented the Shah's march to modernity conspired to further undermine his authority. The demonstrations were widely publicized by a sympathetic media, and the treatment scarcely improved when the Shah traveled to the United States to meet with Carter in November 1977. Thousands of club-wielding, mask-wearing Iranian student protestors caused a scene as the Shah arrived at the White House, echoing the anti-Shah riots that persisted in Iran.[10]

With the Shah's government under assault, Carter offered no assistance—indeed, he actually urged the Iranian *not* to defend himself. Not satisfied with his own efforts at appeasement, Carter was fond of lecturing other leaders with his self-righteous philosophy; now he warned the Shah against using force to quell the opposition.

In his autobiography, Ronald Reagan was blunt about Carter's treatment of the Shah. "Our government's decision to stand by piously while he was forced from office led to the establishment of a despotic regime in Teheran that was far more evil and far more tyrannical than the one it replaced. And as I was to learn through personal experience, it left a legacy of problems that would haunt our country for years to come."[11]

"I was told by officials of the Shah's government," Reagan

wrote, "that after rioting began in the streets of Teheran in 1979, the Shah's advisors told him if they were allowed to arrest five hundred people—the most corrupt businessmen and officials in the government—the revolution fires could be extinguished, and they could head off the revolution. But people in the American Embassy told the Shah to do nothing, and he didn't. Until the very end, he kept telling his staff, 'The United States has always been our friend and it won't let me down now.' "[12]

As Reagan went on to note, the Shah trusted us and followed our advice in dealing with the rioters—to his enormous detriment. Then, when he was forced to escape Iran as a result, Carter's administration was reluctant even to offer him sanctuary for personal medical treatment. For a foreign leader who had been a loyal ally of the United States for more than thirty-five years, it was a cruel betrayal. But it was also profoundly contrary to the national interests of the United States—because our virtual abandonment of the pro-Western Shah paved the way for his overthrow.

Former Secretary of State Alexander Haig, a regular on *Hannity & Colmes,* knew the Shah personally. Although Haig admits there were human rights problems under the Shah, he calls him "an essentially benevolent despot who was a good friend of the United States, an implacable enemy of the Left and an obstacle to the religious Right."[13]

And while President Carter didn't seem to care, the Shah's Iran was not only a linchpin to the balance of power in the Middle East—it was also a key to our Cold War abilities. My Fox News colleague, retired Lt. Col. Oliver North, who was active in the service at the time, notes that the Shah's Iran was "one of our key listening posts for monitoring the Soviet space, missile, and nuclear war-fighting programs."[14]

As Jeane Kirkpatrick would observe, "In Iran, the Carter administration's commitment to nonintervention proved stronger than strategic considerations or national pride. What the rest of the world regarded as a stinging American defeat, the U.S. government saw as a matter to be settled by Iranians. 'We personally prefer that the Shah maintain a major role in the government,' the President acknowledged, 'but that is a decision for the Iranian people to make.' "[15] Of course, the Iranian people had little say in the matter—which should have troubled Jimmy Carter, who has always held himself out as a guardian of democracy.

The Shah's overthrow created a leadership vacuum, a gap filled by the Ayatollah Khomeini, one of the most militant anti-American leaders in modern history—largely because Jimmy Carter could not see past his own inclination to moralize over the Shah's transgressions. Carter's ambassador to the United Nations, Andrew Young, symbolized how deeply the Carter administration had misjudged the situation, praising Khomeini as "a religious man."[16]

Apparently Carter expected his neutrality during the Shah's overthrow to win him points with the new regime: the United States rushed to recognize the Ayatollah's government, only to be rebuffed as former supporters of the Shah. From the moment he took control of the country in 1979, the Ayatollah declared that "We will export our revolution to the four corners of the world."[17] His son immediately set about taking over the American embassy—a supposedly spontaneous, student-led event that had actually been in the planning for months.[18] The resulting hostage crisis would haunt Carter until the end of his presidency.[19]

Khomeini's regime, with no experience in government, would rule Iran with an iron fist, wielding its considerable military might against its own vulnerable minorities. The Islamic theocracy

was brutally oppressive to members of the Shah's fallen government and army. But the regime was an equal opportunity oppressor, also murdering sympathizers of competing religious leaders
and the disfavored minorities, executing more than eight thousand
people who were summarily convicted as "enemies of Allah" in
the regime's autocratic courts. In all, some one thousand Kurds and
two hundred Turkomans were murdered, as well as Christians,
Jews, and other minority sects. The regime also destroyed churches
and other sacred properties of the minority religions.[20]

The repercussions of Carter's bungling persisted long after
the man himself left the White House. In 1991, the Ayatollah's son
declared that "After the fall of Marxism, Islam replaced it . . . and
as long as Islam exists, U.S. hostility exists, and as long as U.S. hostility exists, the struggle exists."[21] Iran became what the *Washington
Post* columnist Charles Krauthammer would call the "motherland
of revolution," an "orchestrator of disorder."[22] What was once
America's strongest ally in the Gulf had become the number one
radical Islamic terrorist state in the world.

At the end of the day, it is in trials such as these that we find
the measure of our leaders, especially our presidents. When it
comes to our national security, a president's "war face," as General
Patton put it, is all that matters. No president in this century has
had a less convincing war face than Jimmy Carter. Cloaking himself in the banners of peace and nonviolence, he proved unwilling
to confront evil when circumstances required decisive action—and
thousands of Iranians, among others, paid the price. To those who
suffer under the despotism born of his appeasement, Carter's Nobel Peace Prize must seem a cruel joke.

Of course, the final chapter on the bloody theocracy in
Iran—one third of President Bush's "axis of evil"—has yet to be

written. But in the years after the ayatollah's rise to power, Carter's folly would help to usher in our other great nemesis in the Middle East: Saddam Hussein.

BLAME CONSERVATIVES FIRST

In recent months, liberals have delighted in pointing out that during the 1980s the Reagan administration did business with Saddam Hussein's Iraq. Yet the truth is that during that period the United States was forced to play the hand the Carter administration had dealt. It was Carter who left us without an ally in the newly unstable Persian Gulf, and it is his administration, not Reagan's, that should be blamed for leaving America no choice but to align itself with Iran's neighboring enemy, in order to prevent Iran, a terrorist powerhouse, from winning the war.

Indeed, it was the fall of the Shah in January 1979 that directly precipitated the rise of Saddam Hussein. By June of that year, with a frightening Shiite Muslim uprising occurring right next door, Saddam—a Sunni Muslim by clan, and a killer through and through—seized absolute power in Iraq.[23] In fact, the Iran–Iraq war, as Margaret Thatcher points out in her autobiography, was started by Saddam Hussein because of the perceived weakness of the Ayatollah's Iran, which was not only preoccupied with revolutionary chaos, but had rejected a powerful friend in the United States.[24]

Saddam was further tempted to invade Iran because its high-ranking military officers had been displaced in the revolution and its formerly powerful military was disorganized and weakened. But he underestimated Iran's resilience, and its resolve. What he hoped would be an immediate rout was the beginning of an eight-year military marathon between the two countries, resulting in millions of deaths for both and very little territory exchanging hands. In the process, America joined other Western nations in providing aid to Iraq. Though aware of Saddam's brutality,[25] the Reagan administration was anxious to bring stability to the region, and chose what it perceived to be the lesser of two evil regimes.

Carter's betrayal of the Shah, which led to the enabling of his enemies, demonstrates that the dangers of appeasement aren't something consigned to the history books. They're with us in the modern age. And the pattern is always the same: instead of confronting evil at critical junctures, appeasers decline, mostly with the false hope that things aren't as bad as they seem, that problems will solve themselves. It's certainly desirable to avoid war when you can, but not at the price of slavery, oppression, or simply deferring more disastrous consequences until a later day.

As Carter's example confirms, appeasement doesn't prevent wars; it only leads to more dangerous wars, more death and destruction. The same is true today: if President Clinton had been aggressive with al Qaeda in 1993 when it first attacked the World Trade Center, those thousands of people killed on 9/11 might still be with their families today.

And, as we've noted, the appeasers usually fail to recognize the error of their judgments. Not only are they loath to apologize or answer for their miscalculations, they continue to preach from the same discredited script. In September 2002, as war with Saddam seemed increasingly likely and the president of the United States could have used the endorsement of former presidents—or at least silence from those who held differing opinions—Jimmy Carter went public with his criticism. Writing in the *Washington Post,* once again Carter tried to warn America away from war. The title of the piece, "The Troubling New Face of America," says it all; true to form, Carter pegged *America,* not Saddam Hussein, as the problem.[26]

"Fundamental changes are taking place in the historical policies of the United States with regard to human rights, our role in the community of nations and the Middle East peace process," Carter wrote, "largely without definitive debates (except, at times, within the administration)." In such a crisis, most foreign-policy observers might be expected to focus on the threats facing America from abroad—but Carter seemed more concerned with the details of the decision-making process in the White House. "Some new approaches have understandably evolved from quick and well-advised reactions by President Bush to the tragedy of Sept. 11, but others seem to be developing from a core group of conservatives who are trying to realize long-pent-up ambitions under the cover of the proclaimed war against terrorism.

"We have thrown down counterproductive gauntlets to the rest of the world," Carter continued, "disavowing U.S. commitments to laboriously negotiated international accords. Peremptory rejections of nuclear arms agreements, the biological weapons convention, environmental protection, anti-torture proposals, and punishment of war criminals have sometimes been combined with economic threats against those who might disagree with us. These unilateral acts and assertions increasingly isolate the United States from the very nations needed to join in combating terrorism."

Carter was adopting what was quickly becoming a familiar party line: that conservatives are unilateralist warmongers who want to export democracy forcibly, through military action. Other liberals have picked up on these themes, accusing Bush and his "neoconservative" advisers and supporters of trying to build an American empire under the guise of fighting the War on Terror.

But Carter and his fellow travelers, once again, are sadly mistaken. In effect, they were arguing for withholding action against Saddam, despite the fact that he had repeatedly defied United Nations resolutions. Would they have preferred to wait until Saddam was ready to threaten us with weapons of mass destruction—or had procured them for the terrorists he supported and harbored? History suggests they would have, with disastrous results.

Published a year after the 9/11 attack, Carter's letter reveals that he's still too preoccupied with America's perceived moral failures to go after the *real* moral transgressions of our enemies. As Carter saw it, America's conservative leadership was unruly, ungrateful, and uncooperative with the world order: "Belligerent and divisive voices now seem to be dominant in Washington, but they do not yet reflect final decisions of the president, Congress or the courts. It is crucial that the historical and well-founded American commitments prevail: to peace, justice, human rights, the environment and international cooperation."

It's amazing to watch Carter cling to the mantle of moral authority, more than two decades after his own moral leadership scuttled American interests around the world. But it's hardly surprising: Appeasers always claim the moral high ground in peddling their do-nothing response to evil. And they save their sharpest criticism for those who have the courage and foresight to confront it, as Ronald Reagan found out during the 1980 campaign. As he comments in his memoirs, "Because I opposed Senate ratification of the SALT II treaty in the belief it had serious weaknesses that would leave the Soviets with a dangerous preponderance of nuclear weapons—I wanted true arms *reduction*—Carter went around the country suggesting I was a warmonger who, if elected, would destroy the world."[27]

Today's liberal elites are carrying on Jimmy Carter's ignoble tradition, as the debate over Iraq has proven.

BLAME AMERICA FIRST

Conservatives have seen through thinking like Carter's for years. Among the first to put a name to it was Jeane Kirkpatrick, in a brave and perceptive speech in 1984. Indeed, it is impossible to understand the Iraq war, which we'll discuss in more detail in the next chapter, without understanding what Ambassador Kirkpatrick referred to as the "blame America first" crowd, which is still with us today.

Kirkpatrick's insight helps explain how liberals manage to overlook the evils of Saddam Hussein's regime while preoccupied by the "evil" of George W. Bush. It speaks to how Democratic presidential candidate John Kerry could co-opt the phrase "regime change" to argue that President Bush should be defeated in the next election. And the self-hatred it represents is utterly at odds with the best traditions of America.

By August 1984, when Kirkpatrick made her speech, the Democrats had already held their convention in San Francisco, and their chosen presidential candidate, Walter Mondale, was running hard at Ronald Reagan. "As each day of the general campaign passed," said Reagan in his memoirs, "I found myself getting angrier at Mondale, whose basic theme was that I was a liar."[28] (Sound familiar?)

When Kirkpatrick delivered her historic speech at the Republican National Convention in Dallas, the Cold War was still in high gear. The Soviets had not yet come back to the bargaining table with the Reagan administration, which was standing firm in its po-

sitions on Strategic Defense and missile deployment in Europe.
Reagan was supporting efforts to defeat communism in countries
like Nicaragua and Afghanistan. A concrete wall would continue to
divide East and West Berlin for another five years. But what drove
liberals and the Soviet Union crazy was that Reagan—derided by
them as the "cowboy" from California—was winning the battle.

At the time, Kirkpatrick was still a traditional Democrat; she
would not change parties until the following year, five years after
joining Reagan's campaign. But even she perceived that modern
Democrats were very different from former Democratic presidents
like Harry Truman and John Kennedy. This new breed of Democrat gravely undervalued American sovereignty and security in the
fight against communism, much preferring to focus exclusively on
domestic politics. Kirkpatrick accused them of focusing too little
on world affairs, underestimating or simply ignoring dangers
brewing abroad.

> The United States cannot . . . be indifferent to the subversion
> of others' independence or to the development of new
> weapons by our adversaries or of new vulnerabilities by our
> friends. The last Democratic administration did not seem to
> notice much, or care much or do much about these mat-
> ters. . . . The Carter administration's motives were good, but
> their policies were inadequate, uninformed and mistaken.
>
> They made things worse, not better. Those who had
> least, suffered most. Poor countries grew poorer. Rich coun-
> tries grew poorer, too. The United States grew weaker.
> Meanwhile, the Soviet Union grew stronger. The Carter ad-
> ministration's unilateral "restraint" in developing and deploy-
> ing weapon systems was accompanied by an unprecedented

Soviet buildup, military and political. The Soviets, working on the margins and through the loopholes of SALT I, developed missiles of stunning speed and accuracy and targeted the cities of our friends in Europe.[29]

Though I lived through that era, it still amazes me that at a time when America's conflict with evil was so clear, so many Americans sought a kind of neutrality—as if it wasn't their fight, as if evil were only a matter of opinion. The media elite was especially guilty of this, abusing their role as "neutral observers" to subtly undercut our great struggle with a system that, given the opportunity, would have enslaved them all.

America's struggle with Saddam Hussein, which gave rise to two wars in twelve years, was marked by the same cowardly behavior among Democrats and the media alike. Liberals, including those at the United Nations, knew well the crimes of this evil man, knew what his regime represented, knew his potential danger to the civilized world—and still hesitated to act.

HUSSEIN: THE RISE OF EVIL

Even as the debate rages on about Saddam Hussein, you get the feeling that some people just don't get it. You see them on *Hannity & Colmes* all the time. They'll call Saddam a "bad guy," then without skipping a beat explain that we should have waited. They know he developed and used chemical weapons against the Iranian army—and against his own people, the Kurds in northern Iraq. But they're more interested in whether the president overstated the case against Saddam in his State of the Union address. What are these people thinking, you ask? We shall see.

The irony is that it won't be long before liberals claim that Hussein's fall was inevitable, just as they now seek to justify their wrongheadedness during the Cold War. But the Soviet Union didn't fall on its own, and neither would Saddam. The Hussein dynasty could have lasted into the foreseeable future. Saddam had two sons who helped him control the levers of terror—trained killers like their father, who would have carried on his reign of terror. Moreover, if Iraq had succeeded in purchasing just one crude nuclear device, Saddam would have wielded enormous power in the Middle East. He would also have posed an even greater threat to America, possessing both the ability and the will to help terrorists unleash such a weapon against our country. No one would have dared invade Iraq under those circumstances—and certainly no revolution could have succeeded from within.

Considering the United Nations' reluctance to deal with Saddam—and considering the many individual nations that were all too happy to do business with him—he could well have lasted long enough to develop his own substantial nuclear weapons program. Remember, Iraq is positioned right next to three of the world's richest oil states: once Saddam managed to obtain a nuclear device, how could he have been stopped from dominating Kuwait, Iran, Saudi Arabia? What could we have done if he had seized access to some 60 percent of the world's oil supply? Saddam and his sons would have had plenty of time to use their oil leverage to change hearts and minds in the U.N.—and among his own neighboring countries, which might no longer look to the United States to protect them. Saddam's track record tells us that such a scenario is by no means far-fetched.

The 1 million men who died in the Iran-Iraq war were only part of the larger portrait of death revealed when Iraq fell in 2003.

Estimates range from hundreds of thousands to a million men, women, and children who were executed and buried in mass graves during Hussein's reign of terror.[30] The unearthing of bodies will no doubt continue for years.

How did such an evil being come to power? Saddam was the head of Iraq's secret police before he rose to "presidential" power in a coup in 1979. In *The Republic of Fear,* his seminal book on Hussein's Iraq, Samir al-Khalil (a pseudonym) describes the ugly reality of Saddam's push for absolute power in Iraq: according to al-Khalil, he executed prominent officials of the al Bakr regime, along with some of their families, after seizing power from them. It is estimated that he ordered the murder of some five hundred leaders of the Baathist Party.[31] For the quarter century that followed, the story of Iraq would be one of rape, torture, death, and destruction, at the hands of a ruthless former hitman.

THE RAPE OF KUWAIT

In 1990 Saddam invaded the tiny nation of Kuwait, the first step in his dream of building a new Babylonian empire. (Not a bad start, considering the oil bonanza he would create by combining Kuwait's huge oil reserves with Iraq's.) But what our enemies haven't seemed to figure out is that aggressive action against American interests is more dangerous when the American president is a Republican than during a Democratic administration. (Doubt it? Consider: Whether faced with the seizing of an American embassy hostage, as Jimmy Carter was in 1979, or the bombing of the World Trade Center, as Bill Clinton was in 1993, Democratic presidents are like weak-willed prosecutors, happy to bargain every capital offense down to a misdemeanor.)

Thankfully, the Democrats weren't in power when Saddam began his mischief in Kuwait. Ronald Reagan had passed the torch to George H. W. Bush, who understood that a righteous nation like the United States had the right to wage war to protect our national security interests, to stop aggression, and to halt genocide.

In the first Gulf War, the United States used its superior military strength to stop an aggressor and protect a victim, successfully driving Saddam's forces out of Kuwait in a matter of weeks. Had the United States been more aggressive, it could have followed them straight to Baghdad, occupying Iraq with little resistance. But the first President Bush declined the opportunity, having achieved his mission of defending Kuwait from Iraq.

In liberating Kuwait, America was impelled by humanitarian motives. One of America's great columnists, Michael Kelly—who was later killed on assignment during the second Iraq war—had been to Kuwait in 1991. He never forgot what he learned about Kuwaiti suffering during the Iraqi occupation. As he reported:

> About 400 Kuwaiti civilians had been killed during Iraq's seven-month occupation, and many more had been brutalized in one way or another—ritualistically humiliated (forced to urinate on the Kuwaiti flag or on a photograph of the Kuwaiti emir, for instance), robbed, beaten, raped, tortured. Some of the subjugation, rape and torture had been professional: the work of Iraq's terrible special security units and aimed at specific individuals annoying to the regime. But more had been the work of enthusiastic amateurs—poor-boy soldiers let loose in a rich land suddenly realizing that if they wanted to make some well-fed banker watch his wife and

daughters get raped, why, they could just go ahead and do it. Shattered people were everywhere. . . .

Tyranny truly is a horror: an immense, endlessly bloody, endlessly painful, endlessly varied, endless crime against not humanity in the abstract but a lot of humans in the flesh. It is, as Orwell wrote, a jackboot forever stomping on a human face.[32]

It's one of the great ironies of modern politics that the Democratic Party has somehow managed to preserve their image as the party of compassion and human rights, when time after time they have refused to rise to the defense of victims of brutal despotism. During the seige of Kuwait, the exact numbers of rapes and murders were in dispute. Was it thousands? Hundreds? Scores? Hussein wouldn't allow anyone into Kuwait to verify the horror stories told by witnesses who escaped. Kuwaitis were suspected of "exaggeration."[33] Despite the urgency of the situation, liberals were frozen in indecision. A nation that had been a friend to the United States was being devoured right before our eyes. And yet because Kuwait was also a nation of substantial strategic value, many American liberals decided that Bush must have had ulterior motives in defending Kuwait. Soon their appreciation of the situation was lost in cries of "No Blood for Oil."

The debate that followed found congressional Democrats urging the president to wait for sanctions to take effect. By now, of course, it's a familiar story: Liberals always prefer to dither and debate, while the plundering proceeds. "History shows that even brutal dictators have been toppled and defeated by sanctions,"[34] Majority Leader Dick Gephardt complained. Who knows how long that could have taken? How many innocent Kuwaitis would have died before sanctions could even cause a dent in Saddam's oil-rich, ruthless regime?

Nevertheless, Gephardt had the support of almost 70 percent of the House Democrats. In a stunningly clueless, classic liberal moment, a young Nancy Pelosi stood up to support Gephardt, but seemed more concerned about potential ecological damage that could result if America went to war with Iraq. "I hope the point will be made," said Pelosi, "that we take very seriously the environmental consequences of our actions."[35]

Environmental consequences? What about the human disaster already happening before the eyes of the world? Can you imagine if a massive army had overrun America from New York to San Francisco, looting everything in sight, murdering innocent civilians begging for mercy, raping wives in front of their dying husbands? How many of us would spend a moment worrying that launching a counterattack might have a negative effect on the ecosystem of the California coastline? I've often wondered if any Kuwaitis heard Ms. Pelosi's speech.

Their diplomatic corps certainly did. "My country is being savaged and destroyed, our women subjected to mass acts of rape, our men and even children are being murdered while these armchair analysts advocate waiting a year or up to 18 months for sanctions to force him out," said Kuwait's ambassador to the United Nations. "Those who favor letting us suffer might at the very least consider calling upon Iraq to permit a human rights observer force to enter Kuwait—which they have refused to do—to protect our people there."[36]

But the Democrats held on to their sanctions for dear life. "By voting for this resolution you are voting for a declaration of war. The American people don't want war," insisted Representative John Lewis, Democrat of Georgia. "What is wrong with being patient? Patience is not appeasement—patience is not a dirty and nasty concept."[37]

"The sanctions against Iraq are working," declared a House Democrat leader, David Bonior, "and now is too soon to declare this policy a failure and to rush to war."[38]

An amazing 179 House Democrats voted to wait, to "let the sanctions work." It was even worse in the Senate, where 82 percent of the Democratic senators wanted to wait, including Ted Kennedy. "It is sad," Kennedy said, "that the United States with all our ideals and all our heritage and all our history has now become the country driving the engine of war, while other nations offer the olive branch of peace."[39]

America driving the engine of war? Talk about blaming America first: Saddam Hussein invades an innocent neighboring country, and somehow *we're* in the wrong. *Excuse me for letting my face get in the way of your boot, Mr. Hussein.*

During the House debate on the war, another Kennedy was reminded of the nobler side of his family tradition. After Rep. Joseph Kennedy of Massachusetts took the floor to deride the Bush administration's "misguided machismo mentality," he was rebuffed by Republican congressman Gerald Solomon, who reminded him of President Kennedy's words during the Cuban Missile Crisis: "My fellow citizens, let no one doubt that this is a difficult and dangerous effort on which we have set out. No one can have foreseen precisely what course it will take, but the greatest danger of all would be to do nothing! The 1930s taught us a clear lesson. Aggressive conduct, if allowed to go unchecked and unchallenged, ultimately leads to war."[40]

In the famous words of his inaugural address, President

Kennedy had declared: "Let every nation know, whether it wishes us well or ill, that we shall pay any price, bear any burden, meet any hardship, support any friend, oppose any foe to assure the survival and the success of liberty." Words for the ages—yet they were completely lost not only on the Kennedys of the 1990s, but on an entire generation of liberal leading lights.

In fact, there are those who actually hold such a perverse view of America that they consider the United States the enemy of peace, the perpetrator of inhumanity. Among these is Ramsey Clark, attorney general of the United States under President Lyndon Johnson. In the early 1990s Clark issued a "report" accusing the United States of war crimes—against Iraq!

According to Clark, the United States:

- Baited Iraq into provoking U.S. military action, paving the way for permanent U.S. military domination of the Gulf;

- Intentionally bombed and destroyed Iraqi civilians;

- Waged war on the environment;

- Forcibly secured control of Iraq's oil resources.

President Bush himself, Clark charged, was personally guilty of war crimes including:

- Obstructing justice and corrupting United Nations functions as a means of securing power to commit crimes against peace and war crimes;

- Intentionally depriving the Iraqi people of essential medicines, potable water, food, and other necessities.[41]

Can you believe such nonsense coming from a former cabinet-level official of the U.S. government? Just as we've seen, appeasers always reserve their most heated rhetoric for their own citizens. Why no such rhetoric against the tyrant who started the whole thing? For the simple reason that the tyrant is the one who must be appeased. In the topsy-turvy world of the appeaser, it's the Churchills, the Reagans, the Bushes who become the dangerous warmongers. When it comes to the Hitlers, the Brezhnevs, the Saddams, pussyfooting is the order of the day.

After U.S. troops entered the Persian Gulf to take on Iraq, the Johnny-come-lately Democrats—most of them, anyway—joined House and Senate Republicans in a nonbinding resolution commending President Bush and supporting the troops. But some Democrats had to be dragged kicking and screaming. Among the reluctant was Congressman Ron Dellums, who said he supported the troops, but opposed the military action and resented both issues being conjoined in one resolution. "I am particularly distressed that we have been presented with an unamendable measure which is designed intentionally to blur the distinction between these two positions," said Dellums.

Nancy Pelosi agreed. "There should be no doubt," she said, "that although we have strong disagreement with the policy here, that there is no disagreement for our support and prayers for the troops and their families."[42]

Then as now, of course, the Democrats were desperate to have it both ways, distancing themselves from the Gulf War but still eager to be seen as "supporting the troops." But when it comes to supporting the military, the Democrats just don't have much credibility; since the disgraceful days of Vietnam, they have rarely missed an opportunity to cut funding, protest military action, and air their lack of faith in the American military's ability to get the job done. Even Al Gore's campaign manager Donna Brazile seems to recognize this. She wrote a column in the *Wall Street Journal* urging her liberal compadres to remember the late Henry "Scoop" Jackson, a Senate Democrat and true freedom fighter who believed in a well-funded military. "If voters continue to see us as feckless and effete," Brazile warned, "they will not listen to our message next year and they will re-elect Mr. Bush."[43]

But antimilitary Democrats clearly controlled (and still control) the party. Among the Democrats who voted against the Kuwait resolution in 1991, several currently hold top leadership positions in the Senate. Joseph Biden of Delaware is the ranking member on the Foreign Relations Committee, Carl Levin of Michigan the ranking member on the Armed Services Committee. South Dakota's Tom Daschle, of course, is the Democratic leader, Vermont's Patrick Leahy the ranking member on the Judiciary Committee, West Virginia's Robert Byrd the ranking member on the Appropriations Committee, and West Virginia's Jay Rockefeller the ranking member of the Senate Select Committee on Intelligence.

Several current Democratic senators were in the House at the time of the 1991 vote, where they voted against the resolution: Barbara Boxer of California, Richard Durbin of Illinois, Charles Schumer of New York, Byron Dorgan of North Dakota, Ron Wyden of Oregon, and Tim Johnson of South Dakota. Boxer, one of the most radical leftists in Congress, argued at the time:

"There's a huge price if we choose this route, even in the best of circumstances. The price is in body bags, in babies killed, in an uncertain, unstable Middle East even after the crisis. In a decade that will be lost as we once again have put our resources into war and weapons and rob our people of what they need in this country. I had a community meeting in my district, I had two in one day. A thousand people came out. I've never seen anything like it. We voted on how they would vote on a resolution to go to war and 95 percent voted no. That's my district in California."[44]

In the Senate, Ted Kennedy raised similar alarms. "Most military experts tell us that a war with Iraq would not be quick and decisive, as President Bush suggests," he said during the Senate debate. "It'll be brutal, and costly. It'll take weeks, even months, and will quickly turn from an air war to a ground war, with thousands, perhaps even tens of thousands, of American casualties. . . . we're talking about the likelihood of at least 3,000 American casualties a week, with 700 dead, for as long as the war goes on."[45]

Boxer and Kennedy were wrong, of course. The ground war against the invading Iraqi army lasted only 100 hours. The total number of American soldiers lost in combat was limited to 148.[46] Kuwait was freed; by the spring of 1991 Michael Kelly was able to walk the streets of Kuwait unmolested and report to America on the stark contrast between tyranny and liberty.

And yet liberals remained unchastened by this latest victory they had refused to support. As soon as the dust had cleared in Kuwait, the Democratic Party changed the channel to "It's the economy, stupid," distracting America's attention from their determined and reckless appeasement. And it wouldn't be the last time.

FIVE

Axis Iraq:
The New Appeasement

There comes a time when soft power or talking with evil will not work—where, unfortunately, hard power is the only thing that works. . . . There are still leaders around who will say you do not have the will to prevail over my evil, and I think we are facing one of those times now.

—COLIN POWELL,
Washington Post, *January 27, 2003*

The more I experience being a parent, the more I understand why little children like traditional fairy tales. Even as an adult, I love them. They may be "stories," but they deal with the basic truths of life—things like courage and fear, hope and despair, loyalty and betrayal. We adults aren't always so in touch with these truths; we're more likely to rationalize them away. We can turn a lie into "opinion," or cowardice into "reasonable caution," or betrayal into "the only sensible thing to do given the circumstances." Our vision seems to have been blurred by the pervasive cloudiness of morality in our culture. But sometimes it's important that we step back, stop overcomplicating things, and see clearly the truth in the experiences we share. As hard as it is for liberals to grasp, there *are* black-and-white issues in this world, not just shades of gray.

Children are too innocent—and too wise—not to size up any new situation they confront with complete honesty and candor. When my son is afraid of the dark, for example, or a thunderstorm, that's a meaningful emotion: there may be no immediate danger, but his basic impulse is right—the dark *can* hide things, lightning *can* strike, so we're right to anticipate danger and take extra care. Moreover, it's only through experiencing fear that we can learn to overcome it. In the meantime, until he's old enough to handle it himself, he knows he can always call in the "big guns," mommy and daddy, to tuck him in and read him adventure stories full of inspiring ideals—courage, heroism, victory snatched from the jaws of defeat.

Of course, great moments in history, like fairy tales, also have a way of distilling things down to their essence. While we're living these moments, we adults can't always appreciate them. It takes time, and sometimes a different perspective, to see them clearly. The story of Sir Winston Churchill, for example, comes into relief only in retrospect: throughout the 1930s he was mocked by his own people for his dire warnings about Hitler, but ultimately it was Churchill, not his detractors, who proved to have sized up the situation correctly. When President Reagan cajoled Mikhail Gorbachev to "tear down this wall," his detractors were horrified not just at his directness, but for being "unrealistic." Until the wall came down, few onlookers ever really recognized that the Iron Curtain could come crashing down.

In the same way, President Bush's grasp of his moment in history transcends the trivial politics of the moment. It seems to me that the story of George W. Bush, the War on Terror, and the end of brutal tyrannies in places like Afghanistan and Iraq is a new chapter in American history—one whose true importance may not even be fully apparent for years or even decades.

As we've seen, though, while Churchill, Reagan, and Bush shared a knack for perceiving and seizing pivotal moments in history, their respective liberal counterparts were wholly blind to those moments. The sad truth is, such obliviousness has characterized the American left for years—from Carter's worthless dithering over Russia and Iran to Clinton's arm's-length approach to terrorism. In every case they have been ardent appeasers, and in every case they've been wrong.

It's not just that liberals fail to see history in the making; they also ignore the lessons of history—even those that should be fresh in our minds. Why? Because their approach toward world events is based on ideology, not on logic—on politics, stalling, and hairsplitting, not on moral judgment.

No matter how much evidence we now have that the Soviet communists were murderous thugs, that the gulag was a place of horrific cruelty, that Soviet spies were actively infiltrating American institutions during the Cold War, liberals continue to romanticize communism—insisting that the communist state was an honorable dream, if only it could have been made to work as Marx intended. No matter how much Saddam Hussein brutalized and murdered his own people, how many times he lied about his WMD programs, how many times he violated his Gulf War treaties and U.N. resolutions, liberals continued to treat him as an honest negotiator—insisting that he could be brought to heel if only he could be given more time.

No matter how often the United Nations airs its intrinsic antagonism and hostility toward the United States, liberals defend each new self-important pronouncement it makes, promoting it as the panacea for every international conflict. Like Rodney King in Los Angeles, they make their cry *Can't we all just get along?* But when it comes to terrorist thugs like Saddam or Osama, of course, "getting along" can mean only one thing: giving up, ceding power.

Sure, sometimes it seems that liberals are beginning to see the light—that they're finally getting it. After the 9/11 attacks they were right there with us, apparently seeing evil as clearly as we did. But in no time they were back to their old ways, wringing their hands over potential quagmires in Afghanistan, and urging patience in Iraq.

But even as America went into the 2002 midterm elections, the Democrats realized that they were facing a real dilemma. Since 9/11, President Bush had earned the American people's trust. He had risen to extraordinary heights as commander in chief in the War on Terror. To this day, despite the continuing challenges in Iraq, he continues to hold the public's confidence. He has earned a reputation as a masterful crisis president, and a defender of our liberties and national security.

For the Democrats, though, every problem is a political problem. And throughout the last two years—through a midterm election dominated by Bush and the Republican Party—they have had to face a difficult truth. If you asked a Democrat what his concerns were, he might say "*My party's got an image problem. We can't shake the idea that we're soft on defense.*" Well, it's not like they're wrong about that—just think back to Michael Dukakis in that tank during the 1988 presidential race. In truth, though, the Democrats' problem goes far deeper than their image—down to the reality of who they are, and how they would run the country. Their miserable track record speaks for itself.

So as the race for 2004 began shaping up, the Democrats were faced with a dilemma: How could they possibly convince the American people that they're worthy of our trust on national security, when that issue is sure to be more important than any other in the 2004 elections? They know they can't capture voters' trust by dismissing the threats to our national security. Nothing could be more politically suicidal. Yet they know they can't afford to alienate their leftist base—even if they wanted to, which is hard to imagine. What to do?

Well, Democrats are nothing if not resourceful. And it didn't take long for them to break out a favorite old strategy to deal with their image problem. They apparently view it as their best chance to shed their image of being soft on defense—without actually having to grow a backbone. They call it "multilateralism." I call it the new appeasement.

As we'll see, the Democrats' big idea is to cultivate an image of sophistication in foreign policy, by advocating that we work more closely with other nations to combat international terrorism. If only we would work through the United Nations, they claim, we could have the cooperation of the entire world, and everything would work out fine. Never mind that America has its *own* national security to worry about. Never mind that nations like France and Germany were courted tirelessly by the Bush administration, even when their demands flew in the face of America's interests. Never mind that our supposedly "unilateral" action in Iraq was actually mounted by a coalition of willing nations.

The Democrats hope to get to the White House by calling George Bush a "unilateralist." Well, I've got two problems with that idea. First of all, the fact that a few other recalcitrant nations won't agree to join your cause doesn't make you a unilateralist—even if those nations are longtime allies. But here's the much more important point: *Unilateralism is no crime,* if it means acting in our own national interest regardless of the stance of other nations. It is our right—no, it is our *duty*—to protect our own interests, regardless of whether other nations are willing to help us. We have never agreed to mortgage away our military to the U.N., or to delegate our national security interests to other nations or international bodies. And no matter what the Democrats might prefer, we *must* never do so—not if America is to remain an independent nation.

But today's Democrats aren't concerned about big-picture ideas like *national security* or *independence.* The only thing that's important to them is finding a way to use their new buzzword—*multilateralism*—to convince America that it can play the foreign affairs game, too. To them, it looks like the perfect way to have their cake and eat it, too: they get to waffle and stall when it comes to national defense, while spinning their cowardice as a "failure to achieve international consensus."

You can dress it up in whatever colorful international garb you want, but appeasement's still appeasement, any way you cut it. The Democrats are fond of complaining about unilateralism whenever it suits their agenda—at least since the Reagan eighties, when a Libyan dictator was snapping at America's heels. Of course, you don't often hear about it when there's a Democrat in the White House; Bill Clinton's "coalition" to wag the dog against

Iraq didn't even extend across Washington to Congress, but his party barely lifted a finger to stop him. No, the Democrats are fair-weather multilateralists—happy to act unilaterally when it suits their purposes, happy to scold Republicans for doing the same when they're trying to score some political points.

They just never learn, do they?

FORESHADOWINGS OF THE NEW APPEASEMENT

You don't hear much about it today, but one of the most telling early terrorist challenges America has faced in the postwar era began back in the late 1970s, when Libya's Muammar Qaddafi began a series of antagonistic incursions into international waters. After Reagan's Republican administration took over the White House in 1980, it moved swiftly and decisively to curb the activity. But the Democrats cried unilaterism—and the voice who was leading the attack was none other than Senator John Kerry, the 2004 presidential candidate and still one of the Senate's most vocal "multilateralists."

Kerry and his party were wrong twenty years ago. They're just as wrong today. And they're wrong for all the same reasons.

Since the 1970s, Qaddafi had been "the most active and visible promoter of state-sponsored terrorism," according to former Attorney General Edwin Meese.

"In the late 1970s, in his role as would-be challenger to the United States, Qaddafi decided to extend the coastal claims of Libya to the waters where [American] maneuvers were conducted. The entire Gulf of Sidra, extending up to one hundred miles from Tripoli and Benghazi, was proclaimed by Qaddafi to be a Libyan lake, off limits to our forces. The Carter government, unfortunately, had meekly rescheduled our maneuvers to stay outside the prohibited area."[1] True to form, Carter failed to confront Qaddafi over the issue even after a siege on the American embassy in Tripoli in 1979.[2]

Within months after taking office, though, Ronald Reagan took a stand. He made it clear that American maneuvers would proceed as they always had before Carter, following the universal guidelines for international waters—no less, no more. Anticipating trouble, the Joint Chiefs of Staff asked President Reagan for clear rules of engagement: What should American pilots do if attacked? Did Reagan's standing orders allow for "hot pursuit"? Reagan's answer? "All the way into the hangar."[3]

The military didn't have to wait long to put Reagan's orders into action. In mid-August 1981, Qaddafi used the American maneuvers as an opportunity to attack. Two Libyan fighters fired on us over the Gulf of Sidra, but were quickly shot down by a pair of American Navy F-14s.[4] It was a significant moment: Successful action creates confidence, and this president had sent a clear signal that he was not afraid to act.

In March 1986, armed with new weapons systems and eager to push back, Qaddafi declared the Gulf of Sidra a "zone of death" for American naval forces. The Libyans fired on American airmen, and once again Qaddafi's forces took a beating. But this time there was an immediate follow-up—using terrorist tactics. On April 5, a Berlin disco popular with American servicemen was bombed, killing one American sergeant and wounding fifty G.I.s. Civilians were also affected, including one Turkish woman who was killed.[5] Well over a hundred others were wounded. After intelligence confirmed that the attack was tied to Qaddafi, President Reagan responded immediately.

This time the "crackpot in Tripoli," as Reagan later called him in his memoirs, had gone too far. "I felt we must show Qaddafi," wrote Reagan, "that there was a price he would have to pay for that kind of behavior, that we wouldn't let him get away with it."[6] Reagan resolved to send U.S. F-111s from Britain over France, and across the Mediterranean, to deliver a surprise attack on Qaddafi's military headquarters and barracks in Tripoli.

But can you guess what happened? Our old friends the French refused to let our planes pass through their airspace, forcing American pilots to fly an extra thousand miles en route to Libya. Reagan saw that France's decision was based on "economic considerations" rather than the higher good. "While it publicly condemned terrorism," he recalled, "France conducted a lot of business with Libya and was typically trying to play both sides."[7] The resulting detour caused substantial difficulty and put the Americans in greater danger; the attack was successful, but two Americans were lost, and some civilian lives were lost in Tripoli due to an errant missile. Nevertheless, Reagan's message was delivered. As he reflected later, "As tragic as the loss of life was, I don't think they were lives lost in vain: After the attack on Tripoli, we didn't hear much more from Qaddafi's terrorists."[8]

But back in the United States, Reagan had a different battle to fight—with the Democrats. "Dissenters complained that Reagan was engaging in unnecessary violence," recalled Ed Meese, "(including unproved charges that U.S. bombs had killed Qaddafi's adopted child), that the raid really had not accomplished anything, and that our retaliation would only spur Qaddafi on to greater acts of terrorism."[9]

And leading the charge was none other than John Kerry. I have to thank one of my listeners for calling my attention to a letter Kerry wrote at the time, criticizing Reagan's confrontations with Qaddafi. It was a typical Kerry performance—full of hedging and conditions, with one foot planted firmly on each side of the fence.

"While I stated that my initial inclination was to support the President," Kerry wrote,

> I pointed out that two essential tests had to be met in determining whether or not the U.S. action was appropriate. First, the United States had to have irrefutable evidence directly linking the Qaddafi regime to a terrorist act and, second, our response should be proportional to the act. The evidence was irrefutable that the Qaddafi regime was behind the Berlin disco bombing which claimed the lives of two innocent victims and injured 200 others. . . .
>
> However, as to the second test, it is obvious that our response was not proportional to the disco bombing and even violated that Administration's own guidelines to hit clearly defined terrorist targets, thereby minimizing the risk to innocent civilians. I believe it was a mistake for us to select as targets areas of heavy civilian concentrations, as well as to include the family and home of the head of state of another country—no matter how repugnant we find the leader.
>
> The fact that the bombing resulted in the deaths of at least 17 civilians certainly undermined the Administration's own justification for the raid. Beyond this point, however, is the fact that we are not going to solve the problem of terrorism with this kind of retaliation. There are numerous other actions we can take, in concert with our allies, to bring sig-

nificant pressure to bear on countries supporting or harboring terrorists.[10]

Sure, I wanted to support the president. But not if it involved any risks. Better to take "numerous other actions, in concert with our allies, to bring significant pressure to bear." Sound familiar? *Sure, I'll vote to support President Bush on the war in Iraq. But not if it involves any political risk to me. And not if it means spending any money. Put me down for yes on the war, no on the funding.*

Kerry went on to condemn Reagan for calling Qaddafi's bluff over the rights to the Gulf of Sidra. He contended that Qaddafi's claim should have been tested in the World Court—and then charged that America, supposedly in violation of international law over the mining of Nicaragua's harbors, didn't have the credibility to make the case in the World Court. *Blame America first, Senator Kerry.* Then came his pitch for multilateralism: if only we had conducted our military maneuvers *jointly* with our NATO allies, we would have been in a much stronger position to object to Qaddafi's actions.

In other words: *If America wants to act with credibility, it cannot act alone.*

There you have it. All the same shameful tactics the senator and his Democratic colleagues are still employing today: appeasing the enemy, blaming America, and insisting on a hollow multilateralism. Needless to say, John Kerry got it exactly wrong—just as he's been profoundly wrong about Iraq today. The Tripoli attack became a famous model for aggressive action against state-sponsored terrorism. Qaddafi had his own door slammed in his face, and he ceased to be a major player on the world stage. Reagan's willingness to confront Libya offers an important historical lesson: That the only language terrorists understand is that of strength and force. (As we know from bin Laden's statements, on the other hand, weakness in the face of terror only invites more terror.)

David Gutmann, a clinical psychologist and an ex-member of the Israeli Hagana, has pointed out that shame-based cultures, found mostly in the Islamic Middle East, "are most likely to attack an enemy who appears weak, rather than strong and threatening. The weak enemy is corrupt, effeminate, and ready to surrender his honor. The enemy's perceived weakness is like catnip to shame-mongers, as they fantasize about the foe's humiliation."[11]

As Edwin Meese observed, "The Libyan episode of 1981 was the first time President Reagan authorized the use of military forces in defense of U.S. interests—and the President never flinched. His message was loud and clear: No longer could Third World despots challenge the United States and depend on America's post-Vietnam guilt complex, or its uncertainty about its global role, to bind our hands. No longer would we act as a 'pitiful, helpless giant,' crippled by internal divisions or ideological confusion."[12]

Of course, Meese wrote this before the Clinton era, when that "post-Vietnam guilt complex" seemed to rear its ugly head again in the form of the president himself. By this point, sadly, it's once again become a central tenet of liberalism: *A confident, independent America is a dangerous America.*

The use of force by a president is not, in essence, a matter of courage or skill. It is a matter of principles, worldview, and character. Remember, even four-star generals don't ultimately initiate military action. They follow orders. Presidents lead—that is, they're supposed to. Presidents embody executive power. They give orders. They make very lonely decisions when it comes to using America's military might. There is no cover for them. No excuses. Presidential candidates who are not willing to take responsibility shouldn't be willing to take the job.

CLINTON'S IRAQ MESS AND SOFTNESS ON TERRORISM

After the Reagan era, things only got worse for the Democrats' credibility. They always seemed to be on the wrong side of history. Reagan won the Cold War, no thanks to the Democrats and their "freezenik" friends. Bush I beat back Saddam, and kept America safe in the early 1990s. Then along came Bill Clinton, who latched on to this double peace dividend—plus an already rebounding economy—and what does he do? He practically ignores national security, for eight long years.

Clinton downgraded and gutted the American military, reducing our navy to dangerously low levels. Yet at the same time he expanded our military commitments—but rarely in an effort to protect our national security interests. During the Clinton era, the military came to be used as a kind of glorified Peace Corps. And when Clinton did respond to real assaults against Americans or our strategic interests he would do so with the proverbial fly-swatter.

Take his halfhearted swipe at Saddam in 1993. In retaliation for conspiring to assassinate George H. W. Bush in 1993, Clinton sent a few token cruise missiles to Saddam's intelligence headquarters in Baghdad. If anything, as *Newsweek* pointed out, Saddam was emboldened rather than deterred by this tepid attack, which was followed by two other air attacks against military targets in 1996 and 1998.[13]

Clinton's entire approach to Iraq was disgraceful. During his administration, as the world knows, Saddam Hussein brazenly and repeatedly ignored United Nations resolutions on weapons of mass destruction. He spent years thwarting U.N. weapons inspectors, and then gave up the pretense and just turned them away altogether. And when he wasn't scheming to procure banned weapons on the black market, Saddam used the years between wars with the United States to wage a brutal campaign of oppression, intimidation, torture, and murder against his own people—a campaign that reduced a once-proud nation to cowering before its all-powerful leader.

These days Clinton seems to be getting a pass for his egregious mishandling of Iraq. During his presidency, though, even some in the mainstream media were calling him to account for it. A full year before President Bush took office, the *Boston Globe*—by no means a conservative newspaper—wrote a startling editorial describing the mess Clinton had made of the Iraqi situation, a failure that was dangerous not only to the American people, but to the whole world. The *Globe* labeled Saddam's unwillingness to inspect and dismantle his weapons of mass destruction as "the most flagrant and protracted failure of President Clinton's foreign policy.

"In seven years," the paper continued, "Clinton has tried to ignore, obscure, and misrepresent the threat from Saddam. Clinton's so-called containment policy has done nothing more than deter Saddam from invading his neighbors again. . . . While Clinton clings to his futile containment policy, seeking to avoid difficult decisions between now and the first Tuesday in November, the threat grows. Saddam's regime enriches itself with smuggling operations and by diverting money from the $10 billion in yearly oil sales allowed under the UN's oil-for-food program."[14]

A few years later, *Newsweek* described the situation Clinton left behind for his successor: "By the time George W. Bush became president in January 2001, Saddam Hussein had every reason to believe he was winning his long war against the United States. At the United Nations, the French and Russians, eager for oil contracts, were pushing to do away with sanctions altogether. The U.N. arms inspectors were gone, and no one was agitating very hard to send them back."[15]

It's hard to refute this. While we were fooling ourselves into believing we had tamed Hussein during the Clinton years, he was growing ever more sadistic and tyrannical. The very core of the Iraqi regime was evil, and it showed every evidence of persisting: Saddam's sons Uday and Qusay, who learned at their father's knee, were taught to watch torture at a young age with the purpose of hardening them to violence. The training was successful: Uday and Qusay grew up to be proficient murderers, taking pleasure just as their father did in watching others suffer and die.

On February 25, 2003, in one of many eloquent speeches made on the House floor supporting the war, Rep. Curt Weldon of Pennsylvania reminded his colleagues of the words of a U.N. human rights envoy: "The brutality of the Iraqi regime was of an exceptionally grave character, so grave that it has few parallels in the years that have passed since the Second World War."

Weldon also read into the record a horrific passage from Kenneth Pollack's *The Threatening Storm:*

> This is a regime that will gouge out the eyes of children to force confessions from their parents and grandparents. This is

a regime that will crush all the bones in the feet of a 2-year-old girl to force her mother to divulge her father's whereabouts. This is a regime that will hold a nursing baby at arm's length from its mother and allow the child to starve to death to force the mother to confess. This is a regime that will burn a person's limbs off to force him to confess or comply, a regime that will slowly lower its victims into huge vats of acid, either to break their will or simply as a means of execution. This is a regime that applies electric shocks to the bodies of its victims, particularly their genitals, with great regularity. This a regime that in 2000 decreed that the crime of criticizing the regime, which can be as harmless as suggesting that Saddam's clothing did not match, would be punished by cutting out the offender's tongue.[16]

None of this was any secret during Bill Clinton's presidency—to human rights groups or to Clinton himself. In true Democratic tradition, though, he took the path of least resistance, standing by while an endless parade of "multilateral"—and toothless—U.N. resolutions failed to solve the problem for him. Saddam's reign of terror continued throughout Clinton's reign of appeasement.

But it wasn't just in Iraq that Clinton fell down on the job. From the first year of his presidency, Clinton telegraphed his attitude and approach toward terrorism around the world. In Somalia, Clinton demonstrated his discomfort with military intervention by sending a limited number of troops into harm's way without proper support, leading to the deaths of eighteen troops and the national shame of seeing the charred body of an American soldier dragged through the streets of Mogadishu. As the columnist Paul Greenberg wrote, "The Clinton administration reacted to the disaster by pulling out, turning tail and giving up, thus sending the wrong signal to every would-be Osama bin Laden in the terrorist netherworld: The United States will run at the first sight of blood."[17]

Clinton had also pledged to install Jean-Bertrand Aristide, Haiti's democratically elected president. On October 12, 1993, he deployed 193 soldiers to Port-au-Prince, where they were met with supporters of Raoul Cedras armed with clubs. To avoid the risk of another Mogadishu, Clinton withdrew the troops, once again severely damaging American credibility. As historian David Halberstam wrote, "Rarely had the United States looked so impotent."[18]

Clinton was comfortable only with combat that was politically low-risk, such as his air war against Serbia at thirty thousand feet. But Clinton's real distaste for actually countering terrorism, rather than just talking about it, was best illustrated by his nonreaction to the 1993 World Trade Center bombing, where six people were murdered and the property damage exceeded a half a billion dollars.[19] Clinton refused to see the obvious—that this was an act of war. Instead he acted like the lawyer he was, sending his federal prosecutors out to capture a few of the conspirators and put them on trial while the broader Islamic terror network continued to fester at home and overseas.

The simple truth is that terrorism was never a priority for the Clinton administration. If it had been, Clinton himself would not have met with Yassir Arafat—the oldest terrorist—more frequently than any other so-called world leader. President Bush, on the other hand, refuses to meet with Arafat precisely *because* he's a terrorist.

The fact is, when Clinton and Gore were in a position to actually do something about terrorism, they chose not to. Clinton was too preoccupied with domestic policy and personal scandal to focus on foreign policy. Fox News contributor Dick Morris, who worked for Clinton in the mid-1990s, has written that Clinton "was never able to see terrorism as a threat apart from the normal course of international relations." In Clinton, Morris saw a classic appeaser, always trying to play the angles rather than taking a stand. "Clinton's tendency to moral relativism," he recalls, "handicapped his ability to set proper priorities. . . . Terrorism was important, but so were relationships with our European allies, civil liberties, budgetary constraints, the price of oil, the starvation of the Iraqi and North Korean peoples, and a host of other considerations, some worthy and others base."[20] As everyone knows, Clinton even refused to accept Osama bin Laden from the Sudanese government—a miscalculation of obscene proportions.[21] If Saddam was emboldened by Clinton's refusal to confront force with force, Osama bin Laden was fully energized by it.

Had Bill Clinton and Al Gore understood the importance of our national security then, it's quite possible that 9/11 could have been avoided. Yet now, in an effort to rewrite history, to divert attention from their legacy and score political points along the way, Clinton and Gore have taken to publicly disparaging President Bush's actions.

The sheer effrontery of this is overwhelming. For Clinton and Gore to question George Bush's wartime leadership is like Neville Chamberlain second-guessing Winston Churchill during World War II. Even Chamberlain, history tells us, had the good sense to throw his support behind Churchill after he was deceived by Adolf Hitler. Bill Clinton and Al Gore have shown no such sense.

Now, in his obsessive quest to rewrite his legacy, Clinton has lamented that he didn't have the big opportunity, the dramatic moment in world events, to exhibit his leadership prowess, the way George W. Bush has with the War on Terror. *If only they'd attacked on my watch,* he seems to be saying, *I would have had my time in the spotlight. I could have had those 90 percent poll numbers.*

But as we now know, it wasn't a question of serendipity. Clinton didn't embrace the issue of terrorism; he ran from it. And we're still paying the price. As Fox News contributor Rich Lowry summarized in *Legacy: Paying the Price for the Clinton Years,* "The September 11 attacks finally gave Clinton the kind of legacy he had yearned for: one that couldn't be ignored, one that was great in its implications. His could no longer be considered an inconsequential presidency. In leaving the country vulnerable to such an attack after eight years in office, Clinton had achieved the distinction of a monstrous, world-shaking failure."[22]

AN "ACT OF WAR"

As we've seen, President Bush's policy toward terrorist states has been decidedly different. In his first State of the Union address, he made clear exactly why it is dangerous to leave rogue nations unchecked in their power. As information discovered in Afghanistan after the overthrow of the Taliban would make clear, a brutal despotism like the Taliban almost inevitably becomes a petri dish of internal violence and festering anti-American sentiment.

"Our discoveries in Afghanistan confirmed our worst fears, and showed us the true scope of the task ahead," said President Bush.

> We have seen the depth of our enemies' hatred in videos, where they laugh about the loss of innocent life. And the

depth of their hatred is equaled by the madness of the destruction they design. We have found diagrams of American nuclear power plants and public water facilities, detailed instructions for making chemical weapons, surveillance maps of American cities, and thorough descriptions of landmarks in America and throughout the world.

What we have found in Afghanistan confirms that, far from ending there, our war against terror is only beginning. Most of the 19 men who hijacked planes on September the 11th were trained in Afghanistan's camps, and so were tens of thousands of others. Thousands of dangerous killers, schooled in the methods of murder, often supported by outlaw regimes, are now spread throughout the world like ticking time bombs, set to go off without warning.[23]

Now, remember, President Bush could have played duck-and-cover word games that night, the way some of his Democratic predecessors had done in challenging circumstances. He could have called the attacks a "crime," as Bill Clinton probably would have. Crimes are a matter of law, after all, and legal machinery grinds slowly; investigations can be a safe haven for those reluctant to act. Or he could have emphasized our "national tragedy" after 9/11, more than our national outrage. Jimmy Carter had a way of using the word "tragedy" that way—not just to acknowledge a moment of pain and great loss, but in a way that suggested passivity. When teens die in a car accident, it's a tragedy. When a tornado kills a young family, it's a tragedy. Tragedies call for mourning, for introspection, for withdrawal.

But this was no mere tragedy. This was an outrage. And President Bush knew this: Outrages call for action.

After all, this was a deliberate attack on America—an attempt to decapitate our government. It was an act of war. In 1941, as everyone knows, Franklin D. Roosevelt called the Pearl Harbor attack "a date that will live in infamy." Though he acknowledged that "very many American lives" had been lost, he didn't dwell on our "national grief" or "unbearable loss." Instead, as a powerful leader, he focused on what "the American people in their righteous might" would do to the Japanese invaders.

Thankfully, President Bush recognized that 9/11 was another act of war. He had the courage to tell us the hard truth, a truth no liberal Democrat in recent memory could have expressed with such straightforward conviction. And he did us another great honor: On behalf of our wounded nation, he showed us that we could shoulder the burden of righting this wrong ourselves. And we did. On the very day that the last of the World Trade Center fires were finally extinguished, ABC News reported that the United States had "crushed the al-Qaeda organization in Afghanistan."[24]

THE AXIS OF EVIL

In that address, President Bush also declared that both the terrorists and the regimes that give them safe harbor would now be the targets of American power.

That was a revolution in American policy, and a welcome one. For those two groups—terrorists and their rogue sponsors—had lived off of each other for much too long, and now we had paid a painful price for their collusion.

This was the speech in which President Bush first used the phrase "axis of evil," bluntly warning enemies and friends alike of

America's unequivocal intention to defeat evil and defend itself. As the president put it that night:

> My hope is that all nations will heed our call, and eliminate the terrorist parasites who threaten their countries and our own. Many nations are acting forcefully. . . . But some governments will be timid in the face of terror. And make no mistake about it: If they do not act, America will.
>
> Our second goal is to prevent regimes that sponsor terror from threatening America or our friends and allies with weapons of mass destruction. Some of these regimes have been pretty quiet since September the 11th. But we know their true nature.
>
> North Korea is a regime arming with missiles and weapons of mass destruction, while starving its citizens.
>
> Iran aggressively pursues these weapons and exports terror, while an unelected few repress the Iranian people's hope for freedom.
>
> Iraq continues to flaunt its hostility toward America and to support terror. The Iraqi regime has plotted to develop anthrax, and nerve gas, and nuclear weapons for over a decade. This is a regime that has already used poison gas to murder thousands of its own citizens—leaving the bodies of mothers huddled over their dead children. This is a regime that agreed to international inspections—then kicked out the inspectors. This is a regime that has something to hide from the civilized world.
>
> States like these, and their terrorist allies, constitute an axis of evil, arming to threaten the peace of the world. By

seeking weapons of mass destruction, these regimes pose a grave and growing danger. They could provide these arms to terrorists, giving them the means to match their hatred. They could attack our allies or attempt to blackmail the United States. In any of these cases, the price of indifference would be catastrophic.

Though he rose above it on such a somber occasion, President Bush might well have pointed out just how dearly a previous administration's indifference had already cost us.

The president took the occasion to single out three nations that had been terrorizing their own people and their neighbors for as long as most of us could remember. Where others had refused to confront them, now Bush was shining the harsh light of truth on these nations—challenging each of them to change their ways, or meet with a day of reckoning.

Iraq, lair of a savage mass murderer. North Korea, antagonist to its democratic sister state for half a century. Iran, an outspoken and aggressive supporter of terrorism since the Carter administration allowed the Ayatollah to slip into power. Each of them with ambitions to develop chemical, biological, and nuclear weapons. Each tolerated for much too long by American presidents unwilling to challenge them—and by foreign leaders much too willing to accommodate them.

America, at last, had made its position clear.

INTERNATIONAL RESISTANCE

That kind of confidence and bluntness on the world scene—backed up, as it was, by almost instant action—is a rare thing these days. And it didn't play that well around the world, especially with international voices willing to turn a blind eye to evil.

The multilateralism lobby had been making itself known through the mainstream media even as the smoke was still rising from Ground Zero. "After a week of unconditional support from abroad," reported the *New York Times* on September 19, 2001, "the Bush administration confronted its first significant difficulties today in building a broad international coalition to support using military power and other means against a still-faceless terror network rooted in Afghanistan and elsewhere. A procession of world leaders was either on the way or on the phone to Washington seeking to convince the White House that only a multilateral approach based on consultation, hard evidence and United Nations support would justify the use of military power in response to the devastating attacks last week."[25]

Imagine that: "unconditional support" for *an entire week* after the most outrageous terrorist attack in history! Before we could even catch our breath, foreign leaders were already swooping in with "conditions" for their participation in the new war on terrorism: "a multilateral approach based on consultation, hard evidence and United Nations support." *Hold it right there, you uncontrollable Americans. Not one more step before clearing it with us.*

Despite these early signals, the Bush administration managed to preserve an international coalition long enough to prevail in Afghanistan. By the following January, though, Bush's identification of the "axis of evil" brought the appeasers back in force. The

French daily newspaper *Le Monde* called Bush's language "alarmist." According to the *Sydney Morning Herald,* President Bush's world-view was "worryingly simplistic and selective."[26] London's *Guardian* newspaper warned, "Sooner or later, Mr. Bush, self-styled universal solider for truth, will have to stop pretending that tragedy gave him a free hand to remake America and the world to fit his simplistic, narrow vision."[27] A French television commentator on LCI, the nation's twenty-four-hour news channel, said that Bush's address was more befitting of "a sheriff convinced of this right to regulate the planet and impose punishment as he sees fit."[28]

"Bush's 'axis of evil' warning sparks fire," said a *Toronto Star* headline. "Furious international reaction to perceived 'threats' from U.S. President George W. Bush highlight the huge gamble he's taking by warning of unilateral American military action unless terrorism is eradicated," the paper reported, adding that in the view of most around the world, "It's one thing to attack those in Afghanistan responsible for the Sept. 11 attacks on the United States, but another thing to tell sovereign nations how to police themselves."[29]

Needless to say, Iran and Iraq were shocked—*shocked!*—to have made Bush's short list. "Little Bush's accusation against Iraq is baseless," sneered Salim al-Qubaisi, the head of Iraq's foreign relations committee. But "such threats do not scare us, as the Iraqi people are well prepared to repel any aggression or foolishness by the American-Zionist administration."[30] Iranian president Mohammad Khatami responded in a cabinet session, charging that Bush "spoke arrogantly, humiliatingly, aggressively and in an interfering way—and worse than anything, it is an insult to the Iranian nation." The American president, apparently, had it all wrong: "We are supporters of peace, a peace based on justice for humanity."[31]

And what news from North Korea? Actions spoke louder than words. As the world would soon learn, Kim Jong Il's rogue nation had already embarked on a new campaign of reckless intimidation, breaking a 1994 agreement with the Clinton administration and jump-starting its own nuclear weapons program.

THE ACCESS OF EVIL

President Bush's Axis of Evil address was not his last word on the new rules of engagement. A few months later he spoke to the 2002 graduating class at West Point, on the two-hundredth anniversary of its founding. West Point is just up the Hudson River from New York City, high on the river's west bank, where Revolutionary War forts once guarded the river. Since 1802, the leaders of the U.S. army have been trained there—the legendary "long gray line" that stretches back through MacArthur and Patton to Grant and Lee.

On that proud anniversary, President Bush confirmed to the world that the old rules of warfare no longer apply—that anyone caught fighting "the last war" will be caught dead. History has given us a weighty challenge: Today, for the first time, even a small nation can wage war anonymously using these diabolical individuals as an almost untraceable "delivery system." All the old rules of retaliation are out the window. We can no longer expect to evade danger simply by "containing" the aggression of rogue nations through diplomacy and sanctions. America could lose a city, and never know who did it. And then lose another city, and then another—with only a few terrorists in our custody. Under these conditions, the old rules of business-as-usual "diplomacy" can only lead to catastrophe.

At West Point, President Bush made clear to the graduating

class of 2002 that the War on Terror would be their generation's war—and a fight like none we've seen before.

"The gravest danger to freedom," he said,

> lies at the perilous crossroads of radicalism and technology. When the spread of chemical and biological and nuclear weapons, along with ballistic missile technology—when that occurs, even weak states and small groups could attain a catastrophic power to strike great nations. Our enemies have declared this very intention, and have been caught seeking these terrible weapons. They want the capability to blackmail us, or to harm us, or to harm our friends—and we will oppose them with all our power.
>
> For much of the last century, America's defense relied on the Cold War doctrines of deterrence and containment. In some cases, those strategies still apply. But new threats also require new thinking. Deterrence—the promise of massive retaliation against nations—means nothing against shadowy terrorist networks with no nation or citizens to defend. Containment is not possible when unbalanced dictators with weapons of mass destruction can deliver those weapons on missiles or secretly provide them to terrorist allies.
>
> We cannot defend America and our friends by hoping for the best. We cannot put our faith in the word of tyrants, who solemnly sign non-proliferation treaties, and then systemically break them. If we wait for threats to fully materialize, we will have waited too long.

President Bush went on to compare our current struggle to the one we faced during the Cold War. Then as now, he noted, our enemies were totalitarians who devalued human life. Moral clarity, he said, would be as critical for our War on Terror as it had been for our prosecution of the Cold War. And without hesitation, he affirmed his own belief in moral absolutes and truth, which are "the same in every culture, in every time, and in every place."

The President's case was unassailable: "Targeting innocent civilians for murder is always and everywhere wrong. Brutality against women is always and everywhere wrong." He reiterated that we were in a conflict between "good and evil," and that America would be unashamed to call "evil by its name." America, he said, would "lead the world" in opposing evil.[32]

THE NEW APPEASEMENT

As far as Iraq was concerned, George Bush's designation of the "Axis of Evil" marked the beginning of a deliberate process to increase pressure on Saddam Hussein, a process that would take a whole year to unfold—a process liberal Democrats would later call a "rush to war." As the president made clear, time was not on our side. A serious WMD attack on just one major American city could cause a devastating loss of life.

And yet, despite all evidence, the buildup to war in Iraq was accompanied by a cacophony of voices committed to undermining President Bush's ability to lead, dividing Americans in their support of the broader War on Terror, and creating or supporting an antiwar candidate to challenge the president in 2004.

The *New York Times* columnist Anthony Lewis was among the first to use the multilateralist bullhorn, in an essay published the very day after the 9/11 attacks. "None of us can pretend to know exactly how to deal with this newly disclosed threat of large-scale, sophisticated terrorism," Lewis wrote. "But some basics suggest themselves. Most important, America should reach out to the rest of the world for a united stand against terrorism. Nearly all countries, whatever their politics, have a common interest in elementary security. China does. Russia does. The world's cooperation is essential if the authors of this attack are to be found and destroyed. The United Nations must demand that all countries deny shelter to terrorists, and help to crush them. Governments that reject that demand will be targets for military action. It is essential, too, that our foreign policy from here on forward eschew any impression of unilateralism. Even our allies have seen an administration uninterested in what others think, ready to impose its views. President Bush would do well to adopt a tone recognizing that America cannot assure security by itself."[33]

And so began the refrain, heard every day since from the left, damning American self-defense as arrogant unilateralism. Sure, Lewis sounds tough in calling for military action against governments that reject demands for cooperation in capturing terrorists. But remember, Lewis was talking about the United Nations making "demands," the United Nations taking "action"—writing the United States out of the script.

Of course, in an era of terrorism there is an obvious, genuine need for global "cooperation." But the new appeasers take their vision of engagement far beyond simple cooperation. The new appeasers insist on U.N. "authorization" as a precondition to American military action. In other words, they would emasculate the United States, and delegate our most vital decisions about self-defense and national security *to other nations*. In practice, this can lead only to limited, inadequate action. And in principle it is intolerable. The day America cedes its defenses to a foreign power is the day we cease to be a sovereign nation.

Yet this is what the Democrats would have us do. *Call in the U.N.!* says the party of Michael Dukakis and George McGovern. *Consult with France and Germany! Under no circumstances, however, may we act alone.*

Initially, most Democrats said they supported the president in his prosecution of the War on Terror. But their obstructionist behavior belies their words. Sure, they voted for the congressional resolution authorizing military action against Iraq. But now an increasing number of them have declared that they meant only to *threaten* war, or to authorize it only as a last resort, after further inspections had been exhausted.

Senator Kerry, apparently anxious to distance himself from his earlier vote in support of the resolution, has claimed that President Bush "circumvented" the process laid out in the resolution, and insisted that the president had promised to work through the United Nations and go to war only as a last resort.[34] His colleague Senator Kennedy, on the other hand, obviously realized that the resolution *did* afford the president the option of going to war. *He* said he would refuse to support the resolution because he favored a longer, more protracted process. "The proposals that we have . . . are basically a one-step process. It says that when you pass that resolution, you are authorizing the president of the United States to effectively go to war."[35]

General Wesley Clark, a Democratic presidential candidate, said in October 2002 that he supported the resolution. In later interviews he backtracked, saying that he would have supported the resolution for leverage against Iraq, but "I would never have voted for it for war."[36]

Liberals have shown similar vacillation and disingenuousness when it comes to Saddam's tyranny itself, condemning his despotic regime, yet *opposing* decisive action against him or condemning terrorism—and blaming America for provoking the attacks. The cynics among us expect our politicians to be two-faced: the Democrats aren't satisfied with fewer than three.

Indeed, one of the most maddening realities of the modern political arena—especially in a presidential election year—is that truth in public discourse is no longer something we can expect from liberal Democrats. The only thing that means anything to them is winning. Without any higher truth to believe in, they allow their politics to be guided solely by ideology and power. This, in turn, makes honest debate almost impossible.

No matter how much liberals try to deny it, the evidence that has emerged from Iraq only confirms what a horrifying threat Saddam Hussein presented to the world. And while the Democrats can blow smoke about the "trumped-up" evidence the Bush administration supposedly concocted to justify the invasion of Iraq, they cannot account for their own inconsistent approach to foreign policy. When Bill Clinton launched his own incursions into Bosnia and Serbia for humanitarian reasons—even though neither nation threatened the United States in any way, or affected our national interests—his party did nothing to stop him. Yet they have opposed and obstructed President Bush's incursion into Iraq on national security *and* humanitarian grounds.

For those of us who admire attributes like leadership, courage, and moral clarity, such behavior may be mystifying. But it opens a window onto the dark character of the new appeasers—the modern Democratic Party.

THE UNITED NATIONS AND THE FRAUD OF MULTILATERALISM

When the Democrats aren't worrying about politics, they're worrying about image. For at least a quarter century, they've been fretful that America's strength may be intimidating some in the international sphere. In the 1980s, Madeleine Albright, later President Clinton's secretary of state, called Ronald Reagan a "lonesome cowboy" for his willingness to take sole responsibility for America's defense.[37] Now, in their desperate attempt to find a hook for their 2004 presidential race, the Democrats are reviving that old, European-inflected song, lambasting President Bush as a Texan given to shooting first and asking questions later.

Al Gore has been among the most prominent Democrats whistling this tune. In September 2002, as the buildup to war was underway, Gore blasted his old rival, claiming that the Bush administration had been guilty of a "do-it-alone, cowboy-type reaction to foreign affairs." And even as he admitted that Saddam was a worthy target, he sounded the tinny bell of multilateralism: "there's ample basis for taking off after Saddam," Gore crowed, "but before you ride out after Jesse James, you ought to put the posse together."[38]

"The posse," for Gore and the others, means only one thing: the United Nations. But what exactly does the U.N. bring to the table in a situation like this? As its track record suggests, not much—besides a wretched legacy of ineffective policies and bungled military operations.

First of all, it's important to remember what the United Nations is—and what it isn't. The U.N. is an international bureaucracy, in which the nations of the world debate and, on occasion, pass resolutions with respect to international issues. The U.N. has the power to send "peacekeepers" into areas of conflict, as it has done in the past. But the U.N. has no credible military force without the backing of the United States. And as a body it has proven highly reluctant to use its own troops—the "blue helmets," as they're sometimes called—for fear of offending any nation or group of nations on the Security Council or in the General Assembly.

But that raises a very troubling issue, always overlooked by those who call for U.N. cooperation: Far from being a bastion of democracy, the U.N. often serves as a forum for rogue nations to cloak themselves in an air of legitimacy. Its membership includes an alarming number of tyrannies and dictatorships, whose leaders could never claim to represent the interests of the people they rule. This is an organization, after all, whose Human Rights Commission is chaired by Muammar Qaddafi's Libya—one of the world's longest-lived and best-known violators of human rights. But surely the United States outweigh's Libya's role on the commission? Nope: in May 2001 America, which has carried the banner of freedom for more than two centuries, was *voted off* the commission.[39]

In practice, then, the United Nations has become a kind of organized forum for appeasement, anxious to obstruct the actions of law-abiding nations while rewarding rogue nations for their illegal behavior.

The U.N. has also proven highly ineffective in rebuilding war-torn nations. In Kosovo, for example, where the ethnic Albanian majority was saved from destruction by U.S. air strikes on Slobodan Milosevic's Serbian forces, the U.N. has failed in its mission to rebuild. As Stephen Schwartz recently reported in the *Weekly Standard,* Muslims in Kosovo "hate the United Nations and the

European meddlers in whose hands their fate was largely left after NATO's bombing ended." According to Schwartz, the international "peacekeepers" were never all that strongly invested in the conflict: they "never supported the NATO bombing of Serbia in the first place, so why should U.N. functionaries care how they carry out a mandate given them for reconstruction?"[40] Four years after the war, Kosovo still faces "lost salaries, a disastrous economy, roads rebuilt and then torn up again, and power cuts, as well as cuts in the supply of water and heat."[41] Those who complain about America's handling of the first few months in Iraq might be wise to take a reality check from the U.N.'s sorry showing in Europe.

The U.N. isn't even good at peacekeeping. Rwanda is a prime example. In 1993, it took the U.N. five months to raise a force of fewer than three thousand troops from the international community to monitor the fighting between the warring sides in Rwanda. A transitional government was supposed to have been installed with U.N. assistance, but faltered. The president of Rwanda, among others, died under suspicious circumstances when his plane crashed while he was returning from peace negotiations with neighboring countries. This ignited an all-out slaughter of the Tutu minority population by the Hutu majority, which controlled the military.

What did the U.N. do? You'll never guess. It passed several resolutions, to no avail. It imposed an arms embargo on Rwanda, and sought to increase its blue-helmet strength to 5,500 troops. But the member states took six full months to volunteer even this small number of troops. Meanwhile, upward of 800,000 Rwandans were being slaughtered—about 10 percent of the nation's population. Another 2 million had become refugees in neighboring countries. And what of the blue helmets? They were forbidden from intervening in the fighting—and in some cases were actually required to watch the slaughter without lifting a finger to stop it.

And while this human catastrophe was occurring, where was the Clinton administration? Samantha Power, an expert on the genocide in Rwanda, describes its negligence: "In reality the United States did much more than fail to send troops. It led a successful effort to remove most of the UN peacekeepers who were already in Rwanda. It aggressively worked to block the subsequent authorization of UN reinforcements. It refused to use its technology to jam radio broadcasts that were a crucial instrument in the coordination and perpetuation of the genocide. And even as, on average, 8,000 Rwandans were being butchered each day, U.S. officials shunned the term 'genocide,' for fear of being obliged to act. The United States in fact did virtually nothing 'to try to limit what occurred.' Indeed, staying out of Rwanda was an explicit U.S. policy objective."[42]

And the same U.S. policymakers whose hands are dirty from the Rwandan disaster are now part of the crowd demanding that George W. Bush defer to the United Nations. President Bill Clinton; General Wesley Clark, who advised Clinton against intervention (a decision he now says he regrets); Madeleine Albright, who was the U.S. ambassador to the U.N.—with the scar of Rwandan mass murder on their consciences, it's hard to imagine how these Democratic standard-bearers still expect their words to carry any moral authority.

The Democratic multilateralists may be brazen in their critiques of President Bush. But their feigned toughness is pure fraud. In their willingness to defer matters of defense to so questionable a body as the U.N. they are neither hawkish nor sophisticated (except in the art of deception). In fact, their way of thinking poses a serious long-term danger to our nation, because the practical result of such "multilateralism" is inaction and endless appeasement.

So the next time you hear the new appeasers utter the word "unilateralist" to denounce President Bush, and "multilateralist" to congratulate themselves as foreign policy gurus, think back to George Orwell and his lessons about the uses of language to conceal meaning. The left may insist that their "internationalist" policy is one of strength and consensus, but in truth it's one of weakness and paralysis.

We can expect the Democratic Party to hold the multilateralist line, though, because it gives them one priceless escape valve: they seize the opportunity to talk big about foreign policy, exploiting the natural human hope for "world peace"—but all along giving themselves an excuse to evade all responsibility for the consequences of a failed policy. Eager to promise greater "security" under a Democratic administration, these consummate politicians are hoping to lure family-oriented middle Americans—"security moms," you might call them—back to the party. After all, what have they got to worry about? If anything goes wrong, and America is unable to defend itself against some future terrorist threat, they can just chalk it up to the slow-moving deliberations of the United Nations.

From leftists at home to globalists in Europe, there are plenty of politicians out there eager to sign on to this new-appeasement policy. It sounded good for Senator Kerry in 1986; it still sounds good to Democrats today. But as long as the United Nations holds to its current makeup—allowing nations like France, with their ulterior motives, to stand in the way of international justice—these politicians will be jeopardizing the security of all Americans.

Ask yourself this: what would have happened if President

Bush had listened to the voices of accommodation, hunkered down Clinton style, and waited indefinitely for Saddam to cooperate fully with the U.N. inspections? If the U.N. had simply refused to enforce its own resolutions, as they did throughout the 1990s? *At best* Saddam would simply have fooled the inspectors until they returned with some spotty, inconclusive evidence, leaving him to continue his bloodthirsty reign for years to come. And at worst, he would have stepped up his proven campaign to procure WMDs, collude with terrorists—and eventually make good on his threats to dominate the entire Middle East. Would President Bush have been off the hook? Perhaps, at least in the short term. But as Bill Clinton is learning now, a president's legacy may depend more on the world he leaves behind than on the legislation he created while in office.

An unchecked Saddam Hussein, in control of nearly two thirds of the world's oil supply, protected by an arsenal of weapons no one dared provoke him to use: that is what we avoided by going to war when we did. It's an image worth remembering as we choose not only our current political leaders, but those in the future as well. Yes, the United Nations has its place in the world. But every American president must take careful measure of just how much actual responsibility America can share with the U.N. while still retaining control of America's national security interests. After all, the U.S. Constitution makes clear that protecting the nation is the number one responsibility of the federal government. It is not the job of any international body. Conservatives understand that. George W. Bush certainly does. And in the uncertainty of these times, that is no small comfort.

Because of George Bush, however, Saddam Hussein's evil reign of terror in Iraq has ended. While Americans still work to preserve the peace in postwar Iraq, for millions of Iraqis—especially the Kurds he tormented for years—George Bush is a hero. They have literally been given back their lives.

If Iraq is allowed once again to slip back into darkness, however, the work of thousands of brave American troops will have been in vain. And that's exactly what will happen if the Democrats have their way. In calling for a democratic, Iraqi-led new government in Iraq, President Bush has decided to fight terror not only with force, but also with freedom. The road that lies ahead is difficult. The Middle East does not have an uncheckered record when it comes to creating free societies. But a democratic republic, emerging from the ashes of Saddam's dictatorship, is the only fair outcome for the people of Iraq.

As the 2004 presidential campaign unfolds, the Democrats will pound away with their politically motivated questions: *Did we have to go to war? Should we have waited a little while longer? Did the president shade the truth? Have we alienated the French?*

The American people should ask a different question: When it comes to protecting American lives, and preserving freedom around the world, whom do you trust to get the job done?

SIX

The Gathering Storm

The vice president has a world view, and it is not the one shared
by members of the East Coast foreign-policy establishment,
men and women of moderation who believe in reason and dia-
logue, who think that problems can be talked out. Cheney believes that the world is a dangerous place, that diplomacy can be
a trap, that force is sometimes the only choice. Many, probably a
majority of Americans, particularly those living in the "red
states" between the coasts, agree with Cheney. More to the
point, so does President George W. Bush of Midland, Texas.

—EVAN THOMAS,
Newsweek, *March 31, 2003*
(during the Iraq war)[1]

How soon we forget.

When I first read the *Newsweek* article quoted above, I paused
for a second. *Can they be serious?* I wondered. Maybe what I was
reading was actually a piece of satire. Maybe Evan Thomas was just
playing dumb to make a point.

But I should have known better. Only eighteen months into the war on terrorism, the mainstream media had already settled back into its old ways. Instead of offering up a serious analysis of the progress and future of the war on terror, *Newsweek* was backsliding into the same old political war games: *Blue America vs. Red America. Diplomacy vs. force. Moderation vs. extremism.* If the voices of the media want to convince us that they're truly objective—that they represent the interests of mainstream America—do they really think it's a good idea to sneer at the "majority of Americans, particularly those living in the 'red states' between the coasts"? To mock them for not falling in line with "the East Coast foreign-policy establishment"?

I wonder whether Evan Thomas and the editors of *Newsweek* really think the world *isn't* a dangerous place. If so, I'm glad they're working there and not in our defense establishment or intelligence agencies. To tell you the truth, I was hoping that the embedded reporters' experience in Iraq would help teach the media a little something about the realities of terror and tyranny. They became eyewitnesses to the actual evil of Saddam's wicked regime—and, by contrast, to the nobility of the American military and its cause.

I wonder, too, whether they really believe diplomacy *can't* turn out to be a trap. Perhaps they've forgotten about Stalin's pact with Hitler, or Clinton's arms treaties with North Korea. And do they think that force can always be avoided? That may be the most disturbing thought of all. If one of America's most widely read news magazines is taking the position that military force is never necessary—*and this in a time of war*—they've not only lost touch with the American people, they've betrayed their fundamental misunderstanding of human nature. The lessons of modern history are clear: Accommodation only leads to escalation. Tyranny cannot be defeated by diplomacy. No brutal dictator will ever be persuaded to give up his dreams of universal power *simply because it's the right thing to do.*

Liberal voices in the media and elsewhere may have spent the past year or so reaching back toward their old, Carter-era notions about appeasing the enemy and avoiding force at all costs. In the meantime, fortunately, the leaders actually responsible for ensuring America's national security were formulating new principles to answer the demands of twenty-first century war.

These leaders—George W. Bush of Midland, Texas, along with Dick Cheney, Donald Rumsfeld, and the entire Bush administration—did indeed recognize that the world is a dangerous place. And they understood exactly how this new kind of war would have to be fought.

At first, at least, it was clear that the enemy would have some unfair advantages. As mercenaries, they are willing to do business with any ruthless dictator who will offer them training, safe harbor, funding, and weaponry. As terrorists, they are willing to lie dormant for years among a civilian population that's entirely alien to them, exploiting the good graces of their host country while plotting to destroy it. As cold-blooded murderers they're then willing to turn around and attack those civilians, having no concern for the values of civilization or the sanctity of human life.

The Bush administration saw early that we could not repeat the mistake of 9/11; we could no longer wait for the enemy to attack us once again. From this point on, we would have to take the action to the enemy, before he had the chance to strike. And we would have to be willing to strike "preemptively" when necessary—at both the terrorists and the nations sponsoring them—in order to preserve our national security.

PREEMPTION

President Bush's West Point address marked the administration's first reference to the importance of preemptive action in the War on Terror. "The war on terror will not be won on the defensive," said Bush. "We must take the battle to the enemy, disrupt his plans, and confront the worst threats before they emerge. In the world we have entered, the only path to safety is the path of action. And this nation will act."[2]

In August 2002, the administration's position was explained further in an address Vice President Cheney gave in Nashville, Tennessee, to the Veterans of Foreign Wars. Cheney strengthened the president's case for preemptive strikes against terrorist targets. "America and the civilized world have only one option," he said. "Wherever terrorists operate, we must find them where they dwell, stop them in their planning, and one by one bring them to justice."

But Cheney also announced that America would extend this new doctrine beyond the terrorists themselves, to include nations with a proven inclination to sponsor terrorism. Cheney argued persuasively that a regime like that of Saddam Hussein posed a real and significant threat to the United States and the rest of the world. In the face of long-standing, detailed evidence of his nuclear, chemical, and biological weapons programs, he said, a preemptive attack was necessary before he had any chance to use them against America and its allies.[3]

"Deliverable weapons of mass destruction in the hands of a terror network or a murderous dictator, or the two working together, constitutes as grave a threat as can be imagined," Cheney told his audience. The liberal voices that opposed the war have always been skeptical of the idea that Saddam and al Qaeda have conspired in any fashion, even despite the detailed intelligence reports that have emerged since the war. But their objection misses the point. The fact is, Saddam and the Islamic terrorists share one primary goal—to destroy the United States. Saddam has expressed admiration for the 9/11 attacks, and bin Laden has praised the Iraqi resistance.[4] And neither side would hesitate for a moment to cooperate with the other if it served their common, murderous ends. With Saddam Hussein's ability to manufacture WMDs, and al Qaeda's ability to deliver them under the radar, surely neither side could resist the temptation forever. Allowing Saddam Hussein to remain in power while the War on Terror raged around the world would be like hoping the engine fire in your car would simply burn itself out before it could reach the gas tank.

It's for that simple reason that the administration took its emphatic position against Saddam Hussein's Iraq—and against any other nation that might harbor and support terrorism. The world had waited a decade for Saddam to comply with the dictates of civilized society, but to no avail. His regime had ignored international pressure, breached United Nations agreements, obstructed weapons inspectors, even endured four days of bombing in 1998. And yet it remained as defiant as ever. America could no longer risk the chance that Saddam would take the next logical step in his permanent war on the West.

Just as important as the administration's new doctrine of preemption, however, were the vice president's remarks on American preparedness for war.

"President Bush has often spoken of how America can keep the peace by redefining war on our terms," said Cheney.

> That means that our armed services must have every tool to answer any threat that forms against us. It means that any enemy conspiring to harm America or our friends must face a swift, a certain and a devastating response. . . .
>
> As we face this prospect, old doctrines of security do not apply. In the days of the Cold War, we were able to manage the threat with strategies of deterrence and containment. But it's a lot tougher to deter enemies who have no country to defend. And containment is not possible when dictators obtain weapons of mass destruction, and are prepared to share them with terrorists who intend to inflict catastrophic casualties on the United States.

"We will not live at the mercy of terrorists," Cheney told his audience. And his message was seconded by Defense Secretary Donald Rumsfeld the following month in a speech to the Metro Atlanta Chamber of Commerce. As Rumsfeld noted, the Soviet-era policy of deterrence could no longer be our only recourse.[5] The policy of preemption, he said, "recognizes that this is a different security environment than before. In the past, the major threat was from conventional weapons. Today, rogue states could supply weapons of mass destruction to terror groups. . . . How do you defend yourself against a terrorist? Do you absorb the attack and then decide to do something about it?"[6]

The conventional weapons of the past, Rumsfeld noted, threatened casualties in the hundreds or thousands. Today, said Rumsfeld, "the question people are debating . . . is how do you feel about absorbing a blow with a weapon of mass destruction, and it's not hundreds or thousands of people [killed], but it's tens of thousands?" With a nation like Iraq, which not only possessed chemical and biological weapons but had shown a willingness to use them against its own people, the dangers of acting were outweighed by the "risks of not doing anything."[7]

"The task," said Rumsfeld, "is to conduct ourselves in a way that when people look back in five, 10, 15 years, they'll be able to say that the people of this generation did weigh those considerations carefully, they [made] correct assessments and judgments that were in the best interests of their people."[8]

Rumsfeld and the rest of the Bush administration were careful to point out the clear distinction between a preemptive strike and an act of unprovoked aggression. In a Department of Defense news briefing that same week, Rumsfeld was asked if he saw the war against Iraq "as a preemptive war against an imminent threat or a preventive war to keep them from becoming a greater threat." Rumsfeld responded that while preemption involved striking first, it should still be viewed as a "defensive" action. "Everyone agrees that self-defense is legitimate, legal, domestically, internationally," he said. "The concept of anticipatory self-defense is also something that goes back historically a long time." Rumsfeld cited President Kennedy's blockade of Cuba during the missile crisis in 1962 as an instance of anticipatory self-defense, remarking that "I think it's not unfair or inaccurate to say that he . . . engaged in preemption."[9]

In the weeks and months to follow, the administration continued its case for preparing the United States for the challenges of war in Iraq and beyond. As Deputy Secretary of Defense Paul Wolfowitz noted in October 2002, Ronald Reagan's vision of strategic missile defense has become only more relevant in the age of terror, with the nations in Bush's Axis of Evil developing long-range missile capability—and the possibility that terrorists could launch a shorter-range missile from a cargo ship off the coast of the United States.[10] By December 2003, Rumsfeld had declared missile defense "now America's highest priority."[11]

But the defining document in America's War on Terror was published in September 2002, in the form of the Bush administration's first formal statement on national security strategy. As an article in *Commentary* noted, "The 'National Security Strategy of the United States' is a document that usually passes unnoticed. Commenting on the most ambitious such statement produced during the eight years of Bill Clinton's presidency, William Safire quipped that it 'has been kept secret by the fiendishly clever device of making it public.' In truth, these reports, which are supposed to be issued annually, and in the name of the President, are always made public and almost always ignored."[12]

In 2002, however, the National Security Strategy statement marked what *Commentary* called "the fullest statement yet" of President Bush's policy on the War on Terror. "What made this document so different from its predecessors was not only its content but its context. Earlier annual reports, the mandate for which had been enacted in 1986 just as the Cold War was winding down, were usually empty exercises because, in the absence of a crystallized threat, 'strategic planning' was itself hopelessly vague." With the emergence of terrorists as an immediate global threat, however, the demands of strategic planning were suddenly, and bracingly, clear.

"The United States of America is fighting a war against terrorists of global reach," the document bluntly stated. "The enemy is not a single political regime or person or religion or ideology. The enemy is terrorism—premeditated, politically motivated violence perpetrated against innocents." In the wake of our victory in Afghanistan, it continued, "our enemies have seen the results of what civilized nations can, and will, do against regimes that harbor, support, and use terrorism to achieve their political goals."

The National Security Strategy laid out a clear battle plan. America would work "to disrupt and destroy terrorist organizations of global reach and attack their leadership; command, control, and communications; material support; and finances." We would "identify and block the sources of funding for terrorism, freeze the assets of terrorists and those who support them, deny terrorists access to the international financial system, protect legitimate charities from being abused by terrorists, and prevent the movement of terrorists' assets through alternative financial networks." And we would "us[e] the full influence of the United States . . . to make clear that all acts of terrorism are illegitimate so that terrorism will be viewed in the same light as slavery, piracy, or genocide: behavior that no respectable government can condone or support and all must oppose."

But the National Security Strategy devoted special attention to the ongoing threat posed by state sponsors of terror. "Our immediate focus will be those terrorist organizations of global reach and any terrorist or state sponsor of terrorism which attempts to gain or use weapons of mass destruction (WMD) or their precursors," it promised. It made two important declarations: that America reserved the right to act first, in "defending the United States, the American people, and our interests at home and abroad by identifying and destroying the threat before it reaches our borders." And, when necessary, we would take action on our own. "While the United States will constantly strive to enlist the support of the international community, we will not hesitate to act alone, if necessary, to exercise our right of selfdefense by acting preemptively against such terrorists, to prevent them from doing harm against our people and our country; and denying further sponsorship, support, and sanctuary to terrorists by convincing or compelling states to accept their sovereign responsibilities."[13]

Finally, the National Security Strategy document called for a reassessment of our military priorities and redoubling of our defense resources. "A military structured to deter massive Cold War-era armies," it argued, "must be transformed to focus more on how an adversary might fight rather than where and when a war might occur. We will channel our energies to overcome a host of operational challenges.

"Innovation within the armed forces," the document promised, would involve "experimentation with new approaches to warfare, strengthening joint operations, exploiting U.S. intelligence advantages, and taking full advantage of science and technology. . . .

"Finally, while maintaining near-term readiness and the ability to fight the war on terrorism, the goal must be to provide the President with a wider range of military options to discourage aggression or any form of coercion against the United States, our allies, and our friends."

It was the most comprehensive statement of America's right to self-defense issued in years. It was also one of the most reassuring documents I've ever read. At last, for the first time since the 1980s, an American president had issued a credible challenge to those who promote evil around the world. "We will defend the peace against the threats from terrorists and tyrants," President

Bush had promised at West Point, in a quote used as an epigraph for the National Security Strategy. "We fight, as we always fight, for a just peace—a peace that favors liberty."

DEATH OF A DICTATORSHIP

Among the "threats from terrorists and tyrants" suggested by the National Security Strategy document, of course, none was more immediate or alarming than that of Saddam Hussein's Iraq. In October 2002, the CIA issued a report labeling Saddam as "intent on acquiring" nuclear weapons, and projecting that the country "probably will have a nuclear weapon during this decade" unless preventive action were taken.

In the first months after the war, of course, the Democrats had a field day with the lack of immediate hard evidence of Iraqi weapons programs. (Frankly, I'm mystified that so many seem to take this as evidence that Saddam never had WMD—when the government obviously believes it's just as likely that he might have shipped them off to terrorists or other rogue nations.[14] To my mind, the fact that no weapons have yet been found in Iraq only gives me greater cause for concern. Imagine if you were a warden going to check on Hannibal Lecter in his cell, and you found it empty: you wouldn't think *"What a relief! Guess we don't have* him *to worry about anymore!"* would you?)

Even in the absence of actual WMD, though, it's important to know that those combing through the remains of Saddam's regime in Iraq have already turned up incontrovertible evidence of *intent*. In October 2003, Dr. David Kay, the chief coalition arms investigator, reported the results of his preliminary inspection to Congress:

■ "A clandestine network of laboratories and safe houses within the Iraqi Intelligence Service that contained equipment subject to UN monitoring and suitable for continuing CBW [chemical and biological weapons] research.

■ "A prison laboratory complex possibly used in human testing of BW agents, which Iraqi officials working to prepare for UN inspections were explicitly ordered not to declare to the UN.

■ "Reference strains of biological organisms concealed in a scientist's home, one of which can be used to produce biological weapons.

■ "New research on BW-applicable agents, Brucella and Congo Crimean Hemorrhagic Fever (CCHF), and continuing work on ricin and aflatoxin were not declared to the UN.

■ "Documents and equipment, hidden in scientists' homes, that would have been useful in resuming uranium enrichment by centrifuge and electromagnetic isotope separation (EMIS).

■ "A line of UAVs [unmanned aerial vehicles] not fully declared at an undeclared production facility and an admission that they had tested one of their declared UAVs out to a range of 500 km—350 km beyond the permissible limit.

■ "Continuing covert capability to manufacture fuel propellant useful only for prohibited SCUD variant missiles, a capability that was maintained at least until the end of 2001, and which cooperating Iraqi scientists have said they were told to conceal from the UN.

■ "Plans and advanced design work for new long-range missiles with ranges up to at least 1000 km—well beyond the 150-km range limit imposed by the UN. Missiles of a 1,000-km range would have allowed Iraq to threaten targets throughout the Middle East, including Ankara, Cairo, and Abu Dhabi.

■ "Clandestine attempts between late 1999 and 2002 to obtain from North Korea technology related to 1,300-km range ballistic missiles (probably the No Dong), 300-km range anti-ship cruise missiles, and other prohibited military equipment."

Any way you slice it, it's hard to deny the evidence of Saddam's intent—not only to develop prohibited weaponry, but to destroy all traces of any weapons programs. "In addition to the discovery of extensive concealment efforts," Dr. Kay told Congress, "we have been faced with a systematic sanitization of documentary and computer evidence in a wide range of offices, laboratories, and companies suspected of WMD work. The pattern of these efforts to erase evidence—hard drives destroyed, specific files burned, equipment cleaned of all traces of use—are ones of deliberate, rather than random, acts."[15]

The Democrats have droned on about the question of "capability" since before the invasion of Iraq. But as the administration has made clear, in the face of overwhelming proof of intent, it would have been foolhardy and dangerous to hold our fire until the Democrats could be satisfied with our evidence of capability. Saddam was working feverishly to produce WMD—just as he had been for more than a decade preceding our attack—and just as feverishly covering up his activities. If we had waited until he had achieved full "capability," it could have been too late.

In the meantime, of course, the news media buried the story of Dr. Kay's alarming findings. Were they that desperate to help the Democrats out with their gotcha politics? Or are they really just completely unable to think outside the box? Since when is the discovery of a "systematic" campaign to destroy evidence of U.N. violations a nonevent?

It's not as though the news could have come as much of a surprise to any reporter who'd been watching the Iraq story for any length of time. After all, Bill Clinton made the same case in 1998 that President Bush has made in 2002 and 2003. In announcing the military's strikes against Saddam in 1998, Clinton told the nation that his goal was "to attack Iraq's nuclear, chemical and biological weapons programs and its military capacity to threaten its neighbors." As Clinton pointed out, Iraq wasn't the only country to have developed WMD, but "with Saddam there's one big difference. He has used them, not once but repeatedly, unleashing chemical weapons against Iranian troops during a decade-long war. Not only against soldiers but against civilians. Firing Scud missiles at the citizens of Israel, Saudi Arabia, Bahrain and Iran, not only against a foreign enemy but even against his own people, gassing Kurdish civilians in Northern Iraq. The international community had little doubt then, and I have no doubt today that, left unchecked, Saddam Hussein will use these terrible weapons again."

Faced with the threat from Iraq, even Bill Clinton acknowledged the importance of preemption. "Heavy as they are, the cost of action must be weighed against the price of inaction. If Saddam defies the world and we fail to respond, we will face a far greater threat in the future. Saddam will strike again at his neighbors. He will make war on his own people. And mark my words, he will develop weapons of mass destruction. He will deploy them and he will use them."[16]

As usual, Clinton talked a better game than he played: The handful of missiles he fired had no lasting effect on Saddam. Apparently his words also failed to make much of an impression among members of his own party—just a few years later, they seemed to have no recollection that Iraq had ever possessed weapons of mass destruction. The "missing WMD" uproar after the Iraq war was so politically useful to the Democrats that they all caught a bad case of Iraqi amnesia.

THE ANTIWAR MOVEMENT

One thing the American left wing never forgets, though, is how to scare up a hysterical protest movement. Having invented the art form with Vietnam, then kept it up with the Nuclear Freeze movement in the Reagan era and (briefly) Al Gore's Florida recount debacle in 2000, they've now returned to form as the party of the antiwar lunatic fringe.

Starting in the months before Operation Enduring Freedom began, the antiwar cabal has made its shrill voice heard throughout the land for the last year or so—and you can bet they'll still be crowing when election time rolls around in November. Today's antiwar movement is just as strident as the Nuclear Freeze Movement during the eighties, with the same streak of mindless pacifism. But the modern antiwar movement is broad-based, including the liberal media, intellectual and academic elitists, the Hollywood left, and many of the extremists in Congress and on the presidential campaign trail.

I go out of my way to debate with members of the antiwar crowd whenever I can, whether on *Hannity & Colmes* or on my radio show. I often make a point of saying that I don't like the expression "antiwar," because it suggests that all the rest of us are "pro-war." The truth is, I don't know any sensible person who is pro-war. But most of the smart people I know are *realists*—we realize that war will be a reality in this world, as long as evil and tyranny conspire to terrorize human beings and stand in the way of freedom.

But most peace activists I've talked to seem oblivious to the dangers of the world. And they're contemptuous of anyone with a realistic outlook. Alarmingly, the antiwar crowd has grown even more extreme and more virulent with the years. In the debate about the war in Iraq, they not only provided intellectual and emotional nourishment to President Bush's Democratic opposition—they also brought aid and comfort to Saddam Hussein.

The rhetoric of the protestors has gotten so outrageous that you really wonder whether they've taken leave of their senses. One of their favorite tricks was to claim that the Bush administration was no more moral than Saddam Hussein's regime. In March 2003, as our troops were preparing to enter harm's way in Iraq, James Carroll of the *Boston Globe* published an essay entitled "America the Destroyer." "Look at what America has become," he wrote. "We are moving on steel treads across a harsh landscape as a creature of destruction, kicking up clouds of unreality through which we see illusions of our efficiency and virtue." Comparing our military campaign to the 9/11 atrocity, Carroll asked, "And what, exactly, would justify such destruction? What would make it an act of virtue? And in what way would such 'decapitation' spark in the American people anything but a horror to make memories of 9/11 seem a pleasant dream?" Carroll went so far as to equate our actions with those of the terrorists: "If our nation, in other words, were on its receiving end, illusions would lift and we would see 'shock and awe' for exactly what it is—terrorism pure and simple."[17]

Even worse was Professor Nicholas De Genova's statement, made at a Columbia University teach-in, that he hoped American soldiers in Iraq would face "a million Mogadishus."[18] The image itself is obscene: the charred bodies of 1 million American soldiers, dragged shamefully through the streets of Baghdad. To express dissent over a war is one thing; to wish such horrific carnage upon America's bravest young men and women is beyond comprehension.

Not surprisingly, De Genova's comment caused quite a firestorm. The professor himself later claimed that his comments were taken out of context. But his defense only revealed how thoroughly De Genova's perspective had been warped by leftist double-talk: "My rejection of U.S. nationalism," he said, "is an appeal to liberate our own political imaginations such that we might usher in a radically different world in which we will not remain the prisoners of U.S. global domination."[19]

Perhaps the most notorious of the academic apologists for Osama bin Laden and Saddam Hussein, though, is MIT professor

Noam Chomsky. On October 18, 2001—little more than a month after 9/11—Chomsky gave a bizarre lecture in which, according to a campus news outlet, he "bored down on the 'propagandist, militarist leaning' in the U.S. media, and what he described as the history of American terrorism in Nicaragua, Chile, Costa Rica, Honduras, Argentina, Colombia, and Turkey, not to mention Vietnam, Laos and Cambodia."

Speaking of 9/11, Chomsky said, "This is the first time the guns have been pointed the other way. For hundreds of years, Europeans have been slaughtering each other and slaughtering people all over the world. But the Congo didn't attack Belgium. India didn't attack England. Algeria didn't attack France. The world looks very different depending on whether you're holding the lash or being whipped by it."

Chomsky also made the claim that "terror, as defined by the U.S. Army manuals, is the driving force of American foreign policy. . . . Here at home, terrorism is seen as what people who are against us do. When America perpetrates violence, it is renamed counterinsurgency or counterterror—terms coined by various U.S. administrations to rationalize its actions."[20]

By August 2002, the level of rhetoric from the antiwar voices was growing so disturbing that the *Wall Street Journal* editorial page took notice. "The Senate began hearings this week over deposing Saddam Hussein," the *Journal* wrote, "which is fair enough. But we think the much bigger news is the way America's antiwar forces are rising from their post-September 11 quietude to stop any U.S. invasion of Iraq. . . . The intellectual left wing of the Democratic Party has begun to agitate against a war, especially in the news and editorial pages of the *New York Times.*"

As the *Journal* noted, the growth of the movement confirmed that old-style liberalism was still on the march in some pockets of American culture. "The left's Vietnam antiwar generation became quieter with the fall of the Berlin Wall, but it never went away. . . . Its intellectuals still rebel at unilateral U.S. self-defense, and especially at the Bush Doctrine of 'pre-emption' against a threat to U.S. interests."[21]

Writing in reaction to the growth of extremist liberal rhetoric, Andrew Sullivan called remarks like De Genova's and Carroll's "a profound moral abdication." Saddam's regime, Sullivan wrote, was "a Stalinist dictatorship that murders its own civilians, that sends its troops into battle with a gun pointed at their heads, that executes POWs, that stores and harbors chemical weapons, that defies 12 years of U.N. disarmament demands, that has twice declared war against its neighbors, and that provides a safe haven for terrorists of all stripes . . . [It] is not the moral equivalent of the United States under President George W. Bush. There is, in fact, no comparison whatever. That is not jingoism or blind patriotism or propaganda. It is the simple undeniable truth. And once the left starts equating legitimate acts of war to defang and depose a deadly dictator with unprovoked terrorist attacks on civilians, it has lost its mind, not to speak of its soul."[22]

But the left had already grown too carried away by their showy theatrics to listen to reason from voices like Sullivan's. A number of American antiwar types converged on Baghdad around January 13, 2003, along with fellow protestors from Italy, Germany, and South Africa. Saddam Hussein was still in power, but these protestors weren't joining forces to call attention to his inhuman regime. Instead, they hoped their activities would encourage European nations not to join the coalition against Iraq, thereby thwarting President Bush's efforts to internationalize his campaign.

Saddam's supporters were all too happy to back the human shield movement: "It helps us to strengthen public opinion in Europe," one said.[23] Indeed, in some cases Saddam's regime offered to pay for the activists' hotel, food, and even airline tickets. The Iraqi government even escorted some of the protestors on tours to show the horrors America inflicted in the first Gulf War and through economic sanctions. Talk about working hand in glove with the enemy.

As the protestors' tactics grew, the broader antiwar movement swelled in the months before the war. On January 18, 2003, hundreds of thousands of them marched in Washington, D.C., to condemn the Bush administration for "rushing into war"—a war they insisted would kill thousands of Iraqi civilians and set a "dangerous" precedent for preemptive military strikes. It was said to be the largest antiwar rally since the Vietnam era. On that same day thousands of other protestors assembled in San Francisco and Tampa. The organizers chose that date because the U.N. weapons inspectors' first major report was due January 27, 2003.[24]

"The antiwar movement is now at a whole new level," said Tony Murphy, a spokesman for International A.N.S.W.E.R. ("Act Now to Stop War & End Racism"), an antiwar organization formed just three days after the September 11, 2001 attacks—apparently ready to protest any American response, before they could even know what it might be.[25] By now the protestors had dug out their old "no war for oil" banners, accusing the Bush administration of attacking Iraq to exploit its oil. One protestor charged that the war "is more about oil than terrorism. After this war in Afghanistan, it seems like Bush just wants to keep going." Other marchers yelled, "We don't want your oil war."[26]

One group of mainly American protestors, calling themselves

the Iraq Peace Team, announced their intention of going to Iraq to act as human shields to prevent American bombing by placing their bodies in the way of likely targets. Iraq's deputy prime minister, Tariq Aziz, preferred to call them "civil defenders";[27] another Iraqi spokesperson encouraged such activity, saying, "If we can prevent the war any way we can, we have the privilege and the right to do it."[28] Of course, neither the Iraqis nor any of the human shield contingent showed the slightest concern that such activity would violate the Geneva Convention's rule against using noncombatants to shield potential targets.

Another group, called Truth Peace Justice, was organized by an anti-American ex-Marine known variously as Ken Nichols O'Keefe and Kenneth Roy Nichols. O'Keefe/Nichols had renounced his U.S. citizenship in 2002, declaring the United States the "#1 Terrorist on the Planet with the political goal of total global domination." In organizing Truth Justice Peace, he included a manifesto declaring that "As thinking people we see the obvious, [that] George W. Bush is far more of a threat to world peace than Saddam Hussein." O'Keefe's group attracted an array of protestors whose motivations ranged from the malicious to the naive. Judith Empson, a fifty-two-year-old British woman, symbolized the deep denial of some of the protestors, dismissing the fact that Saddam's regime had gassed the Kurds in the 1990s: "I don't think one can necessarily say it was a thing deliberately carried out by Saddam Hussein."[29]

Some of these protestors not only held America in contempt, but eagerly sang Iraq's praises. David Hilfiker, a doctor, said, "What the American people are not aware of is that before sanctions, Iraq was highly successful. It had free health care, education was universally available. They had reduced the infant mortality rate."[30]

But the human shields' action was short-lived: Iraq ended up expelling many of them from the country because the volunteers had the idea that they were going to protect locations "essential to the civilian population," and because they criticized the government when they discovered they had been misled. Iraq had apparently hoped to use the shields to protect "more sensitive locations." Other human shields had previously left on their own earlier over a similar dispute when the regime insisted they guard power plants and oil refineries.[31]

Despite having been misled by Iraq, some of the human shields remain unrepentant, and continue to impugn America's motives. Ryan Clancy of Milwaukee, Wisconsin, said he had no intention of paying the fines he faced for violating travel bans to Iraq. "I can't in good conscience give the Treasury Department money for the privilege of having met the people that my country was going to bomb and kill," said Clancy. And Faith Fippinger of Sarasota, Florida, similarly persisted in chastising the United States. "If it comes to fines or imprisonment, please be aware that I will not contribute money to the United States government to continue the build-up of its arsenal of weapons," she said.[32]

In February 2003 antiwar protestors staged a rally in New York City; the result was so pleasing to Saddam that he showed footage of it on his state-run television network over the logo "International Day of Confronting the Aggression." Four separate protest groups joined forces to organize the event: Bay Area Against War, the Not in Our Name Project, United for Peace and Justice, and International A.N.S.W.E.R. On its website the week before the rally, A.N.S.W.E.R. advertised a number of workshops it would be conducting on February 14, 2003, as part of a "Teach-In and Rally in New York City."[33]

The website featured the agenda for the workshops, and

stated its purpose: "Building an anti-war movement that connects the struggle against war on Iraq with the fight for social and economic justice and civil rights at home." Topics to be covered at the workshops would include:

- "The historical background of U.S. imperialism in the Middle East. The threatened U.S. war against Iraq must be understood as a continuation of the exploitative, militarist and colonial policy that the Western superpowers have followed in the region for the last century;

- "The way in which the evolving needs of U.S. imperialism affected its relationship to Iraq, as well as how world events impacted on Iraq's development;

- "The long history of the U.S. government in "regime change," including many instances of overthrowing democratically elected governments;

- "The different ways in which the U.S. government uses racism during times of war to further the war drive. Specifically, we will discuss the role that demonization of Arab and Muslim communities has played in passing new legal measures that will be used against all immigrant communities and the entire population, the racism frequently employed in the corporate media, and the role of racist ideology throughout history;

- "The so-called War on Terror: Where Will the Bush Administration Go After Iraq? [This workshop would] feature speakers from different groups discussing the U.S. threats against and objectives in Korea, Cuba, Iran and other countries on the 'target list.' . . . Speakers will give both the history of U.S. aggression in the country they're speaking on, as well as the more recent targeting of these countries under the guise of the 'war on terror.' We will demonstrat[e] . . . why the antiwar movement must expand politically beyond the current situation in Iraq and oppose U.S. interventions around the world.

■ "The Cost of War at Home: Money for Social Programs Not for War. In order to support a new war on and occupation of Iraq, funds will be diverted from domestic programs for additional military spending, following the pattern of a society that would rather produce missiles than provide healthcare because it makes for greater profit."

Hollywood also contributed its usual share of left-wing agitation against the war. "President" Martin Sheen, star of NBC's *The West Wing,* accused the president of starting the war as a personal vendetta: "I think he'd like to hand his father Saddam Hussein's head and win his approval for what happened after the Gulf War."[34] Comedian Janeane Garofalo has claimed that "There's nothing you could point to in the Bush Administration with pride . . . Nothing. There is no way any rational, reasonable person can say that the Bush Administration has been good for America."[35] And in a statement that betrayed either profound ignorance or irresponsible indifference to the evil of Saddam's regime,

Richard Gere claimed that "there doesn't seem to be any indications [sic] whatsoever that this man poses an immediate threat to anybody."[36]

But one radical voice was more contemptible than most: that of actor Sean Penn. In October 2002, Penn paid $56,000 for an ad in the *Washington Post* excoriating President Bush for suppressing debate on Iraq. In his open letter, he urged the president to stop what he saw as a pattern in which "bombing is answered by bombing, mutilation by mutilation, killing by killing." Claiming he was looking for "a deeper understanding of the conflict,"[37] Penn implored President Bush: "As you seem to be willing to sacrifice the children of the world, would you also be willing to sacrifice ours? I know this cannot be your aim, so I beg you Mr. President, listen to Gershwin, read chapters of Stegner, of Saroyan, the speeches of Martin Luther King. Remind your self of America. Remember the Iraqi children, our children, and your own."[38]

In December, Penn himself visited Baghdad,[39] in what he called an attempt to ascertain the "ground truth" about Iraq's denials that it had weapons of mass destruction. He apparently thought he could discover the truth by having members of the Iraqi regime escort him around the country to show him there were no weapons. As one writer pointed out, Penn was not taken on a tour of Iraq's torture cells, or to the sites where young girls were raped in front of their fathers, or to the Kurdish villages where Saddam had gassed his own citizens. But that didn't keep Penn from moralizing as his trip came to a close: "If there is a war or continued sanctions against Iraq," he crowed, "the blood of Americans and Iraqis alike will be on our hands."[40]

Penn even suggested that he felt some kind of personal guilt over the war: "My trip here is to personally record the human face of the Iraqi people so that their blood, along with the blood of the American soldiers, would not be invisible on my own hands."[41]

When Penn returned to America, though, he discovered that his newfound friends in Iraq had betrayed him. The *Iraq Daily* had published a quote from Penn saying he had "confirmed that Iraq is completely clear of weapons of mass destruction and the United Nations must adopt a positive stance towards Iraq." Penn was outraged, and rushed to deny having made such a statement. He later admitted, through his publicist, that he had been used by the Iraqi regime as a propaganda tool.[42]

Soon the antiwar fever had spread to the houses of Congress, where Democratic leaders who might have preferred to accommodate Saddam grappled over how to vote on a war that was widely popular with the American people. Senator Edward Kennedy of Massachusetts told an antiwar rally that "The administration's doctrine is a call for 21st century American imperialism that no other nation can or should accept."[43] "Naked aggression is not the American way," complained Marcy Kaptur, a Congressional Democrat from Ohio.[44] (Kaptur was later quoted as likening Osama bin Laden to the American Founding Fathers.[45]) And Dennis Kucinich, Kaptur's fellow Ohio Democrat and a 2004 presidential candidate, claimed that "this attempt to foment a war is really against the best interests of America, it is against the spirit of the country, it is against the economic interests of the people."[46]

Some extremist members of the United States Congress even managed to disgrace themselves on enemy soil, playing right into the hands of the antiwar movement and the Iraqi government alike. On a trip to Baghdad during the lead-up to the war, three Democratic congressman, David Bonior, Jim McDermott, and

Mike Thompson, appeared on ABC's *This Week*. "Before you left for Baghdad," host George Stephanopoulos asked McDermott, "you said the president of the United States will lie to the American people to get us into this war. Do you really believe that?"[47] McDermott replied, "I believe they sometimes give out misinformation. . . . It would not surprise me if they came with information that is not provable and they shifted." When Stephanopoulos pressed for a more specific answer, McDermott said, "I think the president would mislead the American people."[48] As George Will would write, "Not since Jane Fonda posed for photographers at a Hanoi antiaircraft gun has there been anything like Rep. Jim Mc-Dermott."[49]

"A THREAT TO ALL [WE] HOLD DEAR"

While these three Congressmen were probably the most ardent antiwar advocates, many of their Democratic colleagues were anything but supportive of the war effort, as we've shown in some detail. The Democratic Party has become hostage to the extreme left wing. But, gratifyingly, a few Democrats—not enough, in my opinion—came forward to speak out against the leftward surge of their party.

Ed Koch, one of New York's most famous Democrats, came to President Bush's defense on *Hannity & Colmes,* saying he had been particularly troubled by the extreme nature of the attacks on the president by members of his own party. Among other things, said Koch, Bush had been called a "fraud," a "liar," a "miserable failure," and a "gang member." "It's outrageous what some of the Democrats are doing in demeaning him with personal invective," Koch said. "He's the president. You can disagree with his policies and at the same time be respectful. . . . But that's not what they're doing. They're trying to demean him in the mud of politics, but they won't succeed."[50]

Not long after Koch spoke out, I was pleasantly surprised when Andrew Cuomo, a liberal Democrat, also sternly rebuked his party. Cuomo, a Clinton administration cabinet secretary, charged today's crop of Democrats with being "lost in time," often appearing "bloodless, soulless and clueless," and "fumbling" their role in the post-9/11 world. In contrast, Cuomo praised President Bush "for recognizing the challenge of 9/11 and rising to it." The president had provided true leadership, Cuomo said, and he and other Republicans "deserved credit" for understanding and "rising" to 9/11. "We [Democrats] handled 9/11 like it was a debate over a highway bill instead of a matter of people's lives."[51]

Sadly, though, Koch and Cuomo were rare sober voices in a party that has been hijacked by the radical left. But at least one very other important voice has emerged from the Democratic Party: Senator Zell Miller, who has taken his colleagues to task in his recent book *A National Party No More*. Miller pledged President Bush his "full support" in cosponsoring the Iraq war resolution, and in his book he uses a story to explain why:

> A few weeks ago, we were doing some work on my back porch back home, tearing out a section of old stacked rocks, when all of a sudden I uncovered a nest of copperhead snakes. . . . A copperhead will kill you. It could kill one of my dogs. It could kill one of my grandchildren. It could kill any one of my four great-grandchildren. They play all the time where I found those killers.
>
> And you know, when I discovered those copperheads, I didn't call my wife Shirley for advice, like I do on most

things. I didn't go before the city council. I didn't yell for help from my neighbors. I just took a hoe and knocked them in the head and killed them—dead as a doorknob.

I guess you could call it a unilateral action. Or preemptive. Perhaps if you had been watching you could have even called it bellicose and reactive. I took their poisonous heads off because they were a threat to me. And they were a threat to my home and my family. They were a threat to all I hold dear. And isn't that what this is all about?[52]

Senator Miller is right: that's *exactly* what this is all about. Unfortunately, though, the antiwar left is here to stay—and so, apparently, is its hold on the Democratic Party, which has become increasingly hostile and antagonistic and decreasingly rational, as we'll see in chapters to come.

At present, two distinct visions for America's security are battling for supremacy within American society: that of President Bush, and that of the Democratic Party—including all nine of its presidential candidates and its other potential contender, Senator Hillary Clinton. The Bush administration's assessment of the challenges we face from terrorists, and their state sponsors, is serious, thoughtful, and *realistic*. The antiwar activists of the Democratic left, on the other hand, have expressed a vision that is naive at best, dangerously out of touch at worst.

The American people have demonstrated in poll after poll that they trust President Bush to lead us through this perilous time. Appeasement-minded Democratic leaders like Jim McDermott, and fringe-element showboaters like Ken Nichols O'Keefe and Sean Penn, may have been able to use the media to gain some attention for their side. But relatively few Americans share their radical worldview. That's why this crowd has been pulling out all the stops to undermine President Bush's credibility since talk of war with Iraq began—and why they can be counted on to keep it up as this election cycle plays itself out.

With their talk of American "terrorism" and "war for oil," the Democrats may think they can draw blood in their cutthroat political battle. But the American people are smart enough to see through their rhetoric. And when the dust settles after the election, the Democratic antiwar lobby may wake up and realize that the blood they were smelling was on their own hands.

SEVEN

Hillary and Bill Clinton

Since the early 1990s, Bill and Hillary Clinton have enjoyed virtually total control over the Democratic Party. Bill Clinton was the first Democrat since F.D.R. to serve two consecutive, full four-year terms as president. Hillary Clinton was the first First Lady to be elected to the United States Senate. The Democratic National Committee (DNC) is filled with Clinton loyalists, current DNC chair Terry McAuliffe chief among them. Fox News contributor Dick Morris, who has advised the Clintons closely, says that they use the DNC "as their private fund, channeling donations to candidates and causes they favor or that favor them."[1]

Ryan Lizza of the *New Republic* shares that view. "Three years after Bill Clinton left office," she writes, "he and Hillary still control what remains of a Democratic establishment: Terry McAuliffe . . . was installed by Clinton. Most of the powerful new fund-raising groups, known as 527s, and the new think tanks, such as the Center for American Progress, are run by the best and brightest of the Clinton administration. As *National Journal* noted in a detailed look at what it called Hillary Inc., the senator's network of fund-raising organizations 'has begun to assume a quasi-party status.' "[2]

In addition to control of the party levers, Bill Clinton insists on maintaining a visible presence on the political stage. He seems to have an insatiable appetite for control and attention, never missing an opportunity to share his policy views (or attack the current administration) in public speeches. He even injects himself into the role of senior adviser to a number of the Democratic presidential contenders,[3] and strategizes with party leaders[4]—partly, perhaps, to satisfy his ego, partly to ensure that he retains ties to whatever candidate becomes the eventual nominee. He simply can't pull himself away from the spotlight. As his former chief of staff, Leon Panetta, has said, "He's someone who never stops eating, breathing, and thinking politics."[5]

Some have speculated that Clinton's persistent presence is preventing the Democratic Party from moving forward, and causing dissension within the party. William Greider, National Affairs Correspondent for *The Nation*—no conservative publication—speculated last year that "If the Democratic Party in exile is ever to find a new voice and sense of purpose, it will first have to get around a peculiar obstacle left behind by the Clinton era: The man did not really go away."[6]

Greider, too, is convinced that Clinton retains an influence on party strategy, policy, and finances. "Bill Clinton is keeping his hand in, also his handsome face and savvy intellect, plus his insider influence as strategist and money-raiser. Many Democrats still hunger for Clinton's magic touch. Others loathe him like the dinner guest who won't leave at a polite hour. But Clinton's active presence and, more important, his concept of how Democrats should govern remain at the party's vital center. This is bad news for those who think a progressive overhaul is necessary for the Dems to again become the majority party."

This is no partisan complaint, but a groundswell of Clinton fatigue emerging from the ranks of the former president's own party. Greider quotes "a former congressman still active in presidential politics" as complaining, " 'He's like a shadow, a bit of an albatross for us, much more divisive than anyone else.' " And Greider reports "another Washington operative, associated with one of the . . . candidates for 2004," as saying that "the Clintons are doing their best to maintain control." Democratic strategist Robert Shrum certainly agrees. "Anybody who dismisses Bill Clinton's presence or power in the American political scene is making a big mistake, he says. "Clinton will be a powerful, visible, influential presence in the Democratic Party and an effective campaigner for Democrats far into the future."[7]

Far into the future indeed. Many political insiders, of course, believe that as soon as it appears politically feasible, the Clintons will attempt to seize power once again, in the form of a Hillary Clinton presidency. Whenever that should occur, it seems likely that the Clintons will play a significant role, and have considerable influence over, Democratic policy—including their attitude toward national security—for years to come. All of which should be a matter of grave concern for Americans who understand the importance of vigilance in the face of evil.

The reasons for apprehension are clear. The events of the Clinton presidency contributed to many of the international problems we now face. And yet the Clintons have managed to elude any real accountability for their actions—while retaining a serious base of support among Democratic voters. Consider this:

In December 2003, a poll cited on NBC's *Meet the Press* showed Howard Dean with 20 percent support among likely voters; Wesley Clark with 15 percent; Richard Gephardt with 15 percent; John Kerry with 14 percent; and Joe Lieberman with 9 percent. When a pollster placed Hillary Clinton's name in the mix, however, Mrs. Clinton had 43 percent support against Dean's 12 percent and Clark's 10 percent![8] Like it or not, the Clintons are the heart and soul of today's (and tomorrow's) Democratic Party.

Though Mrs. Clinton has consistently denied that she is running for president this year, it clearly appears that she is setting herself up for a run in 2008. Most analysts (myself included) believe that Mrs. Clinton stands a better chance at being elected president when she will not have to face an incumbent. At the time of this writing, Saddam Hussein has been captured; the military battles in Afghanistan and Iraq have been won (despite continuing skirmishes on the ground in Iraq); there has not been another major terrorist attack on U.S. soil; and the U.S. economy is on the rebound. President Bush will be difficult to defeat in the 2004 election. Mrs. Clinton is a smart enough politician to recognize this; barring some last-minute convention upheaval, she's not likely to run for president—this time.

During the 2004 presidential election, then, the Clintons may cede center stage to the Democratic nominee. But make no mistake: If that nominee fails to win the presidency, the Clintons will reassume their positions as the face of the party. In preparation for that day, Mrs. Clinton is trying to reinvent herself as a liberal version of Margaret Thatcher—earning her defense bona fides, talking tough, visiting the troops, serving on the Senate Armed Services Committee. As conservatives, we must prepare for the day—probably four years from now—when we must run against the Clintons once more.[9]

What makes Hillary a formidable contender is that she is the one Democrat with the political skills to bridge the current gap between the moderate wing of the Democratic Party and the radical base that is necessary to secure any nomination. She is working to build a record as a moderate hawk by questioning President Bush's policies in the War on Terror. But she may also be the one Democrat who can talk tough on Iraq and still command the support of the party's left wing. This makes Hillary especially dangerous from a political standpoint.

But if their presidency taught us anything, it is that the Clintons' political positions are just that—purely political. They're a form of camouflage, created to help the candidate appeal to a broad base of moderate voters while concealing their true far-left colors. To understand the Clintons' approach to national security and terrorism, we must consider the enduring mistakes of Bill Clinton's policies in the 1990s, along with Bill Clinton's hypocritical rhetoric since 9/11, and the policies Hillary Clinton is now advocating. The record is clear: The Clintons have failed in the past to confront evil, and if given another chance they will fail again. We cannot afford the danger they pose to our nation's security.

BILL CLINTON'S PRESIDENCY

When Bill Clinton left office in 2001, most people probably assumed that his impeachment would be the most enduring black mark he left on history. Yet, as journalists like Fox News contributor Rich Lowry and Richard Miniter have noted, with the events of September 11 it became clear that the Clinton administration's most damaging legacy had nothing to do with his personal moral recklessness. It concerned his utter failure to safeguard the national security interests of the United States by refusing to confront evil with strength and resolve.[10]

Today, Bill Clinton may pine over his lost "opportunity" to shine in foreign policy. But he conveniently overlooks the many chances he had to engage the terrorists. If Clinton had had the courage to recognize and act upon them, he could have seized any number of legitimate opportunities to commence the war on terrorism that America was destined to face.

Consider the record of terrorist attacks on America during Clinton's time in office: Osama bin Laden's attack against American marines in Yemen in 1992. The first bombing of the World Trade Center in 1993. The Khobar Towers incident in 1996. The bombing of American embassies in Kenya and Tanzania in 1998. The bombing of the USS *Cole* in 2000. Each of these took place on Clinton's watch. Yet the Clinton administration largely relegated terrorism to the back burner. In the words of former CIA agent and State Department member Larry Johnson, "the Clinton administration paid lip service to the notion of combating terrorism through some money added, but generally kept it as a very low priority."[11]

When it came to pursuing bin Laden after the Yemen attack, Clinton seemed wholly uninterested. In *Losing bin Laden,* his history of Clinton's record on terror, Richard Miniter notes that "Yemen wanted help tracking down Osama bin Laden. But no help ever came."[12] After the World Trade Center bombing, where six people were killed and thousands injured, President Clinton was asked whether terrorism would change America's way of life.

His response revealed his failure to come to terms with the terrorist threat:

> I certainly hope not. We've been very blessed in this country to have been free of the kind of terrorist activity that has gripped other countries. Even a country like Great Britain, that has a much lower general crime rate, has more of that sort of activity because of the political problems that it has been involved in.
>
> I don't want the American people to overreact to this at this time. I can tell you, I have put the—I will reiterate—I have put the full resources of the Federal Government, every conceivable law enforcement information resource we could put to work on this we have. I'm very concerned about it. But I think it's also important that we not overreact to it. After all sometimes when an incident like this happens, people try to claim for it who didn't do it. Sometimes if folks like that can get to stop doing what you're doing, they've won half the battle. If they get you ruffled, if they get us to change the way we live and what we do, that's half the battle.
>
> I would discourage the American people from overreacting to this. . . . But I would plead with the American people and the good people of New York to right now keep your courage up, go on about your lives. And we're working as hard as we can to get to the bottom of this.[13]

Clinton's words captured his essential attitude toward terrorism, and toward evil: *Don't overreact.* Let the law-enforcement agencies handle those isolated radicals who might seek to harm Americans—certainly no need to trouble the military or the State Department.

And even on the law enforcement side, Clinton was all talk and no action. After promising that he had "put the full resources of the Federal Government" to work on the problem, he made no changes in American policy to prevent future attacks. As Larry Johnson notes, "From the time President Clinton took office until May of 1995, a Presidential Decision Directive, PDD 39, sat in the National Security Council, in the In Box of one of the officials with no action taken. The significance of PDD 39 is that it was the document defining what the missions and roles were of combating terrorism."[14] In fact, it wasn't until after the Oklahoma City bombing that Clinton chose to act on PDD 39. Even the Oklahoma City attack may not have prompted Clinton's belated action, speculates Johnson, had *Newsweek* and *Time* not both posed the question two weeks before Oklahoma: "Is President Clinton Relevant?"[15]

The goal of the bombers in 1993 was to topple one of the Twin Towers onto the other "amid a cloud of cyanide gas."[16] It was later discovered that Ramzi Yousef, the terrorist who executed the 1993 attack, was also plotting to bomb "eleven U.S. commercial aircraft in one spectacular day of terrorist rage."[17] Yousef attempted to engineer the bombs "to be made of a liquid explosive designed to pass through airport metal detectors."[18] In the original investigation into the WTC bombing, Janet Reno's Justice Department failed to share critical information with other national security agencies. If Yousef hadn't accidentally started a fire while working with bomb-building chemicals in a hotel room in the Philippines, attracting the attention of police and the capture of an associate, he might never have been arrested—and America might have suffered a 9/11-style attack during the 1990s.[19]

Though Yousef's terrorist attack was clearly designed to kill tens of thousands of Americans, the Clinton administration's treatment of the bombing sidestepped the larger issue of terrorism, not to mention state sponsorship. It was an approach that must certainly have encouraged our enemies, and only heightened the danger they posed to the American people. As the Iraq expert and Defense Department consultant Laurie Mylroie warned at the time:

> [B]y responding to state-sponsored terrorism solely by arresting and trying individual perpetrators, the U.S. government, in effect, invites such states to commit acts of terror in such a way as to leave behind a few relatively minor figures to be arrested, tried and convicted. Done adroitly, this makes it unlikely that the larger, more important, and more difficult question of state sponsorship will ever be addressed.[20]

Mylroie was correct: other attacks would soon follow.

In 1996, terrorists bombed a U.S. military compound at Khobar Towers, near Dhahran, Eastern Province, Saudia Arabia, killing nineteen Americans and injuring hundreds.[21] In 2000 terrorists attacked the the USS *Cole* in Yemen, killing seventeen more Americans.[22] But again the attacks went largely unanswered. In the case of the Khobar Towers, the Clinton administration once again entrusted the FBI and the Reno Justice Department with investigating the bombing.[23] The administration disregarded any notion that the bombings might be part of a larger operation by hostile nations and organizations to attack America through the use of individual terror cells. This waffling in the face of terror was taken as a sign of weakness by al Qaeda, and only further encouraged and emboldened the terrorists.

In 1998, when al Qaeda terrorists attacked the U.S. embassies in Kenya and Tanzania, killing twelve Americans and more than two-hundred Africans, and injuring nearly five thousand people, Clinton's reaction was predictably muted:

> These acts of terrorist violence are abhorrent; they are inhuman. We will use all the means at our disposal to bring those responsible to justice, no matter what or how long it takes. Let me say to the thousands and thousands of hard-working men and women from the State Department and from our other government agencies who service abroad in these embassies, the work you do every day is vital to our security and prosperity. Your well being is, therefore, vital to us and we will do everything we can to assure that you can serve in safety.
>
> To the families and loved ones of the American and African victims of these cowardly attacks, you are in our thoughts and prayers. Out of respect for those who lost their lives, I have ordered that the American flag be flown at half-staff at all government buildings here at home and around the world. We are determined to get answers and justice.[24]

Clinton, of course, was a talented mourner-in-chief. But his halfhearted promise to "get answers and justice" was never followed up with action. An attack on American embassies is an attack on American soil; two simultaneous, carefully coordinated attacks constitutes a major, warlike assault on America itself. Did Clinton follow these words with strong, decisive action? No. A little less than two weeks later, while vacationing in Martha's Vineyard, Clinton ordered the only military action against al Qaeda of his entire presidency: the launching of one cruise missile attack on terrorist facilities in Sudan and Afghanistan. There were no additional strikes.

Once again, the Clinton administration reserved most of its energies for the legal sphere. Taking its consistently wrongheaded approach to terrorism, Clinton's Justice Department indicted Osama bin Laden and Muhammad Atef in November 1998 for their roles in planning the bombings of the U.S. embassies. The assistant director of the FBI office in New York stated that the indictment showed "the resolve and determination of the entire law enforcement team to bring to justice all those who were responsible for the murder of innocent Americans, Kenyans and Tanzanians on August 7."[25] Instead of enlisting the Department of Defense or the military to answer the terrorist attacks of 1998, Clinton persisted in treating each new event as a criminal violation.[26]

Clinton's refusal to seize Osama bin Laden is another failure that endangered Americans. As has been widely reported, the Sudanese offered to produce Osama bin Laden in 1996. Bill Clinton declined the offer. As Milton Bearden has written:

By 1995 . . . bin Laden's presence in Sudan had become an issue both for the United States and for Saudia Arabia, which by this time had stripped bin Laden of his citizenship. . . .

According to a PBS *Frontline* television interview with Sudanese president Umar Hassan al-Bashir, the Sudanese government offered to keep bin Laden on a tight leash, or even hand him over to the Saudis or to the Americans. The Saudis reportedly declined the offer, for fear that his presence would only cause more trouble in the kingdom, and the United States reportedly passed because it had no indictable complaints against him at the time. In 1996, then, on U.S. and Saudi instructions, bin Laden was expelled from Sudan, and he moved to the last stop on the terror line, Afghanistan.[27]

Presented with multiple opportunities to seize one of the world's most notorious terrorists—a known threat to our country—the Clinton administration chose not to act. It was a pattern that would characterize his entire presidency: The Clinton administration neglected nearly every obvious imperative to act affirmatively to combat terrorism. Under Clinton's leadership, America "failed to secure intelligence files on Bin Laden and his network offered by Sudan. It failed to get Saudi Arabia's cooperation in the investigation into [the Khobar Towers incident]. And it failed to act on [a] warning of the bomb attack on the American embassy in Nairobi in 1998, which killed 213."[28]

As even this brief review of the historical record demonstrates, the terrorist war against the United States and its citizens began more than ten years ago with the murder of our marines in Yemen. In almost every case, President Clinton refused to treat the atrocities as part of a war. He talked tough, but rarely issued retaliatory strikes, preferring either to ignore them or to channel them through the protracted legal system. These failures of the Clinton administration are inexcusable. By treating each new attack as a separate criminal incident perpetrated by individuals, rather than as the work of terrorist cells or the networks and nations that supported them, President Clinton put the safety of all Americans in jeopardy.

President Clinton's lax approach to terrorism is also apparent in his overtures to the infamous terrorist leader Yasser Arafat. It is eye-opening to realize that, among all the foreign leaders with whom he did business in his eight years in office, Clinton played host to Arafat *more often than any other.*[29] While some have elevated Arafat to the status of a statesman,[30] he has a well-earned reputation as a terrorist. As Mort Zuckerman, the publisher of *U.S. News & World Report* and the New York *Daily News,* has written:

> The reality of Arafat as terrorist is written in a terrible record. He formed the al-Aqsa Martyrs Brigade because his experience has taught him that far from marginalizing him, terrorism pays. Let the record show: By November of 1974, Arafat's Palestine Liberation Organization had carried out the massacre of Israel's Olympic athletes, plane hijackings, letter bombs, the assassination of an American ambassador and Jordan's prime minister, the slaughter of 21 Israeli schoolchildren at Maalot, and the killing of 52 Israelis—mainly women and children—in Kiryat Shmona. Yet November 1974 was the month in which he was invited to address the United Nations General Assembly, virtually unanimously. "Asking Arafat to give up terrorism," explains Bernard Lewis, the dean of Middle East scholars, "is like asking Tiger Woods to give up golf."[31]

Ariel Cohen, a *National Review* Online contributor, adds:

> [Arafat] was deeply involved in planning the killings of Israeli athletes at the Munich Olympics in 1972 and March 1, 1973, as well as the assassinations of U.S. ambassador Cleo A. Noel and Deputy Chief of Mission Curtis G. Moore in Khartum. The following year, Arafat's terrorists threw Israeli schoolchildren out of the windows of a school in Maalot. Since then, his henchmen have killed dozens of Israeli children, and trained hundreds of Palestinian children to serve either as human shields or as killers.[32]

And yet Bill Clinton didn't hesitate to rub elbows with an evil actor like Yasser Arafat if there was any chance it might help him accomplish his political goal of establishing a legacy as a Mideast peacemaker. Rather than casting Arafat in irons when he stepped onto the grounds of the White House, President Clinton literally welcomed him with open arms. (It should hardly come as a surprise that, despite all the attention Clinton lavished on Arafat, in the end the Palestinian rejected Israeli prime minister Ehud Barak's near-complete capitulation to his "peace" demands— proof yet again that no good can come of negotiation with terrorists.)

Clinton's paralysis in the face of terrorism was matched only by his negligence when it came to Saddam Hussein's evil regime. Though well aware of the dangers Saddam posed, Clinton did almost nothing to arrest his reign of terror. Oh, but he talked such a good game. Listen to him in 1998:

Now, let's imagine the future. What if he [Hussein] fails to comply and we fail to act, or we take some ambiguous third route which gives him yet more opportunities to develop this program of weapons of mass destruction and continue to press for the release of the sanctions and continue to ignore the solemn commitments that he made? Well, he will conclude that the international community has lost its will. He will then conclude that he can go right on and do more to rebuild an arsenal of devastating destruction. And some day, some way, I guarantee you, he'll use the arsenal. . . . If we fail to respond today, Saddam and all those who would follow in his footsteps will be emboldened tomorrow by the knowledge that they can act with impunity—even in the face of a clear message from the United Nations Security Council and clear evidence of [a] weapons of mass destruction program.[33]

Amazing, isn't it? Clinton *knew* Saddam and his regime were evil! He knew Iraq was rebuilding its WMD program. He even understood that if America failed to show sufficient resolve Saddam would only be emboldened! Yet, with all that insight, what did this president do to protect America? He launched a couple dozen cruise missiles and waged a four-day air campaign. It was hardly a serious effort to thwart the dictator.

I believe with all my heart that the Clinton administration's delays and hesitations, coupled with the ineffectiveness of its fleeting military strikes, paved the way for the attacks of 9/11. I believe that evil people only respect force, and that evil can only be deterred by the credible use of such force. The escalating cycle of terrorist attacks from al Qaeda, and defiance and brutality from Saddam Hussein, proves conclusively that such inaction can spawn only more violence, murder, and destruction.

President Clinton, in short, has taught us all a costly lesson in the perils of modern-day appeasement. In his preoccupation with political matters, and his essential reluctance to view terrorists or brutal dictators as a military threat, he failed to stand up to evil, and in so doing gravely compromised our national security. The fact that he was on record as recognizing the nature of Hussein and bin Laden only makes his refusal to act more reprehensible. Bill Clinton wasn't asleep at the wheel. He just refused to drive—and Americans paid for his folly and lack of leadership with their lives.

BILL CLINTON AND NORTH KOREA

The Middle East isn't the only arena where Clinton's inability to confront evil left America less secure than when he took office. Halfway around the world, another repressive dictator managed to deceive an unsuspecting Clinton administration for years, while furthering a weapons program more intimidating than Saddam's ever became.

North Korea is known as one of the most evil regimes in the world. Its dictator, Kim Jong II, has subjected his people to mass starvation and torture. He has routinely sent individuals to prison camps modeled on the old Soviet gulag system. In 2002, a State Department report summarized North Korea's record on human rights:

> [The North Korean] Government's human rights record remained poor, and it continued to commit numerous serious abuses. Citizens did not have the right peacefully to change their government, and the leadership views most international human right[s] norms, particularly individual rights as illegitimate, alien, and subversive to the goals of the State and Party. There continued to be reports of extrajudicial killings and disappearances. Citizens were detained arbitrarily, and many were held as political prisoners. Prison conditions were harsh, and torture was reportedly common. Female prisoners underwent forced abortions, and in other cases babies reportedly were killed upon birth in prisons.
>
> A human rights dialogue initiated by the European Union in 2001 led to another exchange of views in June 2002 in Pyongyang, but the Government did not acknowl-

edge that international standards of human rights apply to North Korea. The Penal Code is Draconian, stipulating capital punishment and confiscation of assets for a wide variety of "crimes against the revolution," including defection, attempted defection, slander of the policies of the Party or State, listening to foreign broadcasts, writing "reactionary" letters, and possessing reactionary printed matter. Citizens were denied freedom of speech, the press, assembly and association.[34]

Once again, though, President Clinton trusted a corrupt regime enough to accommodate it with a deal that was lucrative for them while doing nothing to protect our security. In 1994, Clinton brokered a deal with North Korea that was ostensibly designed to prevent Kim's government from developing, acquiring, or exporting nuclear weapons. The deal, called the Agreed Framework, essentially required the United States to pay the little nation in exchange for its promise not to produce nuclear weapons. Under the Agreed Framework, North Korea agreed to "take steps to implement the North-South Joint Declaration on the Denuclearization of the Korean peninsula." North Korea agreed to "remain a party to the Treaty on the Non-Proliferation of Nuclear Weapons (NPT) and will allow implementation of its safeguards agreement under the Treaty."[35]

What happened? Kim Jong II took the money and ran. Syndicated columnist Charles Krauthammer described how Bill Clinton was snookered:

> Clinton assured us that [the agreement] froze the North Korean nuclear program. North Korea gave us a piece of paper promising to freeze; we gave North Korea 500,000

tons of free oil every year and set about building—also for free—two huge $2 billion nuclear power plants that supposedly could be used only to produce electricity. Japan and South Korea were induced to give tons of foreign aid as well, Clinton being the committed multilateralist, even in extortion.

It turns out the North Koreans took the loot and lied. Surprise! All the while they were enriching uranium. They now brazenly admit to having a nuclear weapons program and other weapons of mass destruction.[36]

It was another setback for America at the hands of the appeasers. Trust, but don't verify. Talk, give away the farm, demand nothing in return—and don't waste a moment worrying about our security.

But Clinton's dealings with North Korea were not limited to the Agreed Framework. In the waning days of his administration, he sent his secretary of state, Madeleine Albright, to North Korea. Instead of taking the opportunity to condemn the vicious Kim Jong II in person, Secretary Albright demurred. Even the *Washington Post* editors disapproved:

We know, from past example, how influential the United States can be when it chooses to show disapproval for the morally repugnant—and when it chooses not to. When Ronald Reagan called the Soviet Union an "evil empire," we now know that the word traveled from cellblock to cellblock across the taiga, giving courage to dissidents throughout the gulag. When Jimmy Carter and his administration spoke out for freedom in Argentina, political prisoners there were similarly cheered. But when American leaders toast a dictator without a word of disapproval, just as certainly they dishearten those who would fight for freedom.[37]

By the end of their private dinner, though, Secretary Albright and Kim Jong II "were laughing and applauding like old chums."[38] It was a disgraceful performance: A man responsible for the deaths of untold thousands, who maintains an iron grip on his terror-stricken people, who starves his populace to arm his military, socializing with a senior U.S. official even as the murderer's regime was in flagrant violation of a critical arms agreement. This was Clinton-era diplomacy.

Officially, Secretary Albright's visit accomplished the goal of convincing Kim Jong II to "accept the idea" of cutting back his country's missile programs. A senior State Department official stated that Mr. Kim was "accepting the idea of serious restraint on his missile program."[39] But when diplomats use euphemistic phrases like "accepting the idea of serious restraint," what they're really saying is that they haven't accomplished anything. As a result of the Clinton administration's refusal to confront this tyrant, future generations of Americans are now forced to coexist with an isolated, militaristic nation that possesses the most terrible of weapons—and a maniacal dictator who might be willing to use them.

BILL CLINTON'S POST-9/11 RHETORIC

As misguided and irresponsible as he was while in office, Bill Clinton continues to do damage to this country through his self-promoting, meddlesome foreign policy pronouncements now that he has left office. His post-9/11 rhetoric is always carefully calculated. He doesn't criticize Bush's reliance on intelligence information about Saddam's weapons of mass destruction, for example, because he knows he relied on the same information to justify his own strikes. Instead, he hopes to undermine the president by second-guessing his actions in Iraq. When it was expedient for Clinton and his loyalists to support President Bush, he did so—but his support changed with the political winds.

On September 11, Clinton expressed full support for his successor. "The most important thing is we all have to be strong, calm good Americans now and rally behind the president and support the actions he will doubtlessly take in the days ahead—in both rescue and reconstruction of the area and especially in investigating and taking whatever action is necessary." He even disavowed the idea of partisan dissent: "Nobody should be questioning any decisions [Bush] makes. We ought to be hanging in there, giving his national security team the time it takes."[40] It was a rare instance of Bill Clinton rising above politics in the interest of foreign policy; for a moment he seemed to recognize that a nation going to war with a united front is always stronger than one divided against itself.

Unfortunately, Clinton didn't follow his own counsel for long. In trademark form, by 2002 Clinton was resorting to subtle cues and ambiguous language to deliver a series of veiled, yet unmistakable, critiques of President Bush.

During an October visit to Great Britain, he attacked the president in a speech to the Labour Party. As Jonathan Freedland observed in the *Guardian,* Clinton "did it artfully, sometimes in code, but the 42nd president of the United States used the floor of the Labour party conference to unleash an acid critique of the Bush administration."[41] Clinton paid lip service to his "support" for Bush's policies, but as Freedland observed, "that was bland enough to be non-committal. On the specifics, he raised almost every one of the core arguments that have been deployed by the anti-war camp," including the familiar old call for multilateralism:

> Yes, we have to care for the security of our nation. This means, among other things, of course that we have to fight terrorists. But we also have to build a world with more partners and fewer terrorists. Of course we have to stand against weapons of mass destruction—but if we can, we have to do it in the context of building the international institutions that in the end we will have to depend upon to guarantee the peace and security of the world and the human rights of all people everywhere.[42]

Clinton showered lavish praise on the efforts of the U.N. inspectors, declaring that "I still believe we have to stay at this business until we get all those biological and chemical weapons out of there." He voiced his old blame-America-first refrain, telling the room that "the West has a lot to answer for in Iraq. . . . Evidence has now come to light that in the early 1980s the United States may have even supplied him with the materials necessary to start the bio-weapons program."

Perhaps worst, in a spirit of petty partisan mockery he undermined his own nation's government, during a time of war, on foreign soil: The 2000 election, he told the assembled faithful of the British left wing, "was so close in America that they won it fair and square—5 to 4 at the Supreme Court." The line got a laugh, of course; once again Clinton had sacrificed his nation to the celebration of . . . Bill Clinton.

In March 2003, in a statement that undercut Bush's negotiating position, Clinton asserted that the United States should agree to any timetable set by Hans Blix for Iraqi compliance with United Nations demands.[43] And in November, Bill Clinton—shamefully, even for him—came to the defense of Canada's left-wing prime minister, who refused President Bush's direct appeal for support in the war against Iraq. Clinton attacked Bush's firm stand:

> It was a low moment in our long and mostly happy coexistence. And it was uncalled for, because Canada has been such a strong ally of the U.S. in so many areas involving our mutual security, from border control to our duties as NATO members to the campaign against Al-Qaeda in Afghanistan.
>
> The U.S. can win military conflicts alone. But as we see every day in Iraq, building peace requires partners. Moreover, since we cannot kill, imprison, or occupy all our actual potential adversaries, we must find non-military means to make more friends and fewer terrorists. That too requires cooperation with our allies.[44]

It was classic Clinton, lecturing Bush about failing to do something the former president himself refused to do. Bill Clinton never built a coalition to take on terrorism in Afghanistan, to stop North Korea from building nuclear weapons, or to oust Saddam Hussein. He left these problems for his successor, passing the buck to the next White House.

But Bill Clinton wasn't alone in attacking President Bush. His surrogates also took the offensive, their vigor at least equaling his. Former secretary of state Madeleine Albright charged—during a speech in Paris, no less—that "America is much stronger in a multilateral system, we must be on the same side, work with other people in the world. It shouldn't be America versus the others."

Secretary Albright seemed to recognize how inappropriate it was to be questioning American policy while on French soil. "It's difficult to be in France and criticize my government," she said. "But I'm doing so because Bush and the people working for him have a foreign policy that is not good for America, not good for the world."[45]

Albright's predecessor as Clinton's secretary of state, Warren Christopher, trotted out the Q-word in November 2003. "With two soldiers killed on average every day this month, Iraq is a quagmire in which the United States, by the telling of its own secretary of defense, 'slogs' rather than skates." Christopher also implied that the Bush administration had deceived the American people:

> As we now know, the Bush administration's decision to wage war in Iraq was grounded in faulty intelligence and false urgency. Contrary to the impression created by the administration, Iraq was not responsible for the Sept. 11 attacks, and there was no proof that Iraq was in league with al Qaeda. Similarly, Niger did not sell uranium to Iraq, Iraq was not on the cusp of nuclear capability and Saddam Hussein did not have at the ready scores of weapons of mass destruction. In sum, the United States launched a preemptive war without convincing evidence that Iraq constituted an imminent threat to our nation and without any effective plan for dealing with the aftermath of a military victory.[46]

Not surprisingly, Clinton's favorite party man, Democratic National Committee chairman Terry McAuliffe, had beaten them both to the punch. McAuliffe, no stranger to below-the-belt attacks, had taken an outrageous cheap shot at President Bush in September. As the *Denver Post* reported, McAuliffe claimed that the president had made "absolutely ludicrous and insane statements" that endangered our troops, and called on his audience to "urge Bush to 'go tell the parents' of Americans killed in Iraq why the president found it necessary to don a flight suit, land on the deck of a U.S. aircraft carrier and claim 'mission accomplished' when Iraq was not yet secure."[47]

The Associated Press reported that McAuliffe had "criticized the president for going to war with what McAuliffe called trumped-up evidence that Iraq was pursuing weapons of mass destruction."[48] And McAuliffe questioned the administration's use of intelligence in the War on Terror: "From the bogus statements in the State of Union, to exaggerated claims about aluminum tubes to the latest revelations about drones, the Bush administration seems to have engaged in a pattern of deception in their manipulation of intelligence."[49]

Richard Holbrooke, the former U.S. ambassador to the United Nations and assistant secretary of state during the Clinton administration, claimed that "Had the administration 'been more engaged' earlier this year [2003], Turkey would never have objected to US troops basing in, or over-flying, Turkish territory during an Iraq invasion."[50] Critiquing American diplomatic efforts as "beyond my imagination," he charged that "in the annals of American diplomacy this is not America's finest hour."[51] Holbrooke's criticisms were seized upon by Al-Jazeera, the primary news outlet of the Arab world, in its own attempt to discredit and undermine the Bush administration.

Joe Lockhart, Bill Clinton's former press secretary, surfaced to make a particularly laughable complaint about President Bush's Thanksgiving trip to Baghdad. "This is a president who has been unwilling to provide his presence to the families who have suffered," Lockhart said, "but thinks nothing of flying to Baghdad to use the troops there as a prop."[52] It's hard to believe Lockhart had the gall to suggest that Bush's morale-building visit was politically motivated, when his own comments were clearly intended to win political points at the president's expense. This kind of behavior from the old-line Clinton loyalists is really reprehensible: They can't stand to see President Bush so comfortable with, and so beloved by, the military President Clinton had loathed. It's fortunate that the American people recognize rank partisanship when they see it.

Yesterday and today, from Clinton on down, Democratic political players and officeholders are engaged in a determined and systematic effort to undermine President Bush and diminish his credibility as our commander in chief during wartime. Perhaps it's easy to understand what the Democrats are worried about; as 2004 rolls around, they're anxious to divert the public's attention from their own incompetence and perilous mismanagement of foreign affairs during their leader's eight-year term.

All their glib words, however, will never erase their regrettable record.

HILLARY CLINTON

No account of the Clinton presidency, of course, is complete without acknowledging the role of Hillary Clinton. After all, Bill Clinton himself has credited her with advising him on most important matters. From the start they held themselves out as sharing a co-presidency, and you can be sure they'll return to that message as Hillary prepares to throw her hat into the presidential ring.

It's important to remember several things about Mrs. Clinton. Like many of her Democratic colleagues, she is a political animal who routinely camouflages her true liberal nature in her ceaseless quest for power. She must be fully aware that her extreme brand of liberalism is unpalatable to a majority of Americans, but as she grooms herself to assume the mantle of leadership in the Democratic Party, she'll show no compunction about working both sides of the ideological fence. Mrs. Clinton is not to be underestimated: Those who predicted she couldn't win a Senate seat in New York were sadly mistaken. I feared she could, and said so at the time.

If Mrs. Clinton were to be elected president, I believe the result would be a disaster not just for the conservative movement, but for the security of the nation. There's no doubt that a second Clinton administration would continue the practices of the first—shifting focus away from the terrorist threat, appeasing dictators around the world, playing politics at home while our enemies aligned against us overseas. Like her husband, Mrs. Clinton is disinclined, and doubtless unable, to confront the evils America faces in the twenty-first century. Like Bill, Hillary would hesitate and waver in the face of global terrorism. Their boasts of a dual presidency, of "two for the price of one," leave little doubt that they were in sync on most of President Clinton's major policy positions. There's no reason to doubt that Bill's timid attitude toward terrorism was among them.

Indeed, even as recently as late 2003, Hillary has proudly ratified her husband's record. On *Meet the Press* she told Tim Russert, "You know, when I first saw the Bush administration in action, I thought that they wanted to undo everything Bill Clinton had done. Basically, I took that a little personally because I thought that a lot of good had happened during the 1990s."[53] If Mrs. Clinton is going to take credit for "everything Bill Clinton had done," then certainly it's fair to critique for the critical things he neglected to do—like protect and defend the American people from foreign attack.

Mrs. Clinton's policies toward terrorism are suspect, but perhaps even more disturbing are her reckless and self-serving dealings with certain organizations that have longstanding ties to terrorism. From 1982 to 1988, while Hillary was serving as chair of the New World Foundation, she awarded $15,000 to a group called Grassroots International, which in turn distributed funds to the Union of Palestinian Working Women's Committees and the Union of Palestinian Medical Relief Committees—each a branch of the Palestine Liberation Organization (PLO).[54] As David Bar-Illan reported in the *Jerusalem Post*:

> Serving as chairwoman of the New World Foundation in the 1980s, Clinton directed contributions to PLO-affiliated groups. In the White House she entertained pro-Hamas American-Moslem groups, received gifts from them and spoke at their functions. Her advocacy of a Palestinian state in May 1998 was surprising only because it exposed the administration's true sympathies and undermined its position as honest broker.[55]

And we should all remember that uncomfortable moment when, in a well-publicized event, Mrs. Clinton sat by as Suha Arafat, the wife of Palestinian leader Yasser Arafat, decried Israel. As the *Jerusalem Post* reported:

Suha Arafat said that Israel used poison gas against the Palestinian population, which caused the death of women and children from cancer and other horrible diseases, and that Israel poisoned 80 percent of the water used by Palestinians, which also caused widespread disease.

Clinton had her earphones on, listening to the simultaneous translation. As Arafat began reciting Israel's genocidal crimes, Clinton nodded in approval. Then her face froze into a polite smile. When Arafat finished, she hugged and kissed her, uttering not one word of criticism. Only after the White House alerted her to the unfavorable reaction to her conduct did she issue a statement. It did not refer to Suha Arafat but commended President Clinton's plea to all sides (including the US!) to refrain from provocative statements.

Clinton later explained the delay in her reaction by stating that the simultaneous translation was "unclear" and "incomplete."[56]

At the end of her husband's presidency, Mrs. Clinton benefited politically from several last-minute pardons. It's no stretch to believe that the outgoing president's eleventh-hour pardons of the Armed Forces of National Liberation (FALN) terrorists aided Hillary's chances at being elected to the Senate in New York. According to press reports, the Department of Justice took "extraordinary steps to enhance the chances of clemency for a group of imprisoned Puerto Rican terrorists after receiving regular expressions of interest from the White House."[57] Though Mrs. Clinton publicly claimed that she disagreed with President Clinton's decision to grant clemency,[58] it doesn't strain credulity to imagine the Clintons calculating that the release of these terrorists would help her win the support of the New York Latino community.

As senator, Mrs. Clinton has led the charge against President Bush on a number of occasions. On May 16, 2002, Mrs. Clinton unleashed a scurrilous attack on President Bush on the Senate floor. Among other things, she said:

> The pain of 9/11 is revisited every time a scene of the flaming towers appears on the television. It is revisited every time we see a picture of the cleanup at Ground Zero. It is revisited every time the remains of a fallen hero is recovered. And it is revisited today, with the questions about what might have been, had the pieces of the puzzle been put together in a different way before that sad day in September. . . .
>
> As for the President, he may not be in a position to respond to all of those concerns. But he is in a position to answer some of them, including the question of why we know today, May 16, about the warning he received, and why we did not know this on April 16, or March 16, or February 16, or January 16, or December 16, or November 16, or October 16, September 16 . . . or August 16?[59]

On January 24, 2003, seemingly searching for every possible angle to condemn the president, Senator Clinton decried the president's supposed failure to fight terrorism on the home front, accusing him of sending inadequate federal funding to local governments:

> While today, the new Department of Homeland Security opens its doors in Washington, DC, here at this conference,

we are examining the question of how far has our nation come since September 11 when it comes to Homeland Security. What has been done, and what is left to be done? Where are we now, and where do we go from here?

The truth is we are not prepared, we are not supporting our first responders, and our approach to securing our nation is haphazard at best. We have relied on a myth of homeland security—a myth written in rhetoric, inadequate resources, and a new bureaucracy, instead of relying on good old fashion[ed] American ingenuity, might and muscle.[60]

In December 2003, Mrs. Clinton went so far as to declare, "I can't maybe even convey it as strongly as I feel, how dangerous this administration is to the future of our country."[61] Of course, in the worldview of the liberal appeasement lobby, the moral courage of leaders like President Bush has always been dangerous—in much the same way that challenging the Soviet Union appeared dangerous to Ronald Reagan's opponents.

Mrs. Clinton is nothing if not an ambitious politician, and there's no doubt that she is willing to change her message in order to attain power. And to have any chance at securing the presidency in 2008, she knows that she must mask her true liberal beliefs, to cast herself as a plausible wartime leader. After all, liberalism and war leadership have rarely been linked, either in history or in the public mind.

You can be sure that Hillary would be running today for the 2004 election if she believed her chances were strong—or if she believed that one of the existing Democratic candidates had any chance of winning, which might foreclose her presidential ambitions until 2012, when her age might be a liability. In ducking the

2004 race, Hillary avoids challenging an incumbent—historically a difficult assignment, even when the incumbent isn't as popular as President Bush. (In the twentieth century, presidential incumbents have won reelection in ten of fourteen contests.)

Hillary Clinton is certainly right in believing that she will have a better chance in 2008. But we mustn't be fooled by her feigned lack of interest, or by her professed commitment to her senatorial duties. Would she abandon her Senate seat the minute she thought she could win the presidency? In a New York minute.

It's also important to recognize that by 2008 the scandals of the Clinton era will have lost much of their immediacy. The foreign policy failures of Bill Clinton's administration will no longer make fresh political fodder. The Democrats will simply return to their old, generic political script: *George W. Bush has had eight years to solve the world's problems. It's time to give the opposition a try.* Of course, the fact that Bush inherited most of them from Bill Clinton won't get much play.

In the meantime, Hillary Clinton will work hard to manufacture an image of being strong on defense—an image any candidate will have to cultivate in order to run a competitive presidential campaign. Currently a member of the Senate Armed Services Committee, she has called for a greater increase in troops in Iraq, and for an increase in NATO's role in Afghanistan. Mrs. Clinton took a well-publicized trip to Iraq in the immediate wake of President Bush's Thanksgiving visit, and is likely to chase further photo ops of the kind in the years to come. These moves are all designed to accomplish a specific goal—to make Hillary Clinton appear to be a more widely acceptable mainstream candidate. She knows that she already has a core of support in the left-wing Democratic Party base. But she must court Reagan Democrats—the blue-collar, middle-class citizens whose votes she will need to be elected. And to win them over Mrs. Clinton needs to shed the image that she is soft on defense, soft on national security, soft on terror.

Her membership on the Senate Armed Services Committee is useful in helping her to project a more hawkish image. Members of the committee are charged with overseeing the Pentagon and conducting an ongoing "comprehensive study and review of matters relating to the common defense policy of the United States."[62] Senators on this committee are charged with appropriating funds for the Department of Defense, and often travel to locations throughout the world to examine U.S. military operations personally, and to meet the troops.

It was a plum committee for Senator Clinton to join—a critical step in her campaign to remake herself. Once a fire-breathing, 1960s-type antiwar activist, Hillary is well-positioned to be seen as a responsible and thoughtful foreign policy statesman. And she's already making the most of her position. Her November 2003 trip to Afghanistan and Iraq resulted in her appearances on three of the four major Sunday network shows, where she aired her criticism of President Bush's policies. No doubt we'll see all that location footage recycled during her future campaigns.

Senator Clinton's hawkish new tone was also on display in a press release she issued on November 27, 2003. "Every American understood why we had to go out after those who attacked us," she declared.

> There is a great level of support for our mission. I am honored to have the opportunity to spend Thanksgiving with the brave men and women who have put their lives on the line for all Americans. It [is] a wonderful opportunity to convey

to them that the American people are fully behind them as they carry out a very difficult task. I am so proud to represent the brave men and women of the 10th Mountain Division.[63]

Yet Hillary can't help herself: She always wants to have it both ways. When asked by military personnel "how the people at home feel about what we are doing," she began by telling them that "Americans are wholeheartedly proud of what you are doing." Still, she couldn't resist getting in a jab at President Bush: "But there are many questions at home about the [Bush] administration policies."[64] Her criticism of the commander in chief—in conversation with troops on the battlefield—rightfully upset conservatives back home, because it risked demoralizing the troops by implying that public support for their mission was wavering.[65]

About ten days later, on *Meet the Press,* Mrs. Clinton voiced the Democratic party line on the WMD issue. "There was certainly adequate intelligence," she told Tim Russert, "without it being gilded and exaggerated by the administration to raise questions about chemical and biological programs and a continuing effort to obtain nuclear power."[66] She dissociated herself from doubters on the war, saying that "I think that Saddam Hussein was certainly a potential threat," that he "was seeking weapons of mass destruction, whether or not he actually had them." And she called for more troops on the ground. It was such a tough-talking performance that William Safire slyly headlined his column the following day "Hillary, Congenital Hawk."[67]

On their face, such statements suggest a strong posture in the face of the War on Terror. But this is Hillary Clinton we're talking about; it's hard to believe her newly discovered love for the military will last a minute longer than necessary.

To Mrs. Clinton's credit, she understands that post-9/11 America has no interest in electing a commander in chief who is weak on national security. Strangely, this is a lesson lost on most of the current candidates seeking the Democratic nomination for president. But Hillary has been in politics long enough to realize that many Americans see her—perhaps the quintessential liberal Democrat—and her party as soft on defense. And she is willing to sprout the wings of a hawk if it will help her achieve her objective.

The truth, as always, is in a candidate's record, not her rhetoric. And Mrs. Clinton's record convinces me beyond any doubt that a Hillary Clinton presidency would endanger American security and lives—no matter how many trips to the front she takes, no matter how many press releases she issues. Like Bill Clinton, whose claim to be a "New Democrat" helped propel him into office, Hillary Clinton, in her latter-day centrist Democrat mode, can be counted on to slash the defense budget, use the military for social experiments, demoralize the troops, and undermine our intelligence agencies, as soon as she gets the chance.

And you can count on one more thing: if Hillary Clinton is ever elected president, we'll see a return to the co-presidency of the 1990s. Bill and Hillary Clinton are a political team, after all: two for the price of one.

Bill Clinton spent his eight years in the White House dithering over foreign policy, ignoring evil, and appeasing terrorism in all corners of the world. Kim Jong II blackmailed and betrayed his administration. Osama bin Laden planned and set in motion the devastating attacks of 9/11. Saddam Hussein flouted U.N. mandates, raped his own people, and terrorized the Middle East.

For Mr. and Mrs. Clinton, there should be no second chances.

EIGHT

Playing Politics at the Water's Edge

Politics stops at the water's edge. It's a saying often invoked whenever a foreign policy crisis shifts national attention away from domestic disputes and toward matters of our shared national security. When the United States commits troops overseas, or is attacked on its own soil, we must put our internal arguments aside and maintain a united front. We must remember, in other words, that we're all Americans first, Republicans and Democrats second.

When a politician puts his party's interests ahead of the nation's interests, the American public tends to find such behavior irresponsible at best, unforgivable at worst. The partisan squabbling that's typical of any debate about welfare reform, Medicare, school vouchers, or taxes should never enter into American foreign policy—particularly in times of war or national emergency.

Traditionally, both parties have respected this principle. After the Japanese attacked Pearl Harbor and the United States entered

World War II, the formerly isolationist Republicans became committed to winning the war. While they had minor disputes with F.D.R. over the conduct of the war, they didn't try to slander him for causing the Japanese attack with his economic embargoes of the Japanese. This bipartisan spirit continued into the Cold War, when Democrats like Harry Truman and John F. Kennedy confronted the communist threat to freedom and liberty, with the support of Republicans in Congress. Throughout most of the twentieth century, Democrats and Republicans were loath to leverage foreign-policy disagreements for short-term political gain.

Unfortunately, during our own critical period in American history, when our way of life is under direct attack, this is no longer the case. As I recently discovered, liberal Democrats have been trying to hijack one of the Senate's most important committees for their own purposes, putting politics ahead of our nation's security.

Now, let me say from the start that I'm no opponent of open and honest debate, even over questions of foreign policy. After all, I make my living debating important issues with people from all over the political spectrum. I would never claim that an earnest difference of opinion about foreign policy is unpatriotic. When the Democrats argue that we should be spending more time and energy on homeland defense in the War on Terror, for example, they're making a legitimate argument. I happen to disagree with them; after all, we're spending unprecedented sums to secure our shores. But I also believe that our first priority should be going after the terrorists where they live—and that we should be allocating substantial resources, as we now are, to that mission. But believing otherwise doesn't necessarily make you unpatriotic; in my view, it just makes for bad policy.

But when it comes to debate during wartime, I think one

principle is clear: The only responsible argument is one that's made in good faith. The Democrats have violated that principle. As their recent behavior suggests, some of the party's most prominent members have stooped to using partisan tactics for political gain—at the expense of U.S. security.

As my radio and television audience knows, I recently uncovered evidence of a deliberate and systematic plan, orchestrated by the Democrats, to discredit and undermine President Bush and the War on Terror. And what shocks me most about this discovery is that the plan emanates from what should be the most trustworthy sector of our government: the members of the United States Senate.

In the earliest days after the attacks of September 11, the Senate stood united behind President Bush. Democrats and Republicans stood together on the steps of the Capitol and sang "God Bless America." By a margin of 98–0, the Senate passed a resolution authorizing the president to "use all necessary and appropriate force" against the terrorists and any nation that provided safe harbor or support to them.[1] Senator Carl Levin, a Democrat from Michigan, stated that "we must be united at home and that means standing up to those who practice hatred."[2] Senator Jay Rockefeller, a Democrat from West Virginia, declared that "In this dark hour we all stand with President Bush and the military and intelligence leadership of this nation in search for propagators of this great evil, and for an appropriate and strong response."[3] And in the months that followed, Congress voted overwhelmingly to authorize the use of military force in Afghanistan and Iraq.

Flash forward two years. The Taliban has been successfully routed from Afghanistan. Saddam Hussein has been driven from power. Afghanistan and Iraq are no longer sponsoring terrorists.

Citizens of these nations no longer live under the evils of tyranny. The seeds of the democratic process have been planted in these nations. President Bush's vision for a more peaceful, stable and democratic world is beginning to come true.

One of the reasons we went to war in Iraq was to deprive Saddam Hussein of the ability to manufacture or use weapons of mass destruction, or to distribute them to other terrorists. As President Bush pointed out, we could not wait for the threat that terrorists could acquire weapons of mass destruction (WMD) to become imminent—for then it would be too late. The United States had to act preemptively, before more Americans were harmed.[4]

In March 2003, American troops stormed across the Kuwaiti border into Iraq. Within a month, the United States had removed Saddam Hussein from power and began to establish a new provisional government. But though American forces uncovered mobile biological weapons laboratories,[5] elements of a nuclear weapons program, and much evidence of Saddam's continuing interest in acquiring prohibited weaponry,[6] they did not immediately uncover actual weapons.

Spurred by reports that the intelligence community may have misled the White House and the public about Iraq's WMD capabilities, the Senate Select Committee on Intelligence (SSCI) began a review of prewar intelligence. The committee sought to complete two tasks: first, to "evaluate the intelligence underlying pre-war assessments of Iraq's WMD capability"; second, to "evaluate the accuracy of those assessments by comparing them with the results of the ongoing search for prohibited weapons."[7] The committee's review included, among other things, examining the "quantity and quality of U.S. intelligence on Iraqi weapons of mass destruction," analyzing "the objectivity, reasonableness, independence, and accuracy of the judgments reached by the Intelligence Community," and "determining whether those judgments [by the intelligence community] were properly disseminated to policy makers in the Executive Branch and Congress" as well as "whether any influence was brought to bear on anyone to shape their analysis to support policy objectives."[8]

In the spirit of apparent bipartisanship, SSCI press releases included statements from both its chair, Senator Pat Roberts, and its vice chair, Senator Jay Rockefeller. Roberts and Rockefeller stated that they shared a "*joint* commitment to continue the Committee's thorough review of U.S. intelligence," and that the SSCI "would use whatever tools of oversight it deems necessary to complete its work."

In these joint statements, the SSCI was only reaffirming the tradition of nonpartisan work for which it had been known since its establishment in 1976. In its nearly thirty-year history, the committee has been involved in evaluating the most sensitive national security issues, from our intelligence community's ability to validate Soviet compliance with the SALT II and INF treaties, to the issue of trading arms for hostages during the Iran-Contra Affair. During the 1990s the SSCI even worked to redefine the role of the director of Central Intelligence.[9]

For obvious reasons, the work of such a committee must be protected from the corrupting influence of political agendas—a principle its members have customarily held in the highest regard. In 1998, then-Vice Chairman Bob Kerrey pointed out that the very structure of the group is unusual in the Senate: "It is organized to be bipartisan, with a Vice Chairman instead of a Ranking Member and a division of only one member, regardless of the make-up of the floor." SSCI members, he said, prided themselves on putting the interests of America ahead of politics: "The national security requires U.S. intelligence activities to be effective, to be efficient, and to be consonant with American law and American values. Only a bipartisan committee, rising above momentary political advantage, can accomplish this task." As Kerrey pointed out, even some of the Senate's most renowned partisans had managed to participate without compromising their work:

> The Intelligence Committee has a heritage of statesmen leaving politics at the door of the Committee room and keeping politics away from their deliberations. Our standards were set by Dan Inouye, Barry Goldwater, Pat Moynihan, Birch Bayh, Dave Durenburger and others who put the national security oversight mission of the Committee ahead of politics.[10]

More recently, Senator Zell Miller of Georgia has stated that the SSCI "should unquestionably be above partisan politics." He further describes the sensitive nature of the information the SSCI deals with and the role the SSCI should play. "The information it [SSCI] deals with should never, never be distorted, compromised or politicized in any shape, form or fashion. For it involves the lives of our soldiers and citizens. Its actions should always be above reproach."[11] And independent policy analysts agree with Senators Kerrey and Miller. As Frank Ciluffo of the Center for Strategic and International Studies observes, "In general, the intelligence committee doesn't get too political. It is pretty bipartisan because national security matters are of greatest importance to our country and don't really have a place for politics."[12]

But today's Democratic Party is a different animal. In a party led by Tom Daschle, Terry McAuliffe, Dick Durbin, Jay Rockefeller, Chuck Schumer, and Hillary Clinton, every position is a political position. And now, apparently, they've decided to put politics above all else—even our national security.

On Tuesday, November 4, 2003, I obtained a copy of a memorandum apparently written by a Democratic staff member of the SSCI, describing the Democrats' plans to use the committee's ongoing review of intelligence activities for their own political purposes.

Think about that for a moment. We are at war. James Woolsey, the former director of Central Intelligence, has described our campaign against terrorism as World War IV, following the first and second World Wars and the Cold War.[13] American soldiers are in harm's way in all corners of the world. The members of the Senate Select Committee on Intelligence are entrusted with the critical task of overseeing the work of the U.S. intelligence community—in order to ensure the security of our citizens and soldiers, at home and abroad.

As this memo demonstrates, though, the Democratic members of the SSCI have other, more sinister priorities. Their clear intention is to use the committee's information-gathering powers for the purposes of undermining the president and other members of the Bush administration. This is more than mere rudeness, more than everyday partisanship; it's a blatant abuse of their public trust. And it's an alarming reflection of how far the Democratic Party will stoop to conquer their political enemies.

The memo reads as follows:

We have carefully reviewed our options under the rules and believe we have identified the best approach. Our plan is as follows:

1) <u>Pull the majority</u> [party—i.e., Republican committee members] <u>along as far as we can on issues that may lead to major new disclosures regarding improper or questionable conduct by Administration officials.</u> We are having some success in that regard. For example, in addition to the president's State of the Union speech, the Chairman has agreed to look at the activities of the Office of the Secretary of Defense (e.g. Rumsfeld, Feith and Wolfowitz) as well as Secretary Bolton's office at the State Department. The fact that the chairman supports our investigations into these offices, and cosigns our requests for information, is helpful and potentially crucial. We don't know what we will find, but our prospects for getting the access we seek is [sic] far greater when we have the backing of the Majority. (Note: We can verbally mention some of the intriguing leads we are pursuing.)

2) <u>Assiduously prepare Democratic "additional views" to attach to any interim or final reports the committee may release.</u> Committee rules provide this opportunity and we intend to take full advantage of it. In that regard, we have already compiled all the public statements on Iraq made by senior Administration officials. We will identify the most exaggerated claims and contrast them with the intelligence estimates that have since been declassified. Our additional views will also, among other things, castigate the majority [party] for seeking to limit the scope of the inquiry. The

Democrats will then be in a strong position to reopen the question of establishing an independent commission (i.e. the Corzine amendment).

3) Prepare to launch an Independent investigation when it becomes clear we have exhausted the opportunity to usefully collaborate with the Majority. We can pull the trigger on an independent investigation of the administration's [sic] use of intelligence at any time—but we can only do so once. The best time to do so will probably be next year either:

A) After we have already released our additional views on an interim report—thereby providing as many as three opportunities to make our case to the public: (1) additional views on the interim report; (2) announcement of our independent investigation; and (3) additional views on the final investigation; or

B) Once we identify solid leads the Majority does not want to pursue. We would attract more coverage and have greater credibility in that context than one in which we simply launch an independent investigation based on principled but vague notions regarding the "use" of intelligence.

In the meantime, even without a specifically authorized independent investigation, we continue to act independently when we encounter foot-dragging on the part of the Majority. For example, the FBI Niger investigation was done solely at the request of the Vice Chairman; we have independently submitted written questions to DoD [the Department of Defense]; and we are preparing further independent requests for information.

Summary

Intelligence issues are clearly secondary to the public's concern regarding the insurgency in Iraq. Yet, we have an important role to play in revealing the misleading—if not flagrantly dishonest methods and motives—of the senior Administration officials who made the case for a unilateral, preemptive war. The approach outline[d] above seems to offer the best prospect for exposing the Administration's dubious motives and motives [sic].

There it is, in black and white: a frank self-portrait of the Democratic Party in full attack mode—willing and eager to co-opt the business of national security for their own selfish purposes. At the risk of losing all faith in our bipartisan government, let's examine more closely what the memo's anonymous author proposes.

As the memo's closing mission statement suggests, the Democratic architects of this plan see themselves as serving "an important role" on the committee—though not the role they were selected to fill. In their view, their true mission involves "revealing the misleading—if not flagrantly dishonest methods and motives—of the senior administration officials who made the case for a unilateral, preemptive war."

And what precedes that mission statement is a battle plan whose sole objective appears to be "exposing the administration's dubious motives." It is a completely political plan, using the same tactics the Clinton-McAuliffe school of cutthroat politics has been honing for years.

The memo cites three steps that Democrats on the SSCI would undertake in order to undermine President Bush. Their first step? To "pull the majority [i.e., the GOP] along as far as we can on issues that may lead to major new disclosures regarding improper or questionable conduct by administration officials."

That's right: the Democrats intend to *use* their Republican counterparts—to leverage their sincere bipartisan support to conduct a fishing expedition, in search of any information that might reflect badly on the president, the secretary of defense, and John Bolton, a prominent conservative at the State Department.

The cynicism of the scheme is breathtaking. "The fact that the chairman [Republican senator Pat Roberts] supports our investigations into these offices, and cosigns our requests for information, is helpful and potentially crucial," the memo says. It's clear that the Democrats have no actual foreknowledge of wrongdoing: "We don't know what we will find," the memo concedes, "but our prospects for getting the access we seek is far greater when we have the backing of the Majority."

Even more insidious, the memorandum reveals that the Democrats intend to leak whatever they uncover: "(Note: We can verbally mention some of the intriguing leads we are pursuing)." Why "verbally mention"? So they can get word out without leaving a paper trail. And there's the smoking gun: an explicit statement that the Democrats intend to leak details from a highly sensitive investigation—one that involved classified intelligence from such sources as the CIA and the National Security Agency (NSA). A leak from the SSCI can literally jeopardize intelligence sources, which in turn can jeopardize lives.

If that isn't bad faith, I don't know what is.

The second step the Democrats would take would be to "prepare Democratic 'additional views' to attach to any interim or final reports the committee may release." Here, the Democrats reveal how fully their attention has been fixed on finding a pretext to embarrass the administration. The memo reveals that the Democrats have already "compiled all the public statements made on Iraq by senior administration officials," in order to contrast these statements with declassified intelligence estimates.

It's a classic dirty-politics campaign tactic: keep a roster of everything your political enemies—in this case President Bush, Vice President Cheney, Secretary of State Powell, Secretary of Defense Rumsfeld, and National Security Adviser Condoleezza Rice—have said. Then put your team to work gathering all available intelligence, just hoping to unearth some kind of "evidence" contradicting those statements. The only difference is, in this case the "team" is a supposedly bipartisan Senate committee specifically designed to remain beyond the reach of politics.

This second step also reveals how little regard the Democrats have for the actual work of the committee. Rather than investigating all leads with an open mind, the memo makes clear that they have intended all along to use the "additional views" provision to discredit any interim or final reports it might issue—and to "castigate" Republican members in the process! No matter what the SSCI's examination might uncover, the Democrats had only one goal in mind: to damage Senior Bush administration officials with their findings. So much for Bob Kerrey's ideals of fair play.

The third step the Democrats on the SSCI would take was to "prepare to launch an Independent investigation when it becomes clear we have exhausted the opportunity to usefully collaborate with the majority." Again, the bad faith is overwhelming. By the time this memo was written—with the committee's work still in its first stages—the Democrats had already decided that they would eventually abandon their bipartisan efforts and call for an independent investigation. Of course any such independent investigation would be run by Democrats, with unlimited time and resources, lobbing "Intelligence Brief" grenades from the comfort of Capitol Hill whenever it saw an opening to damage the president. And of course any such investigation would run throughout 2004, just as President Bush was up for reelection.

Now, it's important to note that when this memo was written our troops were still gathering intelligence about Saddam's weapons-program plans—as indeed they still are even as I write this. When this memorandum was uncovered, the SSCI was still working with the Bush administration to continue its review of prewar intelligence. Not only had no legitimate conclusions been reached—our soldiers were still engaged in combat! As I've pointed out on my radio show, nothing in this memorandum has to do with strengthening intelligence or national security, which is the job of the SSCI. Instead, the crafters of this memo are attempting to turn the SSCI into a political attack machine—while the president is leading the nation in a war on terrorism, and brave men and women are fighting and dying.

What happened after I went public on my show with this information? Did the Democrats own up to their duplicity? Fat chance.

Senator Jay Rockefeller, the West Virginia Democrat who vice-chairs the SSCI, released a statement saying that he hadn't approved the memo, nor "was it shared with any member of the Senate Intelligence Committee or anyone else." Rockefeller dodged the real implications of the memo, saying only that it "reflects staff frustration."[14] But he did call for an investigation—not into the Democrats' political scheming, but into *whether Republicans were obtaining unauthorized access to the Democrats' materials!*[15] That's right: Rather than apologizing or accepting responsibility on behalf of his party, he took a page from the Clinton playbook and went on the attack. (In an even more Clintonian gesture, from the other side of his mouth he said he believed that "members of the Intelligence Committee can put aside their differences and continue to work through the tough tasks facing them.")

Notice anything missing? Once again, not a word from Senator Rockefeller, or the other Democrats on the SSCI, about what they would actually do to enhance our national security, protect our borders, ensure the safety of the homeland, or improve our intelligence capabilities. When it comes to defeating the enemy, it's not Saddam Hussein or Osama bin Laden they have in their sights. It's George W. Bush.

Senator Pat Roberts, the Republican chair of the SSCI, described the memo as a "slap in the face." Calling the memorandum an "attack plan,"[16] he condemned it as "a giant buzz saw of politics that's very damaging for the country."[17] But Dick Durbin, another prominent Democrat on the SSCI, hardly broke stride: he used the opportunity to call for the creation of an independent commission—one of the very goals outlined in the memo![18] Durbin was just following the same plan they've all been pursuing from day one: No matter how much the administration cooperated with the Democrats, no matter what information turned up, the Democrats were going to use the bipartisan commission as a springboard to their own partisan witch hunt.

Only one Democrat had the guts to condemn the memorandum: Zell Miller of Georgia, who described the plot as "the first cousin of treason."[19]

Since this memo came to light, I have repeatedly offered Senator Rockefeller the opportunity to clear up the origins of the memo. We've invited the chairman to appear on both my radio program and *Hannity & Colmes* to discuss the issue. But though he's been willing to appear on CNN and other programs, he refuses to appear with me on radio or television. The reason is simple: Senator Rockefeller doesn't want to be exposed as the wizard behind the curtain. At first he blamed a staffer for independently drafting the memo out of frustration with the Bush administration. Now we know that Rockefeller himself was the instigator, and he has refused to repudiate its contents.[20]

But Rockefeller himself isn't the only one to blame. As it turns out, the committee is full of unreconstructed partisans.

Barbara Milkulski of Maryland has been described as "an absolute tyrant,"[21] a "partisan bulldog,"[22] and "fiercely partisan and proud of it."[23] In 1998, she was ranked by staffers as the second meanest senator. By 2000, Senator Milkulski had risen to number one on the list of meanest senators.[24]

In July 2003, Michigan's Carl Levin, another committee member, reportedly was so impatient with Senator Rockefeller's vice chairmanship that he directed his own staff to "begin looking into the intelligence used to justify the war."[25] Senator Levin was so eager to attack the president that he was willing to flout the SSCI's jurisdiction over intelligence-related matters. Senator Levin has been characterized by no less an authority of liberalism than ABC's Peter Jennings as "an unabashed liberal."[26]

Senator Dick Durbin, described as "a fiercely partisan Democrat"[27] and "well versed in partisan tactics,"[28] has worked to undermine the goals of the SSCI. Even before the memo surfaced, Durbin was saying that a Democrats-only investigation was inevitable, and accusing Republicans of "protect[ing] the Administration at any cost."[29] Another fact about Senator Durbin: on September 12, 2001, his office issued a press release vowing to hold gas stations accountable in the wake of any price gouging.[30] Did Dick Durbin condemn the terrorists who perpetrated this despicable act? No. Did he voice sorrow over the loss of three thousand Americans? No. Instead, in the aftermath of our national crisis, Senator Durbin appointed himself as high watchman of America's gas stations.

Senator John Edwards also sits on the SSCI. Although he isn't known to be as overtly partisan as Milkulski, Levin, and Durbin, there's another suggestive little detail about Edwards: He's running for president. Certainly he has the most to gain personally from any damaging attacks on President Bush and his administration.

I don't fault these senators for being partisan. Party politics, after all, is part of the strength of our political system. But there's a time and place for that kind of thing—and it doesn't include misappropriating the work of a select bipartisan committee, dealing with classified information, in a time of war. As an American citizen, that's where I draw the line. Apparently the Democratic Party thinks otherwise.

In this context, it may be worth noting another surprising fact: *none of the Democrats serving on the SSCI has any military or intelligence experience.* The Republicans provide a sharp contrast: Pat Roberts served four years in the Marine Corps. Chuck Hagel won two Purple Hearts as an Army sergeant in Vietnam. John Warner served in the Navy in World War II, in the Marine Corps in Korea, in the Nixon administration as secretary of the navy. I know I've said repeatedly that you don't have to serve in the military in order to speak out on military issues. But serving on a government oversight committee requires a deep understanding of our military and intelligence systems. And I frankly think it's bizarre that the Democrats couldn't manage to find one senator with relevant experience in their ranks to serve in this important capacity. It makes you wonder whether the Democrats even understand the sensitivity of the information they're dealing with—or, more darkly, whether they're really interested in anything beyond their own self-serving motives.

Mind you, I don't believe that this memorandum was an instance of rogue behavior by the SSCI Democrats alone. I believe it's part of a larger campaign by the Democratic Party to undermine the Bush presidency and the conservative movement. Consider the way they treated their own leader when it seemed he wasn't initially on board. In July 2003, shortly after the initiation of the SSCI's review, Senate Democrats began whispering that Senator Rockefeller wasn't up to the job. Reports surfaced that "Rockefeller's unwillingness to consult Senate Democratic leaders on his strategy for tackling the White House's potential misuse of intelligence data is raising the hackles of some in his Caucus who fear a lack of a coordinated message could foil Democratic attempts to take full political advantage of the situation."[31] A senior Democratic aide was quoted as saying, "He's not the team player we need him to be."

Moreover, other members reportedly complained to Senator Rockefeller that he "appeared at times to defend Intelligence Chairman Pat Roberts' (R-Kan.) reluctance to initiate a probe." The more cutthroat Democrats on the committee apparently felt that the lack of a unified message could compromise their party's ability to make the most of any possible Bush weakness leading into 2004. In Washington, when a senator begins to hear that his party colleagues are unhappy with his performance, that senator takes note. This memorandum appears to be the natural outgrowth of a Democratic Party leadership that was unsatisfied with the SSCI's direction and sought to develop a strategy to use it for its own ends.

In fact, the Democrats' actual behavior throughout the fall of 2003 demonstrates that they were following the strategies outlined in the memo. Senator Durbin called for the establishment of an independent investigation led by these very "rebel members of the [SSCI]," as the London *Sunday Telegraph* described them.[32] Moreover, speculation began to surface that such an investigation might result in "a high-profile Bush Administration resignation"—speculation no doubt puffed up by Democrats hoping to hurt the president's profile as the 2004 elections neared.

FALLOUT

Again, it wasn't always thus. During World War II, Franklin Roosevelt's secretary of war, Harry Stimson, was a Republican. Secretary Stimson had served in the same capacity for Republican William Howard Taft, and as secretary of state to Herbert Hoover. Roosevelt even managed to put politics so far aside as to name the Republicans' 1936 vice presidential nominee, Frank Knox, as secretary of the navy.[33]

At the height of the Cold War, John F. Kennedy sought advice and counsel from former president Dwight Eisenhower on how best to deal with the Soviet Union. After the debacle of the

Bay of Pigs Invasion, Ike was equally gracious, declining to criticize President Kennedy.[34]

This kind of discipline is needed more than ever now that we are at war again. Unfortunately, once more the Democratic Party has ignored the lessons of history. But before they continue choosing their own ambitions over the national welfare, they might want to think about the serious consequences of their actions.

They might want to consider the fact that their own actions will almost certainly make anyone within the scope of their investigation think twice about sharing intelligence with the SSCI, now and in the future. By making it clear that Democratic committee members will not hesitate to reveal "intriguing leads" by "verbally mentioning"—that is, leaking—them for partisan purposes, the memo has jeopardized its credibility and effectiveness as an oversight body for the foreseeable future. After all, how can members of the intelligence community be expected to deal in an open and honest fashion with committee members, when they know that those members may be plumbing them for sensitive information for the sole purpose of leaking it to the media?

Of course, if the SSCI's channels of information are compromised—if it becomes unable to obtain full and accurate information—we have to question its long-term ability to fulfill its mission, at least with its current membership. But the implications of the Democrats' activities go beyond just damage to the committee's own domestic intelligence-gathering ability. How can the American people trust a body like the SSCI to make objective reports to the Senate, when we know that half its membership is driven by partisan motivations?

And the consequences in the realm of foreign intelligence are even more disturbing. Will our allies be less likely to share intelligence with the United States for fear that it could also be leaked to the media? Will our enemies, including the Hussein loyalists our troops are currently fighting, derive comfort from the fact that American politicians are actively attempting to undermine the president?

As the efforts to build a stable government in Iraq continue, it is increasingly important that the U.S. presence on the ground remain strong, well-funded, and well-supported at home. It has been widely reported that the remnants of Saddam's regime are pursuing a strategy of attrition. Unable to defeat the U.S. army through conventional means, they are attempting to wear down the will of the people of the United States through the use of hit-and-run tactics designed to sap morale among the troops and on the home front. If our enemies can inflict enough damage to succeed in eroding that popular support (and, by extension, government funding), the United States could be forced to pull out of Iraq—allowing Saddam's loyalists a chance to regain power.

Could so many dominoes fall just because of one memo? Maybe not. But don't fool yourself: this one memo is only the tip of the iceberg—a symbol of the attitude of the liberal Democratic Party, which is single-mindedly bent on discrediting the president and winning back the White House—even if it means compromising our national security in the process. If the Democrats succeed in politically damaging President Bush in this nefarious way, I believe the War on Terror itself will be jeopardized, and American lives will be endangered.

As a senator, Harry Truman appreciated the potentially damaging consequences of having a congressional investigation during a time of war or national emergency. Concerned about money that was being wasted in military construction, Truman founded the Senate Special Committee to Investigate the National Defense Program, which investigated the awarding of defense contracts on the eve of World War II. But Truman realized he must act carefully, because of the potential damage to the presidency and "lives it could cost by prolonging the war."[35]

Truman, in turn, was well aware of Abraham Lincoln's troubles with the Joint Committee on the Conduct of the War, which had attempted to micromanage the Civil War. As Lincoln griped, the committee's "greatest purpose seems to be to hamper my action and obstruct the military operations."[36] Confederate General Robert E. Lee apparently agreed, quipping that the committee was worth about two divisions of Confederate troops. During his eight months in hiding, I wonder if Saddam Hussein ever watched CSPAN coverage of the Senate Democrats and thought the same thing.

Shortly after the memo surfaced, Senator Rockefeller expressed a desire to move on, to get the entire affair behind him and resume the business of the SSCI. But how can Republicans expect the Democrats to act in good faith when they have so completely corrupted the stated purposes of the SSCI? The Democrats on the committee have demonstrated that they're not really interested in an honest and fair accounting of the intelligence on Iraq, or any other matter. What they're interested in is finding some slender premise to establish an independent investigation, accountable to no one, to achieve their stated goal: to discredit the Bush administration.

As I've said, this isn't a matter of Democrats trying to promote honest debate on the issues. It's a simple matter of bad faith. As soon as the smoke cleared after 9/11, we began hearing hysterical shrieks from the left that they were being hounded out of the public square, that their rights of dissent and debate were being taken away from them. "I am sick and tired of people who say that if you debate and you disagree with this administration," Democratic Senator Hillary Clinton has famously cried, "somehow you are not patriotic. We should stand up and say we are Americans and we have a right to debate and disagree with any administration."[37]

But Democrats who claim that theirs is the party of earnest dissent should be ashamed of themselves. Want to see real political suppression? Just look ninety miles off the coast of Florida, where Cuba's prisons are full of political dissidents. Despite the overheated rhetoric from the left, no one is being prosecuted for his political opinions. Nobody is going to stop Hillary Clinton from speaking her mind on Iraq or George W. Bush.

When members of Congress threaten to play politics with classified foreign intelligence, however, that is another matter. To protect our very national security, I believe such abuses must be stopped, and the abusers called to account.

Of course, the Democrats could have handled the discovery of this damaging memo in a straightforward manner—the way the Republicans did in an embarrassing incident of their own a short time later. When Republican staffers on the Senate Judiciary Committee were discovered to have stolen a number of confidential Democratic Party files on a computer network, those staffers were immediately placed on administrative leave. Republican Senator Orrin Hatch of Utah condemned their behavior as "improper, unethical and simply unacceptable." Moreover, when confronted with the allegations of wrongdoing on his committee, Senator Hatch launched an investigation, to be conducted by former federal prosecutors.[38] The Republicans took the only honorable approach to misdeeds by their own staff members, investigating the case, denouncing the act, and punishing the perpetrators.

Take the high road? Not Bill Clinton's party. After I first brought the Democratic memo to the attention of the American public, Senator Rockefeller attempted to intimidate me into silence by threatening to have me called before a Senate committee to answer questions about my sources. His goal, of course, was to have me drop the whole story, to spare himself and his colleagues any more embarrassment. But to me, the point isn't to embarrass the Democrats. The point is that their brand of take-no-prisoners dirty politics behavior is not only unconscionable, it's unpatriotic—and with thousands of troops fighting for us overseas, it's dangerous.

I'm sorry, Senator Rockefeller: I will not be bullied or threatened by any government official defending his own inappropriate action or that of his staff. This is a representative republic. You and your colleagues, Senators Durbin, Schumer, and the rest, serve at the pleasure of the American people. You answer to us. And just as you demand access to information that relates to the president, we must demand the same from you.

But I will take the Democrats up on one of their ideas. Since Senator Dick Durbin has made it clear he's a fan of independent investigations, he and his partisan colleagues should have no problem turning their computers, e-mails, files, and other documents— and those of their staffers—over to the FBI or the Senate Ethics Committee, so that our questions about their conduct, and their worthiness to hold public office, can be answered to the satisfaction of the voters who keep them in office.

Somehow I think that's one can of worms they won't want to open.

NINE

The Candidates

The 2004 election will be the first chance America has had to select a president since the events of September 11, 2001. With the economy on the rebound, the major issue in the election will be the War on Terror—and my expectation is that the American people will demonstrate their support of President Bush's policies and performance by reelecting him. Electing a Democrat in 2004 would constitute a rejection of the clear moral leadership the president has displayed since he has taken office. It would also mean endorsing a political party that's assembled one of the most irresponsible sets of presidential candidates since Jimmy Carter, Teddy Kennedy, and Jerry Brown duked it out for the Democratic nomination in 1980. I don't think the American people are going to let that happen.

We're witnessing an almost unprecedented phenomenon in American history: An entire political party has become unhinged. Much of the American left is suffering from what Fox News contributor and psychiatrist Charles Krauthammer satirically describes as "Bush Derangement Syndrome: *the acute onset of paranoia in otherwise normal people in reaction to the policies, the presidency—nay—the very existence of George W. Bush.*"[1] This hysteria has found its way into the vitriolic speeches of the Democratic candidates for president—not to mention the rhetoric of the party's longtime standard-bearers.

Senator Ted Kennedy, in a fit of Oliver Stone–like paranoia, seems to believe the Iraq War was drummed up by a Texas subsidiary of the Trilateral Commission. "There was no imminent threat. This was made up in Texas, announced in January to the Republican leadership that war was going to take place and was going to be good politically. This whole thing was a fraud."[2] Furthermore, Kennedy thinks that unaccounted funds spent on the war effort are being used for a global slush fund. "My belief is this money is being shuffled all around to these political leaders in all parts of the world, bribing them to send in troops."[3] Maybe Bush is using those black U.N. helicopters to deliver the money.

The "syndrome" has also affected some of the long-shot Democrat candidates for president. In July 2003, Senator Bob Graham—who would later become the first Democrat to drop out of the race—was asked if the president lied in the State of the Union address about Iraq's attempts to buy uranium. "I would not use the three-letter word," he said. "I would use the five-letter word: deceit."[4] No one apparently had the courage to tell the senator that deceit is a six-letter word. (I hate to think what it says about the field of Democratic candidates when the only one smart enough to realize he can't beat Bush can't spell, or count.) Before bowing out of the race, Graham charged Bush with "intentionally deceiving Americans about the scale and imminence of the threat from Iraqi weapons in the months leading up to the war," and even raised the idea of impeachment.[5]

Congressman Dennis Kucinich took off his tinfoil helmet and actually went to the House floor to imply that President Bush was a liar: "America faces a crisis of legitimacy of the administration itself, which lied to the American people to get approval for a war."[6] Without a hint of irony, first-term senator and former supermodel John Edwards charged that George Bush is all style and no substance. "This president is a complete, unadulterated phony," he says, as if the presidential race were some kind of schoolyard popularity contest.[7]

The list of Democratic Bush-haters goes on. Democratic elder statesman and foreign policy expert Al Sharpton, in his signature style, equated President Bush's behavior with that of a gangster. If he were president, Sharpton claimed, "I would not run around trying to be the world's bully, and I would not act like a gang leader, like George Bush did, saying, 'Let's get it on,' when I've got troops over there."[8]

Even the DNC's Terry McAuliffe, in a rare moment of lucidity, seemed to acknowledge that there might be something to "Bush Derangement Syndrome" in the Democrat party. "The Democrats disliked Ronald Reagan . . . but I can tell you the visceral dislike that they have for George Bush and his policies is something I have never seen before."[9] Before that very day was out, though, McAuliffe suffered a relapse himself, with his comment about the president's "absolutely ludicrous and insane statements."[10]

I don't feel I'm taking too much risk making light of second-tier candidates like Kucinich, Sharpton, Graham, and Edwards, because there's little chance any of them will serve as president of the United States. Their rhetorical excesses and pandering to the hard-left Democratic base are no threat to the Republic; they're just blowhard ideologues who saw a chance to grab the national stage for their fifteen minutes of fame, and I'm sure none of them ever really saw themselves touring the world in Air Force One.

The rest of the party's candidates, though, are a different matter. Howard Dean, John Kerry, Richard Gephardt, Joe Lieberman, and Wesley Clark: As I write this, each of these men has a real chance of winning his party's nomination. These men I take very seriously. Whichever of them captures the nomination has some chance of becoming president, given the still-considerable power of the Clinton-McAuliffe party machine. You only have to think back to 1992, when Clinton at one point was polling in the thirtieth percentile, running a distant third behind George H. W. Bush and Ross Perot, to realize how far a candidate can surge from behind when the unpredictable factors of national politics start shifting in his favor.

For this reason, it's critical that we examine the statements and records of these leading Democrats as they enter the most serious stage of the election cycle. For what emerges from their words and deeds thus far is a group portrait of five men who are unwilling or unable to confront the great threat that faces our nation.

HOWARD DEAN

> We don't know whether in the long run the Iraqi people are better off.
>
> —HOWARD DEAN, *July 22, 2003*[11]

When Howard Dean talks about the War on Terror, you know you're witnessing the hardcore left in action. Dean is a committed liberal who does not hide his contempt for President Bush; in fact, he thrives on it. And thus far he's been taking it all the way to the political bank. As his political record reveals, if Howard Dean were elected president, the national security interests of our nation would be immediately and seriously jeopardized. A Dean presidency would be a term of appeasement, delay, and hesitation in the face of the enemy. It would roll back our hard-won victories in the war, and spell disaster for our country.

Howard Dean gained traction in the presidential race by denouncing American military action in Iraq. He appealed to the hardcore left by denouncing President Bush's rationale for war. And yet, beyond simply opposing the president, his speeches and official statements say little or nothing about what policy he actually *recommends* for Iraq. This may be no surprise, given that the governor of Vermont has no actual foreign policy experience whatsoever. But it is a matter of concern when it comes to judging whether he has any proven qualifications to lead his country through the most serious foreign crisis of our times.

During a foreign policy speech given at Drake University on February 17, 2003, it became clear that Dean didn't have a deep comprehension for the breadth of the war on terror. Complaining that the president was focusing too much on Iraq and not enough on the War on Terror, Dean charged that President Bush's State of the Union speech "devoted four paragraphs to the war against terror. He [Bush] devoted sixteen to Iraq."[12] With all due respect, if Governor Dean can't see that fighting a war in Iraq is a part of the larger War on Terror—as much as the campaigns in North Africa, Sicily, Italy, and Burma were part of World War II—he has no business being our president.

A speech Dean gave to the Council on Foreign Relations (CFR) on June 25, 2003, continued his display of naïveté when it comes to world affairs. "Americans do not understand how we could have squandered the precious opportunity we had after September 11 to unite the world in opposition to the likes of Osama bin Laden and al-Qaeda," he said. "They are concerned that international support for the war against terror is waning and, along with it, admiration and support for the United States."[13]

I don't know what people Governor Dean is talking to, but I talk to an awful lot of people myself every day, and I don't find that their primary concern is that we've squandered an opportunity to unite the world in opposition to terrorism. But Dean, like so many other Democratic leaders, is preoccupied with process, when he ought to be concerned with results. The issue isn't whether we've *united the world,* but whether we're wining the war on terror. Sure, it would be nice if all nations would join us in our goal of eradicating the terrorist threat. But leadership requires that we don't stew ourselves into inaction if some of them are slow in coming to the table. With or without the support of other nations, it has fallen to America to win this struggle. We'll graciously accept all the support we are given, but in its absence we press on.

Besides, it's not as if America is the lone voice in this wilderness. On his website, Dr. Dean proclaims: "We cannot lead the world by force, and we cannot go it alone. We must lead toward clearly articulated and shared goals and with the cooperation and respect of friends and allies."[14] That all sounds great, and President Bush would probably agree; after all, as the Democrats would rather forget, he *did* build a broad coalition of nations in support of our action against Iraq. And he did lead with clearly articulated goals. The fact that our righteous goals weren't "shared" by nations like France and Germany certainly isn't President Bush's fault. He can't *force* other nations to act with courage. He can only lead, and hope that others will follow.

One of Howard Dean's heroes, apparently, is President Harry S Truman. I can understand that; Truman, as I've said, was a strong old-school Democrat of the kind who would do his party a world of good today. Not surprisingly, though, Dean seems to be taking all the wrong lessons from the Man from Independence.

For one thing, Dean claims to be following Truman's prescription in challenging "Democrats and Republicans alike to come together to build strong and effective international organizations."[15] But the primary goal of our foreign policy cannot be building international organizations, Dr. Dean. Our *primary* goal has got to be to protect the national security interests of the United States, while conducting ourselves morally and in furtherance of liberty and democracy.

Dean has also invoked the thirty-third president's name in an attempt to add pedigree to his left-wing vision of America's place in the world: "Harry Truman had faith as I have faith, and as I believe the American people have faith, that if we are wise enough and determined enough in our opposition to hate and our promotion of tolerance, in our opposition to aggression and our fidelity to law, we will have allies not only among governments but among people everywhere."[16] Opposing "hate" (and promoting "tolerance") in the abstract is a fashionable pastime of liberals today. To me, though, this passive vision of American foreign policy sounds more like Jimmy Carter than Harry Truman. Nobody is questioning America's opposition to hate, our promotion of tolerance. But are we really supposed to wait around until the self-interested nations of Europe are suddenly inspired by our example?

We should count our blessings that President Bush, and not Governor Dean, was in charge of determining the timeline of the war on terror.

Dean's "major" foreign policy address in February didn't seem to make much of an impression, so he felt compelled to make another one in December. Unfortunately, his speech was upstaged by the capture of Saddam Hussein, which hit the news the day before. But Dean's newest round of empty rhetoric probably wouldn't have made many headlines anyway. Anxious to indict the Bush administration in any way possible, he reverted to the tired, discredited platform of multilateralism: "We must not choose unilateral action as our weapon of first resort. Leaders of the current administration seem to believe that nothing can be gained from working with nations that have stood by our side as allies for generations. They are wrong, and they are leading America in a radical and dangerous direction."[17] Of course we should work with our allies, but not when they put their own economic self-interest above the security of freedom-loving people around the world. Dr. Dean should know the difference.

Neither on his website, nor in his foreign policy speeches, has Dr. Dean offered convincing specifics about how he would conduct the war on terror. Instead he spends his time complaining that "increasing numbers of people in Europe, Asia and in our own hemisphere cite America not as the strongest pillar of freedom and democracy but as a threat to peace."[18] Whether or not those numbers are truly increasing—and I don't know that they are—the important point is that such people are *wrong*. In raising the issue, though, Dean implies that he's in agreement with them—that America is "not the strongest pillar," that we're actually "a threat to peace." Just what nation is a stronger pillar? And in what way have we threatened the peace? If his point is that we have threatened peace by deposing a murderous dictator in Iraq, and fighting back against the terrorists who have attacked us, then I shudder to think how Mr. Dean would respond to future attacks against this country.

In his CFR speech, Dean also had the audacity to say that these "increasing numbers of people" are "disturbed that brave men and women in our armed forces are being targeted systematically nearly two months after a war we were told had ended, in a country where we were assured that our troops would be welcome as liberators."[19] But as Dr. Dean surely knows, the president did not say the war had ended, but that major hostilities had ended, which they had. And despite the dire predictions of liberals like Dean—and the denials of the liberal press in recent months—our troops were greeted largely with open arms by Iraqis, much as the capture of Saddam was hailed ecstatically in the streets of Iraq in December. To imply that the terrorist insurrections since that time are tantamount to a counterrevolution by the Iraqi people themselves is not only ludicrous, it's unconscionable. Dr. Dean should be ashamed—but you can be quite sure he isn't.

But the real campaign-defining blunder on Dean's part was a statement he made during an appearance on *Meet the Press* in June. In discussing the fall of Saddam Hussein, Dean offered that "We don't know whether in the long run the Iraqi people are better off. And the most important thing is that we don't know whether we are better off."[20]

Saddam Hussein ruled Iraq for over thirty years. During that time, his regime committed hundreds of thousands of murders; ordered the gassing of Kurds after the 1991 Gulf War; used rape as an instrument of terror; banned all political dissent; and employed kidnapping to suppress dissent. The State Department reports that there have been "tens of thousands of reported disappearances" under Saddam's reign, and that the torture regimen of his henchmen included such grotesque practices as branding, electric shock, beating, removal of fingernails, amputation, and burning with hot irons.[21] Prior to the war, the Iraqi people suffered while Saddam used funds from the "oil for food" program to build his lavish palaces and support his bloodthirsty Republican Guard. For every one of the twenty-four years that Saddam Hussein held power, the Iraqi people lived in absolute fear.

For Howard Dean to suggest that the Iraqi people may not be better off without Saddam, then, has got to make any reasonable American wonder about Dean's grasp of reality. How many Iraqi men and women are currently being tortured and executed under the Iraqi regime? How many Iraqis have been grabbed out of their homes by an oppressive government? In contrast, how many free newspapers have sprung up since Saddam was removed from power? How many people have savored their first taste of freedom in decades?

In October 2003, a videotape surfaced that documented the systematic torture and execution of Iraqi prisoners by Saddam's Republican Guard and Saddam Fedayeen forces. "The punishments include fingers being chopped or shot off," one account reported, "tips of tongues being cut off, wrists being broken by sharp blows from a wooden rod, lashes by whip or cane, a bound man being tossed off a building, [and] a beheading involving a sword and a knife."[22] The tape was thought to have been made within the last few years of Saddam's regime.

Does Howard Dean think these victims and their families were better off under Saddam Hussein?

But Dr. Dean just carries on, the inane comments dropping from his mouth like pearls. "I think he's made us weaker,"[23] he said of President Bush in New Hampshire. Of course, the governor failed to specify just how the president had made America weaker: by removing the Taliban and al Qaeda from Afghanistan? By conducting one of the most successful military operations in history in Iraq? We have demonstrated to the world the overwhelming power of the U.S. military. In a little over three weeks, our army, navy, air force, and marines marched hundreds of miles and removed an entrenched despot. In the subsequent months, our military has shown resolve by rebuilding post-Saddam Iraq. We have captured and/or killed many top terrorists, from Saddam and his sons Qusay and Uday Hussein, to al Qaeda leaders such as Khalid Sheik Mohammed. This has made us weaker?

In New Hampshire Dean also claimed that President Bush "doesn't understand what it takes to defend this country; that you have to have a higher moral purpose. . . . He doesn't understand that you better keep troop morale high rather than just flying over for Thanksgiving." But what's required to defend America, of course, is exactly what President Bush has provided: the sense of purpose, the gravity and determination in the face of evil, that has been his trademark since 9/11. (And when it comes to "higher moral purpose," I'd like to see the good governor present a case that there's any higher moral cause than defending one's innocent countrymen against terrorist attack.)

But Howard Dean doesn't need me to highlight his warped perspective on foreign affairs: he's pretty good at doing it all by himself. During that same New Hampshire speech, he challenged the commander in chief: "Mr. President, if you'll pardon me, I'll teach you a little about defense." Now this I'd like to see. What exactly does a five-term governor of Vermont have to teach a masterful wartime president about defense? What experience does Governor Dean bring to the table? Has he been waging a covert military campaign against maple-syrup smugglers? Is he planning to send a contingent of Vermont Special Forces troops on a raid into Canada to acquire prescription drugs?

In all seriousness, Governor Dean—whose résumé includes time as the lieutenant governor of Vermont, as a legislator in the Vermont House, and as a practicing physician—ought to think twice before presuming to teach President Bush anything about commanding leadership.[24] Especially when our president and his team have already scored decisive victories in our first two battles global war on terrorism. After all, Dr. Dean still has a few basic problems with geography to work out. On a recent appearance on *Hardball* with Chris Matthews, Governor Dean offered this "analysis" of the threat posed by Iran:

> Iran is a more complex problem . . . the key, I believe, to Iran is pressure through the Soviet Union. The Soviet Union is supplying much of the equipment that Iran, I believe, most likely is using to set itself along the path of developing nuclear weapons. We need to use that leverage with the Soviet Union and it may require us to buy the equipment the Soviet Union was ultimately going to sell to Iran to prevent Iran from developing nuclear weapons. That is also a country that must not be allowed to develop nuclear weapons. Much [of] the key to all this is foresight. Let's act now so we don't have to have a confrontation which may result in force, which would be very disastrous in the case of North Korea and might be disastrous in the case of Iran.[25]

Now, for the moment let's put aside the fact that Dean must have missed the papers the day the "Soviet Union" fell more than a decade ago. Far more troubling is his instinct to try to pay off countries that are trafficking in nuclear material and equipment. This is the classic Democratic response to a foreign threat—the same approach that got Bill Clinton in trouble in North Korea: Throw money at it, and hope the villains we're paying off are as good as their word.

Howard Dean's reckless tirades against President Bush and his conduct of foreign policy say more about Dr. Dean than about the president. They tell us that Howard Dean is a complete neophyte when it comes to leadership and world affairs. They tell us that Dean is in no position to lead this nation in the War on Terror. But they also reveal Dean's essential arrogance—in presuming to lecture the president on a subject he has no background in, and obviously no knowledge about.

As a candidate, of course, Dean has to offer his opinions. But Democrats and Republicans alike have a right to expect those opinions to be informed, thoughtful, and reasonable. Instead, they're often hysterical, irresponsible harangues. Given our remarkable successes in Iraq and Afghanistan, you would think that Dr. Dean and his colleagues would be a little more circumspect with their criticism. To most Americans, their complaints are bound to look like nothing more than trumped-up dissent designed to give the loyal opposition something to talk about.

But when we look at the substance of Dean's statements— from his shapeless policy "proposals" for Iraq to his criticisms of President Bush's leadership—what emerges is that Howard Dean has nothing to offer America but "hot" air. Moreover, aside from his poor judgment in foreign affairs, Dr. Dean has displayed a striking viciousness and a deep-seated anger that makes him appear unstable to some; at least one pundit has speculated—jokingly? It's hard to say—that he might have a meltdown during the campaign.[26]

As a recent *USA Today* profile pointed out, "Howard Dean's temper is no secret" in Vermont, his home state. "He has called political opponents 'boneheads' and said they're 'in la-la land.' He's told lawmakers that he would like to see them lose their jobs. One longtime adversary wonders whether he's up to tasks that require tact, such as international diplomacy."

That adversary, Republican state representative Tom Koch, has nicknamed Dean "Governor Shoot-from-the-mouth," and has been quoted as saying, "He has a very short fuse, which on the wrong subject I think could be dangerous." Koch, who has crossed swords with Dean during their careers in Vermont, says he has "a very nervous feeling personally about him and foreign policy. . . . He could say any number of things in the foreign area that could have lasting consequences."[27]

Dean has also shown a tendency toward the bizarre, as evidenced by his willingness to consider the most fantastic and paranoid of conspiracy theories. In December 2003, during an appearance on National Public Radio's *Diane Rehm Show,* Dean raised the idea that the Saudis had given George W. Bush prior notice of the 9/11 attacks. This incredible notion echoes the baseless slander that FDR knew about the Japanese attack on Pearl Harbor but did nothing to stop it.

In a conversation about the Kean Commission—the bipartisan panel looking into the circumstances of the 9/11 attacks—Dean implied that Bush was "suppressing evidence" that would be useful to the commission. Then he made what is probably the most outlandish comment to come from any serious Democratic candidate this year: "The most interesting theory that I've heard so far, which is nothing more than a theory . . . it can't be proved, is that [Bush] was warned ahead of time by the Saudis." Dean left the comment hanging just as it was, without further elaboration.[28] Given a chance later to backtrack on *Fox News Sunday,* Dean simply pleaded ignorance to host Chris Wallace about the theory's truth. "I can't imagine the president of the United States doing that. But we don't know and it'd be a nice thing to know."[29]

Republicans are not the only ones appalled by Dean's comments. As conservative columnist Robert Novak reports, one "35-year Democratic political veteran" told him that "Dean doesn't understand that he's accusing Bush of something worse than an impeachable offense. It's treason."[30] Yet Howard Dean seemed intrigued by the theory that George Bush might be a traitor with the blood of three thousand of his fellow citizens on his hands. Why, because he thinks raising the idea might win him some votes among the conspiracy-nut crowd? Or—far worse—because he actually believes it?

Howard Dean may be his party's frontrunner. He may be a passionate liberal. But in his campaign for the Democratic nomination, he has also demonstrated that he lacks the temperament and maturity of judgment—at the very least—to be the next president of the United States.

JOHN F. KERRY

[I voted] to give the President . . . a legitimate threat of force.

—JOHN KERRY, *April 3, 2003*[31]

We all know by now, of course, that John Kerry served with distinction in the United States Navy during the Vietnam War. As I have said on my radio and television shows numerous times, we are indebted to all our servicemen and servicewomen for their sacrifices. I am the first to thank all our military personnel, past and present, for their service to America.

However, I don't believe that simple military service renders anyone immune from criticism when it comes to foreign policy, and especially to as critical a challenge as the War on Terror. Indeed, it would be irresponsible to permit a veteran's reckless comments on foreign policy and military affairs to go unchecked merely because of his status as a veteran. It would do a disservice to the very causes to which he contributed.

John Kerry of Massachusetts has served as his state's lieutenant governor, and is currently a member of the U.S. Senate. Throughout his career, Senator Kerry has shown himself to be a political animal of the first order. His policies have shifted time and time again with the prevailing winds—especially, we now know, when it comes to running for president. Having begun his political career as an anti-Vietnam liberal, he is now attempting to remake himself into a moderate. He is anything but. And in passing himself off as something he is not—in his constant shifting, waffling, and flip-flopping on the tough questions of the day— Kerry has proven to be guided not by a strong moral compass, but by the shifting sands of pure political opportunism.

In wasn't supposed to be like this for John Kerry. At the outset of the presidential race, he was the favorite. A war hero with foreign policy experience, he seemed like the perfect candidate to take on a wartime president. And yet as the race for the Democratic nomination heated up, his boyhood dream of the presidency suddenly seemed to be slipping from his grasp. The harsh glare of the presidential primary season revealed a man without a coherent philosophy when it comes to waging the War on Terror. In fact, by the end of 2003 his stated positions had become so riddled with inconsistency that it sometimes seemed impossible to know whether Senator Kerry really had a basic position at all.

Take, for example, his "position" on the use of military force in Iraq. Along with seventy-six of his Democratic colleagues, Senator Kerry voted on October 22, 2002, to authorize President Bush to use military force in Iraq.[32] At the time of the vote, Kerry explained why he would be supporting the president. "Let me be clear: the vote that I will give to the president is for one reason and one reason only, to disarm Iraq of weapons of mass destruction if we cannot accomplish that objective through new, tough weapons inspections in joint conference with our allies."[33]

In April 2003, though—as his party's old appetite for antiwar candidates was beginning to rear its head—Senator Kerry seemed to change his tune. He now claimed that he'd voted to authorize the use of force "to give the president a legitimate threat of force to go to the United Nations and form a coalition."[34]

Then, on August 31, 2003, Kerry claimed that he had voted to "protect the security of the country in a way that defended America's values, that defended the troops."[35]

And then, on September 3, Kerry said that "the President didn't need our authorization" in the first place.[36]

So which is it, Senator Kerry? Did you or did you not cast your vote for "one reason and one reason only"? And if so, what was that reason—to disarm Iraq of weapons of mass destruction? To "give the president a legitimate threat of force"? To protect "the security of the country"? Or was your vote unnecessary altogether?

The reason John Kerry has such different reasons for his vote is that he doesn't want to tell the truth. The truth is that he remembered that the politicians who voted against the first Gulf War paid a political price for voting against the use of force. John Kerry, after all, was one of them. And with his own presidential chances hanging in the balance, he didn't want to be caught on the wrong side of history a second time.

But Kerry bet on the wrong horse. His vote in favor of the war ended up hurting him more than an antiwar vote ever would have—among the fervent anti-Bush, antiwar base he have needed to win his party's nomination.

You see, anyone who wants to gain the Democratic presidential nomination must win the allegiance of the party's hardcore left. These are the people who make signs comparing Bush to Hitler, who build effigies of our president and then tear them down as if they were Iraqi citizens tearing down statutes of Saddam Hussein. For such strident ideologues, a "yea" vote on any type of war is a mark against the candidate.

All of which explains why Howard Dean had all the momentum going into the primary season—because from the start he had billed himself as "the candidate who opposes the war." But it also explains why Kerry spent the next full year after his vote waffling. Actually, Kerry was trying to have it both ways. He knew he would need to project a moderate image for the general election, if nominated. But somehow, along the way, he'd managed to forget that no party in recent history has been so dominated by extremists as the Democratic Party is today. And as soon as he saw how his vote on the war was turning off hardcore left-wingers, he started backpedaling—and before long it was clear to everyone that the only thing John Kerry really stood for was John Kerry's own political survival.

Kerry's naked attempt to play both sides has dogged his campaign ever since. That's why, one year later, Kerry chose to vote *against* the president's request for the funding required to finance the war and help rebuild Iraq. "I voted against that $87 billion in Washington yesterday," he proclaimed. "But let me make it clear, I'm for winning the war in Iraq."[37] Can you believe it? How does the senator expect the military to finish the job in Iraq without the necessary funding? Would Senator Kerry deny our men and women in combat the necessary funds for waging war? Even Democratic onlookers were astonished by the vote; it doesn't take a Republican to recognize that Kerry is trying to cast himself as both a "hawk and a dove."[38]

Indeed, some of Kerry's harshest critics have been liberals. As John Pike wrote in *The Nation,* "It is said in the Bay State that it may take extraterrestrial intelligence to figure him out. Kerry has the backbone to fly a plane under a bridge, ride motorcycles at high speed and steer a warship toward enemy fire in Vietnam, beach it and earn the Silver Star, a Bronze Star and three Purple Hearts. Yet he does not have the spine to stick with a politically unpopular opinion, or even reveal his ethnic and family heritage. In Boston they say it is as if Kerry's backbone works for only half his body. Call him the man with half a backbone. . . . For decades Kerry has been singled out for simply saying without conviction or belief whatever will generate media attention and help win elections."[39]

Sometimes Kerry's hypocrisy is so flagrant that it's hard to imagine what he was thinking. After roundly denouncing President Bush for his appearance on the USS *Abraham Lincoln* to welcome home troops from the Middle East, Kerry formally announced his presidential candidacy standing on an aircraft carrier in South Carolina.[40]

Sometimes his stridency brings into question his presidential timber. In a campaign appearance in New Hampshire, Kerry told the crowd, "What we need now is not just a regime change in Saddam Hussein and Iraq . . . we need a regime change in the United States."[41] When I first heard that line, I couldn't believe my ears. Kerry was speaking on April 2—day fourteen of Operation Iraqi Freedom. While our soldiers were fighting and dying to liberate Iraq and safeguard the security of the United States, Senator Kerry—the would-be commander in chief of the United States— was busy undermining the actual commander in chief with a sound bite that was both tasteless and disturbing.

Beyond his rank political opportunism, though, Kerry offers very little difference from frontrunner Howard Dean in terms of foreign policy. Though a veteran member of the prestigious Senate Armed Services Committee, Kerry is just as obsessed as Dean with the ideas of "multilateralism" and "internationalism." On January 23, 2003, he told a crowd at Georgetown University:

> We need a new approach to national security. A bold progressive internationalism that stands in stark contrast to the too-often belligerent and myopic unilateralism of the Bush administration. The blustering unilateralism is wrong, and even dangerous, for our country. In practice, it has meant alienating our longtime friends and allies, alarming potential foes and spreading anti-Americanism around the world. I say to the president, show respect for the process of international diplo-

macy because it is not only right, it can make America stronger. And show the world some appropriate patience in building a genuine coalition. Mr. President, do not rush to war.[42]

When it comes to campaignining, John Kerry might have done better to take his own advice: With his blatant inconsistencies and persistent pandering, it is he who has alienated longtime friends and allies—his friends in the Democratic Party, the ones he was expecting to vote him into the presidency.

RICHARD GEPHARDT

I think this administration has failed in getting at the root causes of terrorism.

—RICHARD GEPHARDT,
Detroit, October 26, 2003[43]

In marked contrast to John Kerry, Richard Gephardt came to Washington in 1977 as a moderate to conservative Democrat. He was against abortion, against school busing, and supported school prayer. In a news release from August 1981, Congressman Gephardt criticized President Reagan for not taking more action to promote those issues.[44] The young congressman Gephardt has been described as "an unabashed abortion critic and social conservative looking for openings to persuade others. He voted early in his career against extending the deadline to ratify the Equal Rights Amendment to the Constitution and for prohibitions on government-backed legal assistance in gay rights cases."[45]

In defense and foreign policy matters, Gephardt was equally moderate. "By the time he went to Congress in 1977," the *St.*

Louis Post-Dispatch reports, "Gephardt's views on defense mirrored his centrist positions on taxes, abortion and other matters. He favored the development of the neutron bomb, the resumption of the production of nerve gas and the reinstatement of the draft. In 1981 and 1982, he voted against efforts to curb funding for the B-1 bomber, chemical weapons and the MX missile."[46]

How, then, did the moderate young Gephardt transform himself into a liberal icon? The simple answer is politics. As the *Washington Post* puts it, "[Gephardt] was elected to Congress as an antiabortion moderate in 1976. He moved to the left later in his career, running for president in 1988 as a liberal aligned with labor."[47] In other words, he did what he had to do to advance his career in the Democratic Party: He followed the party on its steady path toward liberalism.

Gephardt was eager to ascend to a leadership position in the House of Representatives. But when he recognized that his previous positions on both domestic and foreign policy would have disqualified him, he veered leftward. Joshua Muravchik, a scholar at the American Enterprise Institute, confirms that "As [Gephardt] established himself in the House, he became more of a national Democrat." Moreover, as Muravchik reports, "the clear majority of the Democratic caucus was dovish, and they had to either give up their leadership aspirations or move to more dovish positions."[48]

In 1986, when Gephardt was planning his first presidential campaign, he abandoned his antiabortion position. "On any issue of conscience," he has said, "every American must travel their own personal journey and reach their own certainty. At the beginning of my journey in public service, I didn't yet realize the full consequences of my beliefs."[49]

It's not unheard of for a politician to flip-flop on certain issues, such as taxes or even social security. But abortion is a different matter altogether. It involves life and death. I don't claim to know what's in Richard Gephardt's heart. But many observers suspect that his decision to change his stand on abortion was a purely political calculation, another step to the left designed to further his rise in the Democratic leadership. That he could change his mind on such a critical—and essentially moral—issue, ostensibly to serve his own political interests, raises disturbing questions about Dick Gephardt's true priorities.

Representative Gephardt's record on foreign policy is just as troublesome. In 1987 Gephardt denounced President Reagan as pursuing a "rogue foreign policy." As UPI reported at the time, "Gephardt said the Reagan administration will be remembered for its efforts to prepare for nuclear war and said the administration's recent movement toward an arms control agreement with the Soviet Union, is merely the 'last refuge of a presidency that has run out of other ideas.' "[50] As we've seen, history has judged Ronald Reagan to be one of the most visionary presidents of the twentieth century. The chess match he played—and won—with Mikhail Gorbachev was a lesson in the importance of staring down evil. As a leader in Congress in the 1980s, Dick Gephardt had a firsthand vantage point on Reagan's mastery of the game. Yet to him it appeared that Reagan had "simply run out of ideas." What does that say about Gephardt's vision?

In 1991, Gephardt voted against authorizing the first President Bush to use force in the Persian Gulf War. Indeed, he reportedly "spearheaded the opposition in the House" over the war.[51] By the following year, Gephardt must have realized the mistake he had made; though he had run for the Democratic nomination in

1988—even winning the Iowa caucuses—he opted not to challenge President George H. W. Bush in the 1992 race.

But Gephardt would not make the same mistake twice. In 2002 he appeared with President George W. Bush in a Rose Garden ceremony to express his support of a second Gulf War. During the primaries, Gephardt was generally supportive of the use of force in Iraq. But, as the *New Republic* has pointed out, his vote—like Kerry's—was certainly another political calculation: "For one, he is already on the record making the same case as Bush before the war. His advisers also believe that the key to the Iraq issue is consistency, and, since Gephardt came to the debate with a dovish reputation, any backtracking would expose his vote as political opportunism. 'The notable thing here is that he hasn't moved,' says an aide. 'Sounding like a hawk in Washington and a dove in Iowa doesn't make either side happy.' "[52]

There are indications, however, that Gephardt is trying to increase his appeal with the antiwar left. Gephardt has begun to use the phrase "root causes" when discussing the War on Terror. "Root causes" is a term loaded with meaning for liberals, most often used in the criminal justice debate. Liberals believe that if you remove the root causes of crime, such as poverty or absentee parents or drug abuse, then you can end crime. We conservatives, on the other hand, believe that crime is a choice made with free will—that some individuals choose the path of evil, regardless of whether they are rich or poor. Furthermore, just as labeling Hitler or Saddam a "madman" is a dangerous distraction from the reality of their evil behavior, we contend that searching out "root causes" for a crime merely serves to provide the criminal with an excuse for his behavior.

From the very first days after 9/11, the left started talking about the "root causes" of the attacks, asking "Why do the terrorists hate us?" Well, I don't believe there's any answer to that question that could ever explain, justify, or excuse the terrorists' decision to slaughter three thousand people on that day. And anyone who's inclined to waste much time dwelling on such a question just isn't likely to have much grasp on the reality of evil in the world. The search for "root causes" is an invitation to address the grievances of a group whose actions have put them permanently beyond the reach of sympathy or explanation.

And yet there was Dick Gephardt, during one of the Democratic debates, treating the problem of terrorism as if he were Lyndon Johnson fighting the War on Poverty all over again:

> I think this administration has failed in getting at the root causes of terrorism. I think they're just dealing with the symptom of terrorism, and I support those efforts. You've got to stop someone from doing harm to the United States if they are bound and determined to do it. But we have got to get at the root causes.
>
> Let me say this: If we are going to defeat terrorism, we have got to engage in countries across the world. We have got to fight against poverty, we have got to fight against bad governance, and we have got to say to people that are supporting terrorists this behavior cannot stand.[53]

That kind of talk may endear Dick Gephardt to the far left. But it won't do him much good in the real world, where terrorists are committed to our death and destruction.

What his remarks do reveal, though, is that Gephardt's approach to the War on Terror would involve funneling money to the Middle East nations that hate us, trying to reform their governments while asking them to stop supporting terrorism. Maybe Gephardt hasn't caught on: Osama bin Laden is already a multimillionaire. How would an international war on poverty have stopped him? And what's in it for Syria or Iran or any other Arab dictatorship that doesn't want to reform its people and stop harboring terrorists? Like Jimmy Carter getting his olive branch snapped in two by the ayatollah, like Bill Clinton being played for a fool by Kim Jong Il, Dick Gephardt is apparently convinced that sweet talk—and a lot of American cash—can stop a terrorist regime in its tracks. America has seen too much failed Democratic presidential policy in the last quarter century to let that happen again.

Still, Gephardt has managed to hang in there through the first stages of the campaign—largely on the strength of some pretty sad pandering to the Bush-hating left. The eerily affectless Gephardt has repeated the line "This president is a miserable failure" so many times in his stump speeches, it's become his unofficial campaign slogan.[54] Gephardt first used the line "The President's economic program has been a miserable failure" back in January 2003.[55] Nine months later, at a debate in Albuquerque, he extended the idea to the president himself. He must have thought he was on to something, because he repeated the phrase five times that night. He even had his staff set up a campaign website: www.amiserablefailure.com.[56] In Baltimore for another debate, Gephardt and his speechwriters worked overtime and came up with a new twist: "This president's foreign policy is a miserable failure."[57]

Funny, isn't it, how Dick Gephardt seems preoccupied with failure? Makes you almost feel sorry for the guy.

Gephardt must know he's bound to come up short once again in 2004. But he's still beating that dead horse, long after America has stopped listening. After all, Congressman Gephardt is no less a political animal than Senator Kerry. He's been in Washington for close to thirty years, and it shows. Gephardt may have arrived in Washington full of conviction, but slowly and inexorably he sacrificed his principles to his political aspirations. In his latest bid for the Democratic presidential nomination he tried to position himself as the anti-Dean, making a political calculation to support the war in Iraq. But in the process he only alienated the hardcore left that has made Dean the frontrunner for the nomination.

In the end, what does this record of pandering and posturing tell us about Dick Gephardt? The same thing it tells us about John Kerry, his colleague on Capitol Hill: It's one thing to be a politician—a different thing entirely to be a leader.

JOSEPH LIEBERMAN

> I would have gotten off of pride and hurt feelings and gone to the NATO and the United Nations and asked them to join us in securing and rebuilding [Iraq].
>
> —JOSEPH LIEBERMAN,
> *September 4, 2003*[58]

Personally, I like Senator Joe Lieberman of Connecticut. I do believe he has a strong moral compass, and strong convictions. He has consistently supported President Bush in the War on Terror, and there are many issues where we find common ground.

But I don't believe he is the right man for the presidency.

Why? Because, like most of the other Democratic presidential hopefuls, Lieberman believes that only the "internationalization" of our foreign policies can make those policies legitimate. Like his colleagues, he has conveyed repeatedly that his top priority is to form broad international coalitions with nations such as France and Germany to help implement his policies—leaving open the implication that he, like the other Democrats, would be reluctant to act without those nations' support. In a November 2003 interview on Fox, Senator Lieberman said:

> Well, the first thing you do [to gain international support], without going too far back, is that you wouldn't follow the one-sided foreign policy that the Bush administration has followed before we got to the conflict in Iraq. And what does that mean? Get back into the international effort to do something about global warming. Get back into the effort to control arms. Be more supportive of NATO. I mean, that's the context in which a lot of these countries pull back from the Bush administration, and the administration lost its moral authority with them.[59]

Concerning U.S. forces in Iraq, Senator Lieberman said, "It would be great to get Iraqis to be fighting by our side. We ought to have NATO with us."[60] But how would bringing NATO into Iraq improve the situation there? The North Atlantic Treaty Organization was organized during the Cold War to protect Western Europe from the U.S.S.R. Though NATO's role has evolved since the disintegration of the Soviet Union, there is still nothing to suggest that its presence in Iraq would make a qualitative difference in our efforts to help rebuild that nation and suppress further terrorist insurrections.

The British and the Polish already have large contingents in Iraq. Does Senator Lieberman want to cede power or control to the Germans and French? In a major policy speech at the Council on Foreign Relations, Lieberman also argued that the United Nations should have a role in Iraq: "the United States, the United Nations, NATO, and the international civilian administrator I have proposed should start working together to develop a clear process and timetable under which the people of Iraq will shape their own government."[61] When asked in one of the Democratic debates how he would have handled the challenges of postwar Iraq, Senator Lieberman said, "I would have gotten off of pride and hurt feelings and gone to the NATO and the United Nations and asked them to join us in securing and rebuilding [Iraq]."[62]

To solicit the help of other individual nations in furthering the War on Terror is one thing; President Bush has done that. When some nations, like France and Germany, have failed to step forward, he has proceeded without them. But to predicate the defense of our national security on the involvement of international institutions like NATO or the United Nations is to enter dangerous territory. When it comes to the United Nations especially, Senator Lieberman's faith in such a corrupt and ineffective body is entirely misplaced.

In this faith, he is not alone among the Democrats. Richard Gephardt, John Kerry, Howard Dean, and Wesley Clark are all on record saying either that the United States should not have initiated military action against Iraq without the United Nations and that we should seek U.N. support in postwar Iraq. Howard Dean: "I believed from the beginning that we should not go into Iraq without the United Nations as our partner."[63] Richard Gephardt: "When I am president, I will go back to the U.N., I will go to NATO, I will repair these alliances."[64] John Kerry: "We should only go to war because we have to. And we must hold the United Nations up for what it is. If you didn't have it, you'd have to invent it."[65] Wesley Clark: "[America] would go immediately back to Kofi Annan at the United Nations and say let's talk again about what the United Nations or an international organization could do. I remove that occupying power, that authority there. I'd put it under the United Nations or an international organization."[66]

And yet, as we've seen, the United Nations as a body is demonstrably corrupt, peopled heavily by inhuman dictators who cannot be trusted for a moment to act in defense of the greater good, or even the good of their own people. This is the organization whose Human Rights Commission chair, a Libyan official, opened a recent conference by declaring that a war in Iraq would "destroy everything and will certainly violate all human rights and especially the right to life."[67]

As Stephen Schwartz has written, "The U.N. is not the nations of the world united. It is an enterprise located in a building in New York, with satellite operations around the world, employing a certain cadre of people of many nationalities, most of whom are time-servers and ideologues."[68] Schwartz, who has had six years of experience in postwar Bosnia-Herzegovina and Kosovo, describes the U.N. employees he has witnessed as follows:

> They call themselves "internationals," and are generally young and inexperienced, although the heads of their missions tend to be old and uninterested. They have a strong prejudice against privatization, and too many of those chosen for economic responsibilities hail from Sweden and other countries where statist socialism remains the political religion.[69]

So is a blind allegiance to this body what we could expect of a Lieberman presidency? Of a President Dean, or Gephardt, or Kerry, or Clark? In four years, would Iraq be overrun by "internationals" from Sweden? By "human rights" advisers from Libya?

Here's the fundamental difference I have with Joe Lieberman and his Democratic cohorts over the War on Terror: I do not believe the United States should ever surrender its authority over foreign affairs, and especially over matters of our national security, to any international body, and certainly not to this one. If other nations are willing to support our mission, then by all means we should accept their support. But not at the price of forfeiting our leadership. Anyone who looks to the United Nations as a cure-all for our challenges in fighting terror—or, indeed, as a source of legitimacy in any question of foreign affairs—is gravely mistaken.

If Senator Lieberman were elected president, his stated position—that he would insist on U.N. approval before engaging our forces abroad—would cause certain harm to our national interest. No matter how much the United States works with the United Nations, no American president must ever place the interests of that body, or any other nation, above those of the United States.

President Bush has put his entire presidency on the line in the War on Terror. He has been willing to take his own political risks in order to ensure our safety. Joe Lieberman has not proven that he is willing to do the same.

WESLEY CLARK

General Wesley Clark was one of the last individuals to enter the race for the Democratic nomination for president. A career soldier who served as NATO Supreme Allied Commander, commander in chief of the U.S. Southern Command, and director for Strategic Plans and Policy for the Joint Chiefs of Staff, Clark—like John Kerry—is to be commended for serving his country.[70]

Yet in the weeks since he declared himself a candidate, compelling evidence emerged that General Clark had an extremely checkered history in these high positions of responsibility. A review of these charges leaves little doubt that this man is not fit to lead his country, at war or at home.

In June 1999, while serving as supreme allied commander of NATO, Wesley Clark risked confrontation with the Russians when he authorized the use of Apache attack helicopters to block the Pristina airport in Kosovo from Russian troops. The British general under Clark refused the order, and eventually the confrontation was resolved through diplomatic means.[71]

Standing up to the Russians when justified, necessary, and prudent, of course, doesn't bother me at all, but Clark's behavior in this incident seems reckless to me. Why risk igniting a broader confrontation? At that point in the Kosovo war, the NATO bombing had ended. Peace was largely restored. What would possess Clark to take such aggressive action, to risk starting another conflict?

Clark was also a firsthand witness to the tragic ineffectiveness of the United Nations to halt one of the most brutal instances of genocide in modern history. In the summer of 1994, as hundreds of thousands of Rwandans were being massacred, the U.N. peacekeeping force responsible for monitoring the country's reconstituted government failed utterly to stop the murders.[72] Romeo Dallaire, commander of the 2,600-soldier peacekeeping force, sent frantic requests for reinforcements to help stop the bloodbath, but his pleas were rejected. "Not one country on Earth came to stop this thing," Dallaire said. "The Western world provided me with nothing."[73]

At the time, Wesley Clark had been assigned to work with the United Nations to help alleviate the situation. In an interview with Dan Rather, he describes their talks:

> But, Dan, I had been in the Pentagon during the summer of 1994, when 800,000 people were hacked to death by machetes in Rwanda. I was the officer responsible for doing plans and contingencies for the United Nations, and I did a number of those with my staff, and we presented them and we talked about 'em and you know, we stroked our chins and we worried about things and we thought, you know, "Is this gonna be acceptable?"[74]

The next time a Democrat presidential candidate like Wesley Clark demands that the United Nations be brought in to rebuild Iraq, remember how that body reacted to American proposals to intervene. *We presented them and we talked about 'em and you know, we stroked our chins.* That is how the United Nations chose to act, while nearly a million Rwandans were being slaughtered on their watch. Wesley Clark ought to be ashamed of himself for investing any faith in them whatsoever.

Perhaps the most telling evidence of General Clark's unfitness to lead, however, is the low opinion his fellow generals have of him. It's a matter of record that Clark was relieved of his duty in

Europe prematurely, "asked to retire" by Joint Chiefs of Staff chairman Hugh Shelton. In September 2003, Shelton was asked whether he would support Clark as a presidential candidate. "I've know Wes for a long time," he replied. "I will tell you the reason he came out of Europe early had to do with integrity and character issues, things that are near and dear to my heart. I'm not going to say whether I'm a Republican or a Democrat. I'll just say Wes won't get my vote."[75]

Other respected military leaders seconded Shelton's assessment. General Norman Schwarzkopf, the leader of U.S. forces during the first Gulf War, said during an appearance on *Meet the Press:* "I do know that he's always been viewed as being very, very ambitious . . . and when Hugh Shelton said he was fired because of matters of character and integrity, that is a very, very damning statement, which says if that's the case, he's not the right man for president as far as I'm concerned."[76] And General Tommy Franks, former commander in chief of Central Command, gave a similar answer when asked whether he would vote for Clark: "Absolutely not."[77]

It gets worse. According to an in-depth profile that appeared in *The New Yorker* in November 2003, Clark was even distrusted by William Cohen, Bill Clinton's secretary of defense, under whom he served. In 1997, the post of commander in chief of United States forces in Europe came open. This command included the forces of NATO. "Clark was not the Army's nominee for the post, and the Army Chief of Staff, General Dennis Reimer, refused to recommend him."[78] But other, nonmilitary voices advocated on his behalf, and eventually Secretary Cohen offered him the job.

Within two short years, though, Cohen was regretting his decision.

Cohen, according to someone who worked closely with him, had come to regard Clark's hiring as one of the worst mistakes of his tenure at Defense, and the relationship between the two men became so strained that one of the Joint Chiefs still groans at the memory of Cohen's tortured body language when Clark would enter the room. What so vexed Cohen and the Chiefs was not just the fact that Clark had routinely gone behind their backs, or that Clark was so unyieldingly certain of his judgment. They believed that, too often, Clark's judgment was wrong.[79]

It appears they had ample grounds for concern. During the Kosovo conflict, when Clark prepared a battle plan for a ground war and presented it to the Joint Chiefs, they were "starkly unsupportive."[80] General Reimer "made it clear that he considered Clark's plan ludicrous." According to a Clinton administration defense official, Clark's plan "called into question the real military judgment being put behind it." Clark was removed from his position several months later.[81]

In the run for the White House, Wesley Clark's greatest calling card is his military background. Indeed, the Democrats were so overjoyed by the prospect of having a genuine wartime leader for their party that they seem to have overlooked one thing: Some of America's finest generals believed him to be ambitious, inflexible, back-stabbing, and lacking military acumen, judgment, and integrity.

That is not the kind of leader America needs, at this time or any time.

With the capture of Saddam Hussein the war in Iraq is largely over, though we still face challenges in quelling terrorist uprisings there. The War on Terror will continue, at varying levels of intensity. Meanwhile, public interest will soon shift more thoroughly to the choice of candidates in the 2004 presidential election.

As citizens, we have the opportunity to reaffirm our support of a president who has shown the courage to stand alone in defense of our liberties. The Democratic Party will eventually select one figure from among many—Howard Dean, John Kerry, Richard Gephardt, Joe Lieberman, or Wesley Clark—to oppose him. But that candidate, whoever he is, will represent ideas that would actively threaten America's security in this time of continuing despotism and terror around the world.

Howard Dean has demonstrated that he does not possess the requisite foreign policy experience to lead our nation. His liberal policies of appeasement would harm America. He has stated proudly that he would not have protected America by invading Iraq—that, instead, he would have conditioned any such military action on U.N. approval. In some respects, a Dean presidency might set America back even further than the feckless Clinton era—back to the wholehearted appeasement of Jimmy Carter.

Both John Kerry and Richard Gephardt have proven that they lack the strong moral compass that is required to lead our country. Kerry has been inconsistent throughout the debate over war in Iraq, Gephardt throughout his entire political history. Both are products of the Washington establishment; both have proven willing to take whatever position appears politically advantageous at any given time. By now I think it's clear that the American people prefer another kind of leader: One who knows his own mind.

Wesley Clark is dangerous for the decisions he failed to make in the past—standing by while the United Nations refused to stop the genocide in Rwanda—and for the decisions he would make in the future, including ceding control of Iraq to the United Nations. If his fellow generals aren't willing to support him, I see no reason for us voters to do so.

Joe Lieberman is the least appalling of the bunch. Yet even he seems to place his faith in the creation of "international coalitions"—coalitions that would jeopardize American security interests. When Joe Lieberman and his Democratic colleagues talk of using the highly questionable United Nations to aid our efforts throughout the world, I wonder whether they can possibly understand what they're recommending—and the danger it would spell for our country.

When we go to the polls this November, we are weighing in the balance the course of America in these early years of the twenty-first century: whether it will be guided and protected by a strong and courageous leadership, or become mired in policies of appeasement. As George Washington warned, America must not become overdependent on "entangling alliances" with international bodies—national or institutional—whose interests are not our own.

As my audiences know, I am no blind supporter of President George W. Bush. I have often criticized his domestic policies, and I don't believe he is perfect. But as we enter this election year, I do believe he is the right man in the right place at the right time. His qualities echo the best that America has to offer: strength, courage, conviction, the ability to know right from wrong, and a determination to choose the right path.

For the sake of our nation and the world, I hope we as a nation will continue down that path along with him.

What the Future Holds

The War on Terror, as we've seen, has forced America in some ways to reinvent itself: to reassess ideas like defense and homeland security, to rewrite the rules of war, to recognize new kinds of enemies and prepare to confront them.

In this book, I've tried to reawaken our appreciation of the lessons of our past, to help us apply them to the challenges of the future. Perhaps the most important of these concerns the sheer persistence of evil. Whether it takes the fiendishly organized form of Nazism, communism, or other forms of despotism—or erupts around the world in the loose networks we call terrorism—one thing is clear: Evil will thrive, unless it is confronted and defeated.

Human nature dictates that good and evil will always be at war. And the tyrants of the modern era have proven that evil will seize every opportunity to exploit any sign of weakness in a nation or its leaders. When the forces of Europe approached Adolf Hitler with a desperate gesture of appeasement, he was emboldened enough to unleash the most depraved war humanity has ever known. When the

Soviet Union judged that American leaders lacked the strength or resolve to counter their moves, it ordered its tanks into places like Hungary, Czechoslovakia, and Afghanistan. When the United States was reduced to trying to buy North Korea's cooperation in return for arresting its nuclear program, its despotic leader was encouraged to trample his agreements with us. When the Clinton administration failed to retaliate for eight years of murderous attacks on Americans by al Qaeda, the events of September 11 were only a matter of time.

We would be foolish to assume there is any quick fix, any single solution, to the challenges America will face in the continuing battle with our terrorist foes. But keep in mind that the Cold War was a marathon as well, lasting some fifty years. From that experience, we learned that with strong moral conviction, steadfast confidence in the rightness of liberty and democracy, and resolute leadership, freedom can overcome tyranny and terror.

Just as we must look back to learn from our forebears, however, we must look forward to the potential threats in our future—and look outward, to the regions where trouble may already be brewing. The world is filled with such hot spots, most of which will require our focused attention at some point in the next five, ten, even twenty years. From the Persian Gulf to the Far East, from unfamiliar lands like Syria to the targets of terror in our own homeland, the United States can expect once again to confront evil. If we succeed—and I am confident we will—Americans will be safer and freer, but so too will the oppressed peoples of the world.

Our success will be measured in many different ways. We hope the necessity of armed conflict will diminish through the years, as fewer bad actors step forward to challenge us, and the rewards of democracy become apparent in new parts of the globe. With luck we can minimize nuclear proliferation, eliminate nuclear conflict, and erase the shadow of terrorism from the lives of our children.

But our quest to eradicate tyranny or terror will not succeed through weakness. In the coming years, we will periodically face internal opposition from those in our own country who lack the vision and fortitude to oppose evil. For years into the future Americans will engage in a debate on whether we should appease evil—as we did in the 1930s, 1970s, and 1990s—or meet it squarely. Today, the choice we face is between a Democratic Party that sees American power as a source of arrogance and violence, and leaders like George W. Bush, who see American power as a force for peace and security.

In closing, then, let us look briefly outward, to those hot spots where evil may one day challenge us again.

CHINA

The People's Republic of China may not be at the center of American radar screens in these days of turmoil in the Persian Gulf and rising Islamic terror around the world. In the last decade, however, it has become an increasingly stronger and more threatening power in its region. A recent Defense Department report cited China's ambitions to "dominate Asia, compel Taiwan to reunify with the mainland and prevent the United States from interfering with either objective."[1] As such, China constitutes a threat to three of our close allies in the region—Taiwan, Japan, and South Korea. In each case, the United States is obliged by agreement to come to the defense of these free nations. In view of these commitments, China's apparent determination to amass as much military-related technology as it can, as quickly as possible, is troubling indeed.

China, of course, is the only remaining large Communist state on the face of the earth—as well as the largest totalitarian regime. In the language of a recent State Department report, it is "an authoritarian state in which the Chinese Communist Party is the paramount source of power," a country where "citizens lack both the freedom peacefully to express opposition to the Party-led political system and the right to change their national leaders or form of government."[2] Moreover, the Chinese government is "quick to suppress any person or group, whether religious, political, or social, that they perceive to be a threat to government power, or to national stability."[3]

One recurring source of crisis on the Chinese front has been its highly charged relationship with its smaller, democratic neighbor Taiwan. In the last fifty years, while China has stagnated under communism, Taiwan has progressed slowly but surely toward democracy. In 2000, Taiwan underwent its first peaceful transition of power from the Nationalist Party to the Democratic Progressive Party.[4]

But China believes that Taiwan is rightly Chinese territory, and has threatened to use force against Taiwan if any of three situations occurs: (1) Taiwan constructs nuclear weapons; (2) a revolt occurs on Taiwan; (3) Taiwan declares its independence.[5] Eventually, there is every reason to believe, China will take military action to attempt to reunite Taiwan with mainland China. In 2000, Chinese Premier Zhu Rongi declared:

> Some people have made some calculations about how many aircraft, missiles and warships China possesses and presumed that China dare not and will not use force based on such calculations. . . . those people who have made such calculations and who have made such conclusions do not understand and do not know about the Chinese history. The Chinese people are ready to shed blood and sacrifice their lives to defend the sovereignty and territorial integrity of the motherland.[6]

To Chinese officials, defending the "sovereignty and territorial integrity of the motherland" means seizing Taiwan. And on this subject China has done more than talk. It has built a full-scale model of a major Taiwanese airfield and used it to practice assaults,[7] and has "conducted a ballistic missile blockade of Taiwan."[8]

Richard D. Fisher of the Jamestown Foundation reports that China is currently increasing the capabilities of its navy to "advance two goals: 1) increase China's ability to pursue a range of coercive strategies toward Taiwan, including a naval blockade; 2) impede or prevent the U.S. forces from coming to Taiwan's 'rescue.' "[9] Moreover, Dr. Fisher states that China has the goal of sinking a U.S. aircraft carrier. "[In developing the capability to sink a U.S. carrier] Beijing hopes to deter U.S. military assistance to Taiwan, and by actually sinking one, to terminate U.S. attempts to save the island."[10]

Why is this all of immediate concern to America? Because today, for the first time, Taiwan is beginning to assert its independence—and because the Taiwan Relations Act of 1979, in the words of one account, holds that "any threat to the peace and security of Taiwan is of grave concern to the United States. The act explicitly states that the United States is obliged to make available to Taiwan such defense articles and defense services in such quantity as may be necessary to enable Taiwan to maintain a sufficient defense capability."[11] In other words, the United States is committed to take action to defend Taiwan from any Chinese aggression.

But our concern with China should go beyond the issue of Taiwan. China, according to President Jiang Zemin in 1995, views the West, including the United States, as its "chief enemy." As the authors Edward Timperlake and William C. Triplett II have observed, the United States is the main obstacle to China's "ambition to dominate Asia."[12] China has also shown an intense interest in developing its information warfare capabilities: Not only does China's People's Liberation Army (PLA) have the world's second largest information warfare program (next to the United States),[13] but "the American economic, political, and social system is essentially unprotected against a Chinese information warfare attack."[14]

And information isn't the only kind of warfare China is contemplating. As Timperlake and Triplett have documented, the PLA "is targeting the American people with nuclear weapons and is developing entirely new generations of land-, sea-, and space-based strategic weapons systems capable of threatening any location on the planet."[15] At times, China has talked tough concerning nuclear weapons. In 1999, the Chinese Office of the Central Military Command issued a report alluding to a possible nuclear confrontation with the United States over Taiwan:

> During the last crisis across the Taiwan Straits, the U.S. tried to blackmail us with their aircraft carrier[s], but when their spy satellites confirmed that our four nuclear submarines which used to be stationed at Lushun Harbor had disappeared, those politicians addicted to the Taiwan card could not imagine how worried their military commanders were.[16]

The United States Select Committee on China has also reported that "Chinese Agents stole American nuclear secrets to build long-range ballistic missiles that can strike the United States," and that China transferred some of this stolen nuclear technology to North Korea and Iraq.[17]

From its territorial claims on Taiwan, to its buildup of nuclear, conventional, and information warfare capabilities, to its stated aim to dominate its region and take the West as its enemy,

China should already be a major source of concern to the United States—as well as the neighboring democracies it has threatened.

IRAN

With the defeat of Saddam Hussein in Iraq, Iran is poised to become the dominant power in the Middle East. It has a huge population—some 65 million people—along with a relatively strong military and vast oil reserves. Iran's brutal theocracy is hostile to the policies of liberty and poses an enormous threat to stability in a critical region of the world.

Iran is a primary supporter of terrorism—and is actively pursuing the acquisition and development of nuclear weapons it could use to threaten Israel and other American interests.

Iran is one of the three nations President Bush named as the Axis of Evil. It is ruled by a group of Islamic fundamentalists with a deplorable human rights record. According to State Department reports, Iran's human rights violations include "summary executions, disappearances, widespread use of torture and other degrading treatment, reportedly including rape, severe punishments such as stoning and flogging, harsh prison conditions, arbitrary arrest and detention."[18] And, not surprisingly, Iran's regime "significantly restricts citizens' right to change their government."[19]

Iran's continuing support of terrorism is no secret around the world. In July 2003, President Bush charged that "today, Syria and Iran continue to harbor and assist terrorists. This behavior is completely unacceptable, and states that support terror will be held accountable."[20] In 2001, the State Department reports, Iran "remained the most active state sponsor of terrorism," having "long provided Lebanese Hizballah and the Palestinian projectionist groups—notably

HAMAS, the Palestine Islamic Jihad, and Ahmad Jibril's PFLP-GC—with varying amounts of funding, safehaven, training and weapons."[21] It is critical, for the well-being and safety of all Americans, that Iran be prevented from further supporting these terrorist entities.

Just as disturbing as its support for terrorism, however, is Iran's development of nuclear weapons. As Amir Taheri has written in *National Review* Online, "Iran has a nuclear program designed to make such weapons within 18 months. It is like a chef who brings in all that is needed for making a soup but does not actually start the cooking until he knows when the guests will be coming."[22] Mr. Taheri quotes former Iranian President Hashemi Rafsanjai: "In a nuclear duel in the region, Israel may kill 100 million Muslims. Muslims can sustain such casualties, knowing that, in exchange, there would be no Israel on the map."[23] As Michael Ledeen of the American Enterprise Institute has reported, "leaders of Iran's Revolutionary Guards were informed by the country's National Security Council that the country would soon have nuclear weapons."[24] In September 2003, Ledeen reported,

> In recent weeks, Iran's supreme leader, Ayatollah Ali Khamenei, has been receiving many senior clerics for happy embraces. They have come in unusually large number to congratulate him. According to Iranians I talk to, they believe that Iran now has all the necessary components for an atomic bomb or two or three, and all that remains is to assemble the damned things.[25]

There is little question that the ruling mullahs in Iran will continue to support international terrorism. But it now appears that the Iranians are close to finally acquiring nuclear weapons. With such capability they could easily attempt to blackmail the

United States by making a credible threat to destroy Israel, our primary ally in the region. For the sake of that nation—and our own—we must remain stalwart in confronting any threat of aggression, or nuclear proliferation, from the state of Iran.

SYRIA

Syria is critical because of its strategically important location in the Middle East. With Iraq to its east and south, Turkey to the north, Lebanon and Israel to the west, and Jordan to its south, Syria is in a position to exert influence (for good or evil) over the entire region. But Syria is a problematic nation, with past (and continuing) affiliations with terrorist organizations like al Qaeda and despotic nations like Iraq.

As the *Los Angeles Times* has reported, "Syria has functioned as a hub for an al-Qaeda network that moved Islamic extremists and funds from Italy to northeastern Iraq where the recruits fought alongside the recently defeated Ansar al Islam terrorist group."[26] Moreover, Syria has "provided refuge to a range of extremists—Palestinians, Turks, Lebanese, even former Nazis and a renegade U.S. intelligence agent—and denied doing so."[27] According to some experts, "Syria now ranks as the worst Arab country in terms of its ambitions to develop weapons of mass destruction, support for terrorism and human rights abuses."[28] John Bolton, undersecretary of state for arms control, has stressed the threat Syria poses in both its WMD plans and its support for terrorism.[29]

During his rule, Saddam Hussein "used the Syrian conduit, among others, to assure the flow of dual-use equipment for his WMD programs and rearm his military."[30] The author Jed Babbin reports:

Throughout the Iraq campaign, Syria proved a convenient safe haven (at least temporarily) for many of Saddam's fleeing thugs, and maybe even his WMDs. Billions of dollars looted from Iraq are sitting in Syrian banks. And the terrorists that Syria supports were—and still are—sending people, weapons, and money to the Baathist remnants and terrorists who are now killing Americans in Iraq.[31]

Babbin goes on to contend that "Regime change [in Syria] must be our goal, because nothing else will work. The Syrian Baathists will do what their Iraqi brethren did. Stall, talk, whine to the U.N., and continue their business of supporting terrorism."[32] And the Bush administration suspects that "Syria is continuing to develop an offensive biological weapons capability; has stockpiled chemical weapons such as sarin and VX nerve gas and has equipped part of its force of several hundred ballistic missiles with chemical warheads."[33]

Even after the defeat of Saddam Hussein, Syria will remain a threat. As long as Syria is free to fund terrorist activities in the Middle East and perhaps elsewhere, terrorists will continue to wage war against us. The day may well come when action must be taken to rid the volatile Middle East of this repressive, and aggressive, Syrian regime.

NORTH KOREA

The nation of communist North Korea might be described more accurately as the world's largest prison camp—a hyper-militarized dictatorship where one man, the notorious Kim Jong Il, holds absolute power.

Kim has turned North Korea into an economic basket case that is barely able to feed its own citizens. Its enormous and aggressive military can be supported only through the sale of missiles and missile technology, and the trafficking of illegal drugs and counterfeit money. It is a country that is completely unrestrained by the code of conduct of the civilized world.

In a development almost too horrible to contemplate, this evil regime is also believed to have recently developed nuclear weapons. To make matters worse, according to the *Los Angeles Times* "U.S. intelligence officials . . . believe North Korea has an untested ballistic missile capable of reaching the western U.S."[34] Given its history of supplying weapons to rogue states like Libya and Syria, North Korea has earned its ignoble place in the Axis of Evil. Its instability, its economic duress, its egomaniacal dictator, and its nuclear capabilities, all conspire to make it a continuing threat to the United States and the world at large.

Any predictions about North Korea's future conduct must focus on the personality of Kim Jong Il. There is an ongoing debate whether this dictator's erratic behavior is the result of insanity or a calculated ploy. "Diplomats and escaped dissidents talk of a vain, paranoid, cognac-guzzling hypochondriac," a BBC report noted. "But analysts are undecided whether his eccentricities mask the cunning mind of a master manipulator or betray an irrational madman."[35] The debate persists, in large part because the West has so few opportunities to deal with him. He is a recluse in a nation that has intentionally separated itself from the rest of the world.

There is no doubt, however, that North Korea has the means and will to threaten its neighbors. Its "People's Army" is one of the world's largest, with 1.17 million troops. (The United States, by comparison, has 1.4 million troops spread all over the globe.)

Over the past few decades, North Korea's troops have been moved closer to the American and South Korean forces along the Demilitarized Zone (DMZ).[36] "Of the 1 million troops in the army," according to one account, "about 700,000 are stationed within [62 miles] of the DMZ. In addition, North Korea has more than 6 million reservists."[37] North Korea also has 100,000 troops in its special ops forces, which makes it the largest special forces element in the world.[38] And the North Koreans have had no compunction about using these forces:

> Since the Korean War, the North has repeatedly gone on the attack: kidnapping Japanese and South Korean citizens; digging tunnels through the bedrock below the DMZ into South Korea, tunnels big enough for an invasion force to pass through at a rate of ten soldiers a minute; sending an assassination team to Seoul to kill the President; bludgeoning to death with axes two American officers in the Joint Security Area of the DMZ; blowing up and killing seven senior members of a South Korean delegation to Burma (four cabinet members, two top Presidential advisers, and an ambassador); initiating countless naval battles with Southern ships, resulting in numerous fatalities; sending a submarine to land commandos in the South; launching a missile over Japan. The list goes on.[39]

In short, the North Koreans have been in active conflict with the South for decades.

North Korea's economy has been described as "close to meltdown."[40] "Millions are suffering from acute shortages of food caused by industrial collapse."[41] North Korea suffered massive starvation in the 1990s, after the Soviet Union, its ally and source of support, ceased to exist. "As many as 2 million North Koreans are thought to have died from starvation since the mid-'90s. And 42 percent of children are chronically malnourished."[42]

As the State Department's national security chief John Bolton has noted, however, Kim Jong Il has not had to suffer like the people he oppresses. "While he lives like royalty in Pyongyang, he keeps hundreds of thousands of people locked in prison camps with millions more mired in abject poverty, scrounging the ground for food. For many in North Korea, life is a hellish nightmare."[43] Given this grand economic failure, what supports the massive North Korean military machine?

The answer: missiles, drugs and counterfeit currency.[44] North Korea has been building its own Scud missiles since the 1980s. The Taepodong 1, a "super-missile" based on Scud technology, was test-fired over Japan in 1998, shocking the world. There are now indications that North Korea has developed a Taepodong 2 with a range of nearly five thousand miles, which could reach the western United States. The North Koreans have also made modifications to Scuds to enable them to carry chemical and bacteriological warheads. It is estimated that North Korea has five hundred Scud missiles of various types. And these programs have been a source of cash as well as firepower for Kim's isolated nation: since the 1980s, North Korea has raised cash by exporting missiles or missile technology to Yemen, Iran, Libya, Syria, Pakistan, and Egypt.[45]

In April 2003, Australian authorities seized a North Korean freighter off its coast that was carrying 110 pounds of pure heroin. This incident was only the most recent evidence of North Korea's state-sponsored drug trade. "North Korean diplomats have regularly been caught since the 1970s smuggling drugs in diplomatic packages through China, Russia, Laos, Egypt and elsewhere. Defectors from North Korea have described government efforts to grow opium for heroin production in the country's rugged mountains."[46] Japan and Taiwan have also charged that North Korea smuggles amphetamines to their countries.[47] At base, North Korea qualifies as a state-run criminal enterprise.

The future of North Korea looks bleak, and that is very dangerous for its neighbors and the world. Kim Jong Il's successful attempt to blackmail the Clinton administration for support in the 1990s was likely a direct result of his country's economic problems. And while food shortages have receded somewhat since the 1990s, some diplomats in Pyongyang believe that the economic crisis has gotten so severe that "central rule has broken down."[48] The collapse of the North Korean economy may already be under way.

Given this current crisis, Kim Jong Il could very well attempt nuclear blackmail in the future, or engage in further attempts to hawk WMD on the world market. The United States has already fought one war against North Korea, at great expense in American lives and resources. If we are to to avoid another such confrontation, America may have to arm its allies in the region, including Japan, with nuclear weaponry sufficient to keep North Korea contained long enough for its government to collapse altogether.

This, in turn, will require us to abandon the misguided Carter-Clinton practice of bilateral U.S.–North Korean negotiations—and phony deals in which we support Kim's regime in exchange for false promises to stop its nuclear program. Instead, a coalition of South Korea, Japan, Taiwan, and even China and Russia might be assembled to exert pressure on North Korea. (Ironically, though this is one place where multilateralism may be invaluable, Democrats don't seem to agree.)

In any event, the burgeoning strength and instability of North

Korea poses a sobering threat to American security and interests—
and our government must respond by increasing our military capabilities to meet the challenge. Despite significant recent increases
in military spending, American forces are spread thin thanks to the
budget slashing of the 1990s. If we fail to restore our defensive
strength, it will be at our own risk.

AL QAEDA

Before September 2001, few Americans were aware of this shad-
owy terrorist group. But long before al Qaeda made its direct attack on U.S. soil, it already had a history of attacking America, her
people, and her interests overseas. Osama Bin Laden himself declared in a notorious 1998 statement that it was the duty of all
Muslims to kill American citizens, military or civilian, along with
our allies around the world.

Like the Japanese in World War II, however, al Qaeda has
learned the consequences of awakening the sleeping giant. The
United States has already killed or captured many key members of
al Qaeda's leadership. Osama bin Laden is either dead or on the
run. And al Qaeda's ability to carry out new attacks has been seriously undercut.

Still, we have not seen the end of al Qaeda. It continues to re-
cruit new members, and execute its deadly plans, around the world.
And it is the nature of this diffuse and clandestine group to operate
at skeletal strength; after all, it only took a handful of terrorists on
9/11 to unleash the hell that killed so many of our countrymen.

Today, there are many indications that new attacks may be in
the works. As John Hartley, a former director of Australia's Defence
Intelligence Organisation, has written, al Qaeda's eviction from

Afghan training camps may have been a setback for its activities, but it has not brought them to a halt. "Although Al-Qaeda has had its operational significance curtailed, it still inspires a secretive terrorist network that shows an ability to respond to changing circumstances. The recent use of surface-to-surface missiles, the discovery of a lethal toxin in London, the recruitment of non-Arab Muslim converts and the intentions to deploy militants to Iraq attest to this contention."[49]

Larry Medford, the FBI's executive assistant director for counterterrorism and counterintelligence, agrees. In his estimation, al Qaeda's power has diminished, but it is still potent. "While we think they are clearly downgraded and their abilities are not what they used to be, they are still a very, very serious threat, and the reason they are a threat is that they are absolutely focused and committed to attacking America," Medford told CNN in November 2003.[50]

Recent headlines continue to track al Qaeda and its operations around the world. Evidence has suggested that al Qaeda operatives planned the suicide bombings in Istanbul, Turkey.[51] An al Qaeda suspect was in Canada seeking nuclear material to create a dirty bomb, a conventional explosive device rigged with radioactive material that could contaminate a large area for years.[52] In June 2003, an unclassified CIA report revealed that al Qaeda was prepared to use nuclear, biological or chemical weapons. "Al Qaeda's goal is the use [of such weapons] to cause mass casualties," as Bill Gertz writes.[53] Furthermore, they "may try to launch conventional attacks against the nuclear industrial infrastructure of the United States in a bid to cause contamination, disruption and terror." A recent CIA assessment contends that al Qaeda has decided to step up its attempts to overthrow the House of Saud, the Saudi royal family, which would cause oil prices to soar and severely harm the U.S. economy.[54] These scenarios are too chilling to contemplate.

The question remains: If its key leadership has been neutralized, what explains al Qaeda's continuing viability? The answer most likely lies in the organization's franchise-like structure, which absorbs sympathizers and allows it to carry on without direct supervision from above. In a 1999 interview with PBS's *Frontline,* the Saudi dissident Dr. Saad Al-Fagih noted that Osama bin Laden's group includes both a core group of acolytes and a looser group of sympathizers that number in the thousands:

> And then you have the [wider group]. In thousands, maybe tens of thousands, who are sympathetic to bin Laden and who look at him as their father, and arrange themselves in small groups here and there. A very loose network with that hierarchy. You can never eradicate them. . . . Each small group has its own chain of command, its own logistics. Now they wait for somebody like bin Laden to give them moral support and give them directions. They might try to contact him to get advice from him. But they don't belong to him like a special organization with a pyramidal structure or anything like that. He does have a small core of followers[,] probably in the hundreds. But some . . . have estimated the number to be 600 or 700. But the danger for the west or for Saudi Arabians—for the regime in Saudi Arabia—is not only this 600 people. The danger lies with all those small groups.[55]

These smaller groups may be the crux of the problem. Since America's effective attack on al Qaeda's top leadership, intelligence analysts believe, the group's surviving leaders have "franchised" their style of violence to terrorist groups around the world, creating a new challenge for counterterrorism officials. It's been esti-

mated that some twenty thousand people from forty-seven countries were trained in the group's Afghanistan training camps; today,
those "graduates," united by that shared training experience,[56]
have "fanned out" across the world to lead smaller, like-minded
terrorist groups, which have proved harder to track and defend
against.[57] Some of these terrorists are in sleeper cells in the United
States and Canada, poised and waiting to strike:

> U.S. authorities said sleeper cells also operate in at least 40
> states from Florida and New York to California and Washing-
> ton State—living low-profile lives, often in ethnic communi-
> ties. The September 2002 arrest of seven members of a
> terrorist cell in Lackawanna, N.Y., just south of Buffalo, was a
> first major clue to their existence. Between 2,000 and 5,000
> operatives are said to be in the United States, many of whom
> are hiding in ethnic communities throughout the country,
> populated by millions of foreign immigrants, including illegal
> aliens for which the U.S. government cannot account.[58]

No matter how many direct followers he actually has, Osama
bin Laden remains effectively the leader of an untold number of
committed fanatics in the U.S. and around the world, each of them
committed to our violent destruction. Only time and vigilant action will eradicate their evil influence on the world.

ISRAEL AND THE PALESTINIANS

The first principle in any responsible evaluation of the Israeli-
Palestinian conflict is this: Israel is not only our closest ally in the
Middle East, it is one of our most important allies of all. America

and Israel share common values and beliefs. We have an important strategic interest in assisting Israel, based on our long partnership. And as one of the historical birthplaces of Western civilization, the state of Israel deserves every protection we can offer.

Today, perhaps more than ever before, Israel is fighting for its life. With the Arab world primed to move against it, Israel needs our support. And I firmly believe that we must allow its prime minister, Ariel Sharon, to do what is necessary to protect his citizens. It would be deeply wrong for us to adopt one standard for our own efforts in fighting terrorism, and to judge Israel by another.

Whether practiced by Republican or Democrat presidents, however, U.S. policy in recent years has turned on the mistaken contention that Israel must continue to cede precious land to the Palestinians in exchange for promises of peace. And yet, as we have seen with so many other corrupt regimes, the Palestinians continue to break their promises. Since the Oslo Accords of 1993 and before, the Palestinians have broken their promises often enough that it seems certain they had no intention of honoring them in the first place.

This duplicity can be set directly on the doorstep of the Palestinian Authority (including Yasser Arafat)—a group that is committed to destroying Israel, not coexisting with it.

Through the history of this conflict, Israeli attempts to appease the Palestinians have resulted in more violence, not less. Indeed, the current round of violence can be traced directly back to an Israeli peace offer. In July 2000, Israeli prime minister Ehud Barak met with Yasser Arafat, the Palestinian leader, at Camp David. Despite intense political pressure from home, Barak practically begged Arafat to accept a Palestinian state. Yet, as the *Washington Post* reported, Arafat turned down the most extraordinary concessions:

The summit's failure, coupled with the extraordinarily far-reaching proposals that were on the table when Palestinian leader Yasser Arafat walked away, [generated] shock waves in Israel, among the Palestinians and throughout the Middle East.

Barak's willingness to divide Jerusalem—described by a variety of sources, including Israelis, Palestinians and Americans who attended the talks—has had a particularly big impact. The proposal would have allowed Arafat to proclaim the capital of his independent state in Jerusalem, fulfilling his life-long nationalist ambition.[59]

Arafat walked away from the offer of a lifetime—and returned home to declare a new intifada, or uprising, a few months later. More than 6,700 Israeli casualties have followed, including nearly 900 deaths. This latest cycle of violence has seen the emergence of a grotesque new wrinkle: Palestinian children being recruited to become suicide bombers to kill Israeli civilians. Arafat has condoned and encouraged this chilling development.

[A]ccording to a source who works in the PA-controlled areas and who spoke on condition of anonymity, hundreds of children aged 11–15 are being trained in paramilitary camps in the Gaza Strip and West Bank. The camps are run, not only by Islamic Jihad and Hamas, but also by PLO Chairman Yasser Arafat's Fatah faction.[60]

Despite every effort to approach him as an honest broker, Arafat has repeatedly proven a corrupt and bloodthirsty terrorist whose only goal is the total destruction of Israel. The fact that he walked away from Barak's offer of peace should have convinced the world that he will never be serious about peace with Israel. And his will to continue the intifada against Israel, unfortunately, is matched by more than adequate means:

> According to Aharon Ze'evi, Israel's chief of military intelligence, as of last year, Arafat had a net worth of $1.3 billion. . . . If that sum seems incredible, consider that the European Union alone has sent Arafat and the PA an average of $150 million every year for the past decade. Also, the Arab League has donated $1 billion since 2000.[61]

Arafat continues to fund the violence directly. "An ally at a meeting of Palestinian leaders once asked, 'Where is the money for the Intifada?' " the *Weekly Standard* recently reported. " 'Here I am,' replied Arafat."[62] Arafat's resources will allow him to maintain his war against Israel for the foreseeable future.

The Arab-Israeli struggle has almost drawn the United States into war before. In 1973, Egypt and Syria launched a surprise attack on Israel on one of the holiest days of the Jewish calendar. Israel suffered tremendous losses, and many doubted its survival. The United States rushed to resupply the Israelis. The Soviet Union, which had been supplying the Arab armies, threatened to bring troops to the region as "peacekeeping forces." Only when President Nixon brought the U.S. military to Def Con (Defense Condition) 3, its highest alert status in peacetime, did the Soviet Union back down and Israel was saved.[63]

Since the Yom Kippur War, many Arab dictators have tried to claim the mantle of leadership of the greater Arab world by promoting hatred and violence against Israel. Libya's Muammar Qaddafi and Iraq's Saddam Hussein are recent examples. A large-scale Middle East war would throw the world economy into a tail-spin, propelled by skyrocketing oil prices and investor fears. But if the United States continues to restrain Israel's ability to defend itself effectively against many of the same terrorist forces that threaten America, the real risk, to my mind, is that Israel itself could fall.

And if that should happen, the result would be not only a major strategic loss—but a knife close to the heart of Western civilization. Many of the forces aligned against Israel are the very same ones that seek America's annihilation. Israel must survive, and the United States must ensure its survival. The best avenue toward minimizing direct U.S. involvement to defend Israel is for the United States to lift the restraints on Israel, let her defend herself, and openly embrace her as an ally in the War on Terror.

During the Cold War, Ronald Reagan invoked John Winthrop's vision of America as a "shining city upon a hill," a beacon of hope to freedom-loving people everywhere. Today, as George W. Bush has alerted us, freedom and fear are once again at war. These early days of the conflict have seen seasons of outstanding victory—the routing of the Taliban, the fall of Saddam—and days of lasting loss. But Americans have proven strong, and the world must recognize that we will prevail.

Still, we cannot prevail tomorrow without courageous leadership today. Our leaders will choose how we meet the challenges of the future—with strength and conviction, or with cowardice and accommodation.

We, in turn, will choose those leaders. In doing so, we must remember, we are choosing our future.

In 2004, and the many years to come, I pray that America will make the right choice.

AFTERWORD

As I write this, it is with feelings of confidence and relief. As we all know, the 2004 election was a hard-fought race. As I said many times on the radio, on *Hannity & Colmes,* and in the hardcover edition of this book, there was more at stake in this election than there had been in decades, perhaps within our lifetime. And the good news is that the results proved the American people understood the stakes. They knew the importance of the themes I've heard them talk about so many times: the continuing threat from terrorists and the states that support them, the importance of vigilance, and the danger of appeasement.

Of the two contenders for the Oval Office in 2004, each man ran a race that truly reflected his character. The Republican incumbent, George W. Bush, ran as the leader he has proven himself to be in his first four years in office: strong of voice and certain of his convictions, he led the American people to the polls in record numbers to return him to office for a second term. Democratic nominee John Kerry, on the other hand, emerged as a far different figure: a man of much-celebrated "nuance" and constant contradiction, who tried to position himself as a mili-

tary hero but ultimately emerged as no more than an oppor-
tunist.

The best man won. And the American people are safer for it.

The election of 2004 did, indeed, generate stronger voter turnout
than we've seen in years; more people voted for President Bush
than have ever voted for a single presidential candidate in our history. What was it that drove so many voters to the polls? Many
commentators have concluded that the election turned on the so-
called "moral issues" such as abortion or gay marriage. Indeed,
some exit polls seemed to support that conclusion. But we know
that exit polling, which is often based on skewed sampling, is suspect. Furthermore, to lump a number of loosely related concerns
under the category of "morals issues" may be a way of stacking
the deck, of unfairly inflating their significance in deciding the
election.

Don't get me wrong, I think that the majority of the American people did feel a revulsion for the left's determined effort to
undermine traditional values in this country. Indeed, the unani-
mous affirmation of traditional marriage in the eleven states where
the issue was on the ballot sent a strong message from red-state
America that ordinary Americans are not quite ready to relinquish
control of society to those who reject their sacred institutions.

But when you consider how many disparate issues were
usually collected by pundits under the "moral issues" umbrella, it
becomes clear that the voters' ostensibly second-highest priority—
national security—far outstripped all other concerns. Personally, I
knew this instinctively from the first day of the campaign. Bill
Clinton's war room was famous for coining the slogan "It's the
economy, stupid" to remind his team that economic matters are

almost always most important to voters. But there is one major exception to that rule—in times of war, no issue transcends the safety of our homeland. And make no mistake: During the entirety of the campaign—as we are today—we were at war.

During the 2004 campaign, John Kerry's running mate, John Edwards, tried to ratchet up the perceived urgency of the economic issue; from time to time Kerry joined in. But they failed every time, for a number of reasons. First of all, the economy was performing very well. We've been experiencing robust growth, relatively low unemployment, and very low inflation and interest rates. Kerry and Edwards argued that it was a jobless recovery, but the data didn't support their rhetoric. They carped about the growing deficit, but the American people understand that much of that number is immediately traceable to the costs associated with 9/11 and the military commitments that followed.

And of course the Democrats couldn't resist drawing on that old standby of theirs—the rhetoric of class warfare. According to John Kerry and John "Son of a Mill Worker" Edwards, Republican support for tax cuts had nothing to do with stimulating economic growth, or limiting the burden on average Americans' incomes. Their timeworn party line, gleefully articulated by the Democratic duo, was that Republicans wanted to fund all their other unworthy projects—from the war in Iraq to the Evil Dick Cheney's Halliburton schemes—on the backs of the middle class and poor.

Once again, none of their propaganda and demagoguery worked. The American people aren't that easily fooled. And today, more than ever, American voters are deadly serious—about the security of their children and the future of their country. They know we're in the middle of a war that we need to win.

But if there was one fatal error the Democrats made that en-sured the president's victory on election night, it was the man they chose to represent them—and the long list of mistakes he made along the way. If America owes John Kerry a debt of gratitude to-day, it's less for his controversial service to his country in Vietnam than for keeping the war issue on the front burner in 2004—and demonstrating, time and again, why his party was the wrong one to lead the country in the War on Terror.

The faintly ludicrous spectacle of John Kerry stepping up to the podium at the Democratic National Convention and inform-ing the country that he was "reporting for duty" did the presi-dent's campaign a wildly important favor: It ensured that military and defense matters would be front and center for the duration of the race. Not only did Kerry's declaration place his highly dubious Vietnam record at issue; it simply confirmed what everyone al-ready knew, and the Democrats couldn't deny—that defense issues, and particularly the War on Terror, were the defining issue on Americans' minds.

In shamelessly presenting himself as a war hero, Kerry was presumably trying to offset the inevitable attention to his record as a consummate dove who was constitutionally ill-equipped to be commander in chief during wartime. But in accepting the nomi-nation he had already awakened a sleeping giant in the Swift Boat Veterans for Truth, a group of men who had seen John Kerry's true character up close. Most of these veterans had refrained from commenting on Kerry's war record for years, until he won the De-mocratic primary and it looked like he might actually have a chance to become the leader of the American armed forces—the very body of soldiers and sailors he had trashed as a class when he came home from Vietnam and tarred them all as war criminals.

Having served with him overseas—and then witnessed his despicable betrayal after he returned—these men knew that John Kerry not only lacked the "right stuff" to lead the country in wartime, but would be a disastrous commander in chief.

What the Swift Boat Veterans revealed—or reminded us—about Kerry was devastating, and it forced the Democrats even deeper into their defensive posture. They tried various tactics to stop the bleeding, from maligning the character of John O'Neill to concocting elaborate conspiracy theories tying the veterans' organization to the president's campaign. They even tried to resurrect the thrice-refuted charge that President Bush had been AWOL for his Texas Air National Guard Duty in the early 1970s. In the end, of course, there was no fire behind the smokescreen. And along the way, in his eagerness to bring down the president, one of the icons of the liberal media elite managed to bring down only himself. Dan Rather's resignation as anchor of the *CBS Evening News,* after the forged documents scandal that embarrassed both him and *60 Minutes II,* marked a real moment of reckoning for old-line liberalism. After all, the American people don't need CBS to tell them about President Bush's character, or his fitness to lead the military. From that tragic day of 9/11 forward, they had seen him do it firsthand.

Still John Kerry pressed on, piling up misstep after misstep in his bid for the White House. Trying desperately to hold together his always-fragmented party—from the antiwar Dean contingent to the more conservative Southern Democrats—he had too many masters to serve, and it showed: He managed to tie himself in knots every time he opened his mouth about Iraq. The Democrats grew angry at the term "flip-flopper," but with lines like "I actually voted for the $87 billion before I voted against it," Kerry brought it on himself.

The best defense the Democrats—and their supporters in the mainstream media—could mount was to try to present Kerry as a "deliberative" man, a "thinker," decorated in nuance, who was compelled to change or refine his sophisticated positions on the war whenever new facts became available. All of that was utter psychobabble. Kerry was no more deliberative than President Bush. After all, this was the guy who, before the ink was dry on the 9/11 Commission Report, was demanding that the president implement each and every one of its recommendations sight unseen. Nor was Kerry a consistent or principled leader. During the Clinton administration he had sounded as hawkish about Saddam Hussein as President Bush would later become, and after 9/11, when the public was clearly behind the president's stated intention to attack Iraq, Kerry voted for the resolution giving the president unfettered authority to do so. But then when Howard Dean had his brief flare-up of support during the primary season, Kerry scrambled to do an about-face and realign himself with his true allies: the antiwar element of his party. To explain the shift, he spun a yarn about how President Bush had duped him into supporting the war by "distorting the evidence" of Iraq's WMD program, and by promising not to use military force until all diplomatic options had been exhausted. In fact, Kerry had had access to the very same intelligence on Iraqi WMD as President Bush. And by pretending he'd been tricked about the intelligence, Kerry simply made himself look foolish. Right down to the last days of the race—even during the debates, where he showed tinges of silver-tongued erudition—he was unable to present a consistent, or convincing, case for how he would proceed if elected. Should we be withdrawing our troops immediately from "the wrong war at the wrong place at the wrong time," or stay until we were able to stabilize and democratize the nation? He never did explain how he could reconcile his positions—and the media never asked him to.

No, Kerry was neither deliberative nor sophisticated. In the final analysis, he was just expedient—a career politician who shifted his positions based purely on political calculation.

The election that resulted was a glorious victory for conservatives across America. The Republican Party's commitment to our national security, as embodied in President Bush and the strong-defense, family-values platform he ran upon, resonated with American voters. The American people were not about to allow this curious Boston Brahmin to "report for duty." Instead they handed him his hat—and handed George W. Bush a clear mandate.

I am personally gratified at this evidence that the public still appreciates the evil forces we face in the world, and understands that these forces cannot be appeased, but must be confronted. I'm also heartened at the Republican majorities in both houses of Congress, which will help give the president the latitude he needs to confront the terrorists on the only terms they understand: superior force. The increased number of African-Americans and Hispanics voting Republican, and the Democrats' post-election disorientation and endless self-evaluation, are all signs that the Republican majority is here to stay.

Having said all that, though, I want to issue a major caution against complacency. In politics and governance, nothing is permanent. Circumstances can change overnight, especially in the midst of prosecuting a war. Liberals were soundly defeated in this election, but they were not destroyed, and the last time I checked—despite their threats—they haven't moved to other countries. They sometimes visit foreign lands (when they vacation in the red states), but they're still among us, and they are desperate to regroup. The liberal spirit may be temporarily deflated, its armies may be discouraged, but it will be back and with a vengeance, eager to capitalize on any difficulties we encounter in the Iraq War or elsewhere in the ever-evolving War on Terror.

Right now, we have al Qaeda on the run. As of this writing, we have averted additional terrorist attacks on America's mainland following 9/11. Our intelligence agencies are sharing and utilizing information in a more effective fashion. We remain vigilant against further attacks, though we realize that we cannot remain immune forever. Though we've had great difficulties in stabilizing Iraq against a tireless enemy supported by thug regimes, including neighboring Iran, we have done a remarkable job training Iraqi troops to take over this war, and are proceeding, undeterred, toward democratic elections there.

As we approach the formalization of Iraqi self-rule, the terrorists, who have a vested interest in preserving the instability and chaos, and preventing the institution of democracy from gaining a foothold in the Middle East (beyond Israel), can be counted on to ratchet up the violence, in utter desperation. The death toll on our side is bound to increase, and the antiwar forces here will milk that for all it's worth.

In the meantime, other great dangers loom behind the borders of Iran and North Korea—especially when it comes to nuclear weapons. Even as our resources are stretched overseas, these twin menaces will not adjust to our timetable. With the death of Yasser Arafat, the Israeli-Palestinian struggle is also extremely precarious—not to suggest, of course, that he was a stabilizing or peaceful influence. Russia and its former fellow Soviet states remain in a state of violent flux. Saudi Arabia continues to home-grow terrorists by the thousands. The French and Germans remain stubborn about protecting their own relationships with foreign powers—even highly questionable ones. And the United Nations remains a corrupt institution, whose role in the world grows darker every day.

At home, the left and its mouthpieces in the mainstream media continue to hammer the president at every turn—no matter what he does. His appointment of the eminently qualified Condoleezza Rice as secretary of state was met with near-racist jibes of derision from the left, who say she will be nothing but a "yes-man" for the ever-dictatorial President Bush. (These shameful slurs, of course, recall similar comments hurled at Colin Powell, who was lambasted as an Uncle Tom when President Bush appointed him to his cabinet.)

Also forever in the left's sights is Defense Secretary Donald Rumsfeld, whose refusal to bow before them and tolerate their naysaying has earned their permanent wrath. To them he is evil personified, the man who virtually ordered the abuse at Abu Ghraib while deliberately stripping the armor from our military vehicles in Iraq so as to endanger our troops.

All of which only goes to prove that the election of 2004 was just the latest battle, not the entire war. Despite the Republican victory and the public's positive referendum on the Bush record, the left remains focused on assaulting him at every turn. We must continue to fight not only our terrorist enemies, but the persistent obstructionism of the left, which—as I've said in these pages—sees evil at best through obscured lenses. Victory may be sweet, but our challenges have just begun.

As I write this, we are entering a new year. A new Bush administration is taking shape in Washington, ready to work with our allies to bring terrorists to justice around the world, and our Congress to improve the American way of life at home. Three years have passed since the terrorists hijacked our peaceful way of life, but our borders remain well-guarded and secure. Though still volatile, Iraq is nearing its first free elections in modern times. Right now, our troubles may seem miles away. But in what direction? Four years from now, if we stay the course, we may have far more peace in the world than we have today. The promise of democracy may have spread from the free elections in Iraq to other nations in the Arab world, where it is still all too rare. The other nations of hottest concern—Iran, North Korea—may realize that America is serious about preserving peace in the world, and that our willingness to act is as strong as our beliefs.

And yet there is always the risk that pressure from the left— or the cowardice and fickle support of our European allies—may lead us down other, more treacherous paths. If two years from now we lose focus, as can so easily happen in midterm elections, and let control of one house of Congress pass to Democratic hands, then by 2008 we might find ourselves returned to Bill Clinton's America: complacent, mired in petty domestic squabbling, asleep at the switch . . . while the next threat of terror lurks just over the horizon. With Iran, the Ukraine, the Middle East, Saudi Arabia, all potential tinderboxes, would you trust the safety of America's children to the discredited principles of the Democratic Party, which still looks for guidance to the likes of Howard Dean? Or to a Kerry-style politician like Hillary Clinton, whose conveniently "conservative" stances on the war and illegal immigration seem more opportunistic than ever?

Now is not the time to take chances. Now is the time to remember the reasons we all cared so much about voting in

2004. And to make sure that the leaders we chose have the chance to make good on their promises. Because the strides we make in the first decade of the twenty-first century may well determine the survival of the American people in the years and decades that follow.

NOTES

IN THE SPIDER HOLE

1. "Iraqi Press: Nation 'Swimming in Sunshine,' " Worldnetdaily.com, December 16, 2003.

2. "Democrats Mostly Pleased by Arrest, Bush's Democratic Rivals Mostly Pleased by News of Saddam's Arrest; Lieberman: 'Praise the Lord,' " Associated Press, December 14, 2003.

3. Ibid.

4. Ibid.

5. Howard Dean, "Fulfilling the Promise of America: Meeting the Security Challenges of the New Century," Speech at the Pacific Council, Los Angeles, California, December 15, 2003.

6. "Saddam Caught! Former Iraqi Leader Discovered Hiding at Bottom of Hole by Home Near Tikrit," Worldnetdaily.com, December, 14, 2003.

1. TERRORISM, DESPOTISM, AND LIBERALISM

1. Patrick McMahon, "Taunting of Suicidal Woman Shocks Seattle," *USA Today,* August 30, 2001.

2. Robert E. Pierre, "Pharmacist Admits He Diluted Drugs," *Washington Post,* February 27, 2002, p. A02.

3. Hawke Fracassa, "Ex-Priest Says It Was '2-way Thing,' " *Detroit News,* August 28, 2002.

4. *The Works of John Adams—Second President of the United States* (Boston: Little, Brown, 1854), vol. IX, p. 229.

5. Joseph Carroll, "Seven in 10 Are 'Extremely' Proud to Be Americans This Independence Day, Public Divided on Whether Founding Fathers Would Be Pleased, Disappointed with the U.S. Now," Gallup News Service Poll Analyses, July 3, 2003.

6. George W. Bush, "State of the Union Address," White House Official website, January 29, 2002.

7. David L. Greene, "Bush Turns Increasingly to Language of Religion," *Baltimore Sun,* February 10, 2002.

8. Daniel Philpott, "Iraq's Future Lies in Secrets of its Skeletons," *Chicago Tribune,* July 27, 2003; Tim Potter, "Mass Grave in Iraq Unearths Anguish," *Wichita Eagle,* May 15, 2003.

9. George W. Bush, "National Day of Prayer and Remembrance for the Victims of the Terrorist Attacks on September 11, 2001," White House Official website, September 13, 2001.

10. George W. Bush, "President Bush's Address to a Joint Session of Congress and the American People," White House Official website, September 20, 2001.

11. Patrick E. Tyler and Jane Perlez, "World Leaders List Conditions on Cooperation," *New York Times,* September 19, 2001.

12. Ronald W. Reagan, "Farewell Address," *Facts on File World News Digest,* January 13, 1989.

13. John F. Burns, "Bin Laden Taunts U.S. and Praises Hijackers," *New York Times,* October 8, 2001.

14. R. W. Apple Jr., "On the Home Front, Nagging Uncertainty About Consequences," *New York Times,* October 8, 2001.

15. Editorial, "The Ground War Begins," *New York Times,* October 20, 2001.

16. Tom Raum, "Some Important Bush Goals Met," Associated Press, November 25, 2001.

17. William Raspberry, "Consequences of War," *Washington Post,* March 3, 2003.

18. "Iraq: An Alternative to War," New York *Newsday,* January 29, 2003, available in revised form at www.nybooks.com/articles/16086.

2. EVIL ON THE RECORD: THE HOLOCAUST

1. Victor Davis Hanson, "What Would Churchill Say?" National Review Online, October 1, 2001.

2. William L. O'Neill, *A Democracy at War: America's Fight at Home & Abroad in World War II* (Cambridge: Harvard University Press, 1995), pp. 10–15.

3. Martin Gilbert, *Churchill* (New York: Henry Holt and Company, Inc., 1991), p. 599.

4. Gerhard L. Weinberg, *A World at Arms: A Global History of World War II* (New York: Cambridge University Press 1994), p. 258–62.

5. Ibid, p. 262.

6. William L. O'Neill, *A Democracy at War: America's Fight at Home & Abroad in World War II* (Cambridge: Harvard University Press, 1995), p. 6.

7. David E. Sanger, "The Bushes Tour Auschwitz," *New York Times,* June 1, 2002.

8. Rob Evans and David Hencke, "Hitler saw Duke of Windsor as 'no enemy,' US file reveals," *The Guardian,* January 25, 2003.

9. Edward Renehan Jr., "Joseph Kennedy and the Jews," History News Network, April 29, 2002, http://hnn.us/articles/697.html.

10. Louis L. Snyder, *Hitler and Nazism* (New York: Bantam, 1967), pp. 130–31.

11. Claude Lanzmann, *Shoah* (New York: Pantheon, 1985), p. 69.

12. Ibid, pp. 69–70.

13. Ibid, p. 124.

14. Ibid, pp. 119–20.

15. Ibid, p. 104.

16. Joachim Remak, *The Nazi Years: A Documentary History* (New York: Simon and Schuster, 1969), p. 155.

17. Ibid, p. 149.

18. Ibid, p. 155.

19. Ibid, pp. 159–60.

20. William L. Shirer, *The Rise and Fall of the Third Reich* (New York: Simon and Schuster, 1960), p. 100.

21. Paul Johnson, *The Birth of the Modern: World Society 1815–1830* (New York: HarperCollins, 1992), p. 811.

22. Ronald Reagan, *Speaking My Mind* (New York: Simon and Schuster, 1989), p. 100.

23. Jack Kelley, "Iraqis Pour Out Tales of Saddam's Torture Chambers," *USA Today,* April 13, 2003.

24. "Expert: 300,000 in Iraq's Mass Graves," Associated Press, November 8, 2003.

25. Stephen F. Hayes, "Case Closed," *Weekly Standard,* November 24, 2003.

26. Alice Miller, *For Your Own Good* (New York: Noonday Press, 1990), cited in Daphne Merkin, "If Only Hitler's Father Had Been Nicer," *New York Times,* January 27, 2002.

27. Erica Goode, "Stalin to Saddam: So Much for the Madman Theory," *New York Times,* May 4, 2003.

28. " 'Helter Skelter' Beating Stuns Philly," Associated Press, June 19, 2003.

29. Maryclaire Dale, "Judge Denies Juvenile Status for 15-Year-Old Murder Suspect," Associated Press, November 20, 2003.

30. Maryclaire Dale, "Teen's Grisly Beating Shocks Philadelphia," Associated Press Online, June 19, 2003.

31. Mark Lilla, "New Rules of Political Rhetoric, *New York Times,* February 24, 2002; Susan Sontag, "Real Battles and Empty Metaphors," *New York Times,* September 10, 2002.

32. Remak, *The Nazi Years,* p. 40.

33. Gilbert, *Churchill,* p. 598.

34. Ibid.

35. Ibid, p. 600.

36. Ibid, p. 599.

37. Shirer, *The Rise and Fall of the Third Reich,* p. 421.

38. Ibid, p. 423.

39. Gilbert, *Churchill,* p. 600.

40. Gilbert, *Churchill,* p. 598.

3. FIGHTING COMMUNISM: THE REAGAN WAY

1. David Remnick, "Seasons in Hell: How the Gulag Grew," *The New Yorker,* April 14, 2003; David Harsanyi, "Deep Inside the Soviet Gulag," *Globe and Mail,* May 10, 2003.

2. National Review editors, "Solzhenitsyn: Still Telling the Truth," *National Review,* November 21, 1994.

3. Alexander I. Solzhenitsyn, "Harvard Graduation Speech 1978: A World Split Apart," *National Review* Online, June 8, 2003.

4. Ronald Reagan, *An American Life* (New York: Simon and Schuster, 1990), p. 265.

5. Robert G. Kaiser, "Carter's Campaign Stalls; Behind the Rhetorical Dust, Divergent Views on America's Path," *Washington Post,* October 8, 1980, p. A1.

6. Ibid.

7. Ibid.

8. Paul Johnson, *Modern Times: The World from the Twenties to the Nineties* (New York: HarperCollins, 2001), p. 719.

9. Richard E. Pipes, Letter to the Editor, *New York Times,* January 10, 1980, p. A22.

10. Eric Black, "Winning the COLD WAR; Instead of Blowing Up, Communism Simply Caved in Like a Hollow Log," *Star Tribune,* October 26, 1999, p. 1A.

11. Internet Modern History Sourcebook, "The Brezhnev Doctrine, 1968," Paul Halsall, August 1997.

12. Johnson, *Modern Times,* p. 718–19.

13. Kaiser, "Carter's Campaign Stalls," *Washington Post,* October 8, 1980, p. A1.

14. Adam Clymer, Information Bank Abstracts, *New York Times,* January 4, 1980, p. 12.

15. Brian Crozier, *The Rise and Fall of the Soviet Empire* (Rocklin, Calif.: Prima Publishing, 1999), p. 513.

16. Stephane Courtois et al., *The Black Book of Communism* (Cambridge, Mass.: Harvard University Press, 1999).

17. Jeane J. Kirkpatrick, *Dictators and Double Standards* (New York: Simon and Schuster, 1983), p. 23.

18. Kaiser, "Carter's Campaign Stalls," p. A1.

19. Ronald W. Reagan, "Time to Recapture our Destiny," July 17, 1980, www.reaganfoundation.org.

20. Peter Schweizer, *Reagan's War* (New York: Doubleday, 2002), p. 191.

21. Margaret Thatcher, "Courage," Remarks Before the Heritage Foundation's "Leadership for America" Gala, December 12, 1997, reprinted at http://www.centerforsecuritypolicy.org/index.jsp?section=papers&code=97-P_196at2.

22. Reagan, *An American Life,* p. 234 (50 percent statistic), 294 (quote).

23. Dinesh D'Souza, *Ronald Reagan: How an Ordinary Man Became an Extraordinary Leader* (New York: Free Press, 1997), p. 143.

24. Ibid.

25. Winston Williams, "Military Spending: Debate Is Growing," *New York Times,* March 19, 1987.

26. Reagan, *An American Life,* p. 296.

27. Mona Charen, *Useful Idiots* (Washington, D.C.: Regnery, 2003), p. 142; Lawrence Wittner, "The Surprising Effect of the Nuclear Freeze Movement on the Administration of Ronald Reagan," History News Network, November 17, 2003.

28. Week in Review, "Adding Up the 'Zero Option' Will Take Time," *New York Times,* November 22, 1981, p. 1.

29. Lee May, "Reagan Blames 'Iron Triangle' for Nation's Ills," *Los Angeles Times,* December 14, 1988, p. 1.

30. Andrew E. Busch and Elizabeth Edwards Spaulding, "Awakening from Orwell's Nightmare," *Policy Review,* fall 1993, p. 71.

31. Stephen F. Knott, "Reagan's Critics," *The National Interest,* summer 1996.

32. Ibid.

33. Ibid.

34. Ibid.

35. Busch and Spaulding, "Awakening from Orwell's Nightmare," p. 71.

36. Ibid.

37. Edwin Meese III, "The Man Who Won the Cold War: Ronald Reagan's Strategy for Freedom," *Policy Review,* summer 1992, p. 36.

38. Walter Isaacson, "Reagan for the Defense: His Vision of the Future Turns the Budget Battle into a Star War," *Time,* April 4, 1983, reported by Laurence I. Barrett and Douglas Brew/Washington.

39. David Martin, *Policy Review,* winter 1986; CBS Evening News, Tuesday, November 12, 1985.

40. Sam Donaldson, *This Week with David Brinkley,* Sunday, November 17, 1985.

41. William R. Doerner, reported by Erik Amfitheatreof/Moscow and Johanna McGreary/Washington, "Putting It on the Table: Star Wars Is the Big Obstacle as the U.S. and Soviets Return to Geneva," *Time,* March 11, 1985, p. 12.

42. Leslie H. Gelb, "The Mind of the President," *New York Times,* October 6, 1985.

43. Reagan, *An American Life,* p. 639

44. Meese, "The Man Who Won the Cold War," p. 36.

45. Ibid.

46. Ibid.

47. Ibid.

48. Lou Cannon, "Naivete: The Verdict at Reykjavik," *Washington Post,* October 20, 1986, p. A2.

49. Thatcher, "Courage," reprinted at http://www.centerforsecuritypolicy.org/index.jsp?section=papers&code=97-P_196at2.

50. Steven R. Weisman, "Reagan's First 100 Days," *New York Times,* April 26, 1981, p. 51.

51. "Adding Up the 'Zero Option' Will Take Time," *New York Times,* p. 1.

52. Ronald Reagan, *Speaking My Mind* (New York; Simon and Schuster, 1989), p. 98.

53. Ibid., p. 99.

54. Ibid., p. 107.

55. Ibid., p. 110, 119.

56. Steven Rattner, "Britons Reassured by Reagan's Visit," *New York Times,* June 10, 1982, p. A17.

57. Ibid.

58. Reagan, *Speaking My Mind,* p. 168.

59. Ibid., p. 176.

60. Ibid., p. 180.

61. Busch and Spaulding, "Awakening from Orwell's Nightmare," p. 71.

62. Peter Schweizer, "WWRD?," *National Review* Online, October 15, 2002.

63. Anthony Lewis, "Onward, Christian Soldiers," *New York Times,* March 10, 1983, p. A27.

64. Dennis Prager, "What Makes a Liberal?" Creators Syndicate, Inc., August 12, 2003.

65. Strobe Talbott, "Rethinking the Red Menace; Gorbachev Is Helping the West by Showing that the Soviet Threat Isn't What It Used to Be—and, What's More, that It Never Was," *Time,* January 1, 1990, p. 66.

4. IRAQ I: WAR AND APPEASEMENT

1. Winston Churchill, *The Gathering Storm* (Boston: Houghton Mifflin, 1948), p. 16.

2. Martin Gilbert, *Churchill* (New York: Holt, 1991), p. 861.

3. Ibid., p. 545.

4. Paul Johnson, *Modern Times: The World from the Twenties to the Nineties* (New York: HarperCollins, 2001), pp. 710–12.

5. Chuck Morse, "Carter Sold Out Iran—1977–1978, City Metro Enterprises, 2001.

6. Ibid.

7. While civilian trials and the right of free assembly would certainly have been preferable in such circumstances, President Carter obviously failed to take into account (or didn't care about) the difficult situation the shah was in and how his enemies would exploit these newfound civil liberties to further weaken his authority.

8. Elio Bonazzi, "Double Standards and Deception: How the Left Treats Iran and the Middle East," retrieved from Iranianvoice.org, September 4, 2003

9. Morse, "Carter Sold Out Iran."

10. Ibid.

11. Ronald Reagan, *An American Life* (New York: Simon and Schuster, 1990), pp. 218–19.

12. Ibid., p. 218.

13. Alexander M. Haig Jr. with Charles McCarry, *Inner Circles: How America Changed the World* (New York: Warner Books, 1992), p. 536.

14. Oliver L. North with William Novak, *Under Fire: An American Story* (New York: Zondervan, 1991), p. 45.

15. Jeane J. Kirkpatrick, *Dictators and Double Standards* (New York: Simon and Schuster, 1983), p. 28.

16. Michael Ledeen, "The Willful Blindness of those Who Will Not See," *National Review* Online, February 18, 2003. Johnson, *Modern Times,* p. 713.

17. David Reynolds, *One World Divisible: A Global History Since 1945* (New York: Norton, 2000), p. 392.

18. Ibid., p. 391.

19. J. M. Roberts, *Twentieth Century, The History of the World, 1901 to 2000* (New York: Viking, 1999), p. 684.

20. Johnson, *Modern Times* p. 713.

21. Reynolds, *One World Divisible,* p. 595.

22. Charles Krauthammer, "Iran: Orchestrator of Disorder," *Washington Post,* January 1, 1993, p. A19.

23. Samir al-Khalil, *The Republic of Fear: The Inside Story of Saddam's Iraq* (New York: Pantheon, 1989), p. 70.

24. Margaret Thatcher, *Margaret Thatcher: The Downing Street Years* (New York: HarperCollins, 1993), p. 91.

25. Johnson, *Modern Times,* pp. 713–14.

26. Jimmy Carter, "The Troubling New Face of America," *Washington Post,* September 5, 2002, p. A31.

27. Reagan, *An American Life,* p. 220.

28. Ibid., p. 327.

29. Associated Press, "United Nations Representative Jeane J. Kirkpatrick's Speech as Delivered Aug. 20 [1984] to the Republican National Convention, in Dallas," www.cnn.com/ALLPOLITICS/1996/conventions/san.diego/facts/GOP.speeches.past/84.kirkpatrick.shtml.

30. Mark Fineman and John Hendren, "Garner Believes Hussein Killed Up to 1 Million; Former Head of the Iraq Rebuilding Effort Offers the Highest Estimate Yet of a Civilian Death Toll," *Los Angeles Times,* July 3, 2003, p. 10.

31. Samir al-Khalil, *The Republic of Fear: The Inside Story of Saddam's Iraq* (New York: Pantheon, 1989), pp. 70–72.

32. Michael Kelly, "Who Would Choose Tyranny?" *Washington Post,* February 26, 2003, p. A23.

33. Judith Miller, "Standoff in the Gulf; Atrocities by Iraqis in Kuwait: Numbers are Hard to Verify," *New York Times,* December 16, 1990, p. 1.

34. The Hotline, "Dems '92: Will Anti-War Vote Come Back to Haunt Them?" American Political Network, Inc., January 18, 1991.

35. "Confrontation in the Gulf; Day 3: Remarks in Congress During the Last Hours of Debate," *New York Times,* January 13, 1991.

36. Miller, "Standoff in the Gulf," p. 1.

37. "Congressional Debate Over 1991 Gulf War Remembered," *All Things Considered,* National Public Radio, January 13, 1996.

38. "Wartime Grapevine," *Fox Special Report with Brit Hume,* Fox News Network, September 30, 2002.

39. Senator Kennedy's remarks here were transcribed directly from a video of his speech of January 12, 1991. In the *Congressional Record* two phrases appear in different form: "It is sad" is transcribed as "It is said," and the phrase "driving the engine of war" has been altered to read "that beats the drums of war."

40. *The MacNeil/Lehrer NewsHour,* January 11, 1991.

41. Commission of Inquiry for the International War Crimes Tribunal, retrieved from http://deoxy.org/wc/wc-crime.htm.

42. Leonard Curry, "House Commends Bush and Troops on the War," *San Francisco Chronicle,* January 19, 1991.

43. Donna Brazile and Timothy Bergreen, "What Would Scoop Do?" *Wall Street Journal,* May 21, 2003.

44. "United States House of Representative Debate on the Persian Gulf Crisis and the Use of Force Excerpt of Remarks by Representative Barbara Boxer (D-CA)," Federal News Service, January 11, 1991.

45. "Confrontation in the Gulf: War and Peace: A Sampling from the Debate on Capitol Hill," *New York Times,* January 11, 1991, p. A8.

46. "The Unfinished War: A Decade Since Desert Storm," retrieved from http://www.cnn.com/SPECIALS/2001/gulf.war/facts/gulfwar/.

5. AXIS IRAQ: THE NEW APPEASEMENT

1. Edwin Meese III, *With Reagan: The Inside Story* (Washington, D.C.; Regnery, 1992), p. 201.

2. Retrieved from http://reference.allrefer.com/country-guide-study/libya/libya129.html.

3. Meese, *With Reagan,* p. 202.

4. Ibid.

5. Ronald Reagan, *An American Life* (New York: Simon and Schuster, 1990), p. 517.

6. Ibid, p. 518.

7. Ibid, p. 519.

8. Ibid, p. 520.

9. Meese, *With Reagan,* p. 203.

10. Letter from John Kerry to constituent, May 19, 1986.

11. David Gutmann, "Only U.S. Strength Can Defeat Islamism," *The View From Abroad,* December 2003.

12. Meese, *With Reagan,* p. 204.

13. Evan Thomas; with John Barry, Michael Isikoff, Richard Wolffe, and Michael Hirsh in Washington, and Christopher Dickey in Amman, "The 12 Year Itch," *Newsweek,* March 31, 2003, p. 54.

14. Editorial, "Iraq's Growing Threat," *Boston Globe,* February 13, 2000.

15. Thomas "The 12 Year Itch," *Newsweek,* p. 54.

16. "The Need For Further United Nations Action on Iraq," House of Representatives, February 25, 2003, p. H1324, retrieved from http://www.house.gov/curtweldon/feb25hussein.htm.

17. Paul Greenberg, "The Ghosts of Mogadishu," Tribune Media Services, August 16, 2002.

18. David Halberstam, *War in a Time of Peace* (New York: Scribner, 2001), p. 273.

19. Rich Lowry, *Legacy: Paying the Price for the Clinton Years* (Washington, D.C.: Regnery, 2003), pp. 299–302.

20. Dick Morris, *Off With Their Heads* (New York: ReganBooks, 2003), p. 124.

21. For more on this, see Sean Hannity, *Let Freedom Ring* (New York: ReganBooks, 2002), pp. 16–20.

22. Lowry, *Legacy*, p. 333.

23. George W. Bush, "President Delivers State of the Union Address," January 29, 2002, retrieved from www.whitehouse.gov.

24. Peter Jennings with John McWethy, "Fires out at World Trade Center; New Death Total for World Trade Center Victims; Hunt Continues for Osama bin Laden," ABC *World News Tonight*, December 19, 2001.

25. Patrick E. Tyler and Jane Perlez, "A Nation Challenged: The Diplomacy; World Leaders List Conditions On Cooperation," *New York Times*, September 19, 2001.

26. Arlene Getz, "Cool and Cooler," *Newsweek*, January 30, 2002.

27. Editorial, "George Bush's Delusion: Tragedy Does Not Give America a Free Hand," *The Guardian* (London), January 31, 2002.

28. Suzanne Daley, "A Nation Challenged: The Allies; Many in Europe Voice Worry U.S. Will Not Consult Them," *New York Times*, January 31, 2002.

29. William Walker, "Bush's 'Axis of Evil' Warning Sparks Fire," *Toronto Star*, January 31, 2002, p. A13.

30. Ibid.

31. Ibid.

32. George W. Bush, "President Bush Delivers Graduation Speech at West Point," June 1, 2002, retrieved from www.whitehouse.gov.

33. Anthony Lewis, "A Different World," *New York Times*, September 12, 2001.

34. Amy Fagan, "Bush Sidestepped Process on War in Iraq, Kerry Says," *Washington Times*, July 21, 2003.

35. Thomas Eichler, "Leaders of Democrats in Congress Support Strong Steps on Iraq; Daschle, Gephardt, Others Appear on Sunday Talk Shows," U.S. Department of State, Office of International Information Programs, October 6, 2002.

36. Scot Lehigh, "Clark's Scrambled Message on Iraq," *Boston Globe*, October 24, 2003.

37. Jay Nordlinger, "Albright Then, Albright Now," *National Review* Online, no date given.

38. Carla Marinucci and John Wildermuth, "Gore Blasts Bush's 'Cowboy' Iraq Policy," *San Francisco Chronicle,* September 24, 2002.

39. CNN.com, "U.S. Ousted From U.N. Human Rights Commission," May 3, 2001.

40. Stephen Schwartz, "U.N. Go Home," *The Weekly Standard,* April 14, 2003.

41. Ibrahim Rexhepi, quoted in ibid.

42. Samantha Power, "Bystanders to Genocide," *Atlantic Monthly,* September 2001.

6. THE GATHERING STORM

1. Evan Thomas, with John Barry, Michael Isikoff, Richard Wolffe, and Michael Hirsh in Washington and Christopher Dickey in Amman, "The 12 Year Itch," *Newsweek,* March 31, 2003.

2. Adam Entous, "Bush Warns U.S. Cadets of Unprecedented Threats," Reuters, June 1, 2002.

3. Dana Milbank, "Cheney Says Iraqi Strike Is Justified, Hussein Poses Threat, He Declares," *Washington Post,* August 27, 2002.

4. Paul Wolfowitz, "On Iraq," Remarks at the Fletcher Conference, October 16, 2002; transcript of bin Laden tape, retrieved from http://news.bbc.co.uk/2/hi/middle_east/3204230.stm.

5. Jim Garamone, "Rumsfeld Answers Questions on Iraqi Threat," American Forces Information Services, September 27, 2002.

6. Jim Garamone, "Rumsfeld Says Link Between Iraq, al Qaeda 'Not Debatable,' " American Forces Information Services, September 27, 2002.

7. Ibid.

8. Garamone, "Rumsfeld Answers Questions on Iraqi Threat."

9. Donald Rumsfeld and General Pace, "DoD News Briefing," September 26, 2002.

10. Paul Wolfowitz, "On Missile Defense," Remarks to Frontiers of Freedom, October 24, 2002.

11. Gerry J. Gilmore, "Space, Missile Defense Essential to Defense, Rumsfeld Says," American Forces Press Service, December 10, 2003.

12. Joshua Muravchik, "The Bush Manifesto," *Commentary,* December 2002, p. 23.

13. "The National Security Strategy of the United States of America," retrieved from www.whitehouse.gov/nsc/nss.html.

14. Associated Press, "U.S. Warns Syria on Weapons of Mass Destruction," *USA Today,* May 7, 2003.

15. James Taranto, "The Inspections Are Working," Opinion Journal.com, October 3, 2003.

16. Bill Clinton, "Attack on Iraq; Transcript: 'We Are Delivering a Powerful Message to Saddam,'" *New York Times,* December 17, 1998.

17. James Carroll, "America the Destroyer," *Boston Globe,* March 5, 2003.

18. Andrew Sullivan, "A Million Mogadishus,' Those Antiwar Leftists Who Equate Bush with Saddam and Cheer U.S. Military Setbacks Bring Moral Squalor to Their Cause," *Salon,* March 29, 2003.

19. Margaret Hunt Gram, "De Genova Teach-in Comments Spark Controversy," *Columbia Spectator,* March 31, 2003.

20. http://web.mit.edu/newsoffice/tt/2001/oct24/chomsky.html.

21. "The Antiwar Party," OpinionJournal.com, August 2, 2002.

22. Sullivan, "A Million Mogadishus."

23. Rajiv Chandrasekaran, "Activists Bring War Protests to Baghdad," *Washington Post,* January 14, 2003.

24. Manny Fernandez and Justin Blum, "Thousands Oppose a Rush to War, Chill Doesn't Cool Fury Over U.S. Stand on Iraq," *Washington Post,* January 19, 2003.

25. Ibid.

26. Ibid.

27. "US Warns Iraq On Human Shields," *The Age,* January 16, 2003.

28. Chandrasekaran, "Activists Bring War Protests to Baghdad."

29. Michelle Goldberg, "Saddam's Shields," *Salon,* February 21, 2003.

30. Scott Peterson, "Few But Proud: US Antiwar Activists in Iraq," *Christian Science Monitor,* December 17, 2002.

31. " 'Human Shields' Booted After Criticizing Iraq's Instructions," Associated Press, March 13, 2003.

32. "Human Shields Face $15,000 fines," Reuters, August 13, 2003.

33. Retrieved from http://www.internationalanswer.org/campaigns/f15/f14nyc.html.

34. "Celebs Take Anti-War Stance," Associated Press, December 11, 2002.

35. Elizabeth DiNovella, "Q&A: Janeane Garofalo Won't Back Down," *The Progressive,* April 30, 2003.

36. "Richard Gere Slams Bush on Iraq Policy," WorldNetDaily, February 10, 2003.

37. "Sean Penn Visits Bagdad for 'Insight'; Actor Searching for 'My Own Voice on Matters of Conscience." Worldnetdaily.com, December 14, 2002.

38. Scrapbook, "The War Room Redux, Sean Penn, and More," *The Weekly Standard,* December 30, 2002.

39. Scott Peterson, "Few But Proud."

40. Roger D. Carstens, "Fast Times on a Bagdad High, Sean Penn Offers Himself as an Iraq Propaganda Tool," *National Review* Online, December 17, 2002.

41. Transcript: Brit Hume, Bret Baier, Jonathan Hunt, "Political Grapevine, Daschle Accuses Republicans of Lower Taxes for the Rich Conspiracy, Sympathy for Iraq Builds Up," *Fox Special Report With Brit Hume,* December 16, 2002.

42. Scrapbook, "The War Room Redux."

43. James Carroll, "Antiwar Then, Antiwar Now," *Boston Globe,* October 8, 2002.

44. James Hulse, "Some in Congress, Recalling Vietnam, Oppose War," *New York Times,* September 21, 2002.

45. Carl Limbacher/NewsMax Staff, "Rep. Kaptur 'Happy' She Praised bin Laden; Media Give Her a Pass," NewsMax.com, March 10, 2003.

46. Hulse, "Some in Congress, Recalling Vietnam, Oppose War."

47. *This Week,* ABC News, September 29, 2002.

48. John H. Cushman Jr., "Threats and Responses: Politics; Congressman Says Bush Would Mislead U.S.," *New York Times,* September 30, 2002.

49. George F. Will, "Baghdad Bonoir," *Washington Post,* October 1, 2002.

50. Ed Koch, *Hannity & Colmes,* Fox News, September 11, 2003.

51. Fredric U. Dick, "Andy Slams 'Lost' Dems Over 9/11," *New York Post,* October 22, 2003.

52. Zell Miller, *A National Party No More* (Atlanta: Stroud & Hall, 2003), pp. 197–98.

7. HILLARY AND BILL CLINTON

1. Dick Morris, "Clintons Replacing Democratic Party, with Howard Dean on Rise They Fear Losing Control of Purse Strings," Worldnetdaily.com, November 25, 2003.

2. Ryan Lizza, "Campaign Journal, Outside In," *New Republic,* November 24, 2003.

3. William Greider, "Still Clinton's Show?" *The Nation,* February 17, 2003.

4. Liz Marlantes, "Once-fading Clinton Star Shining Brighter Among Demos," *Christian Science Monitor,* June 16, 2003.

5. Marlantes, "Once-fading Clinton Star Shining Brighter Among Demos."

6. Greider, "Still Clinton's Show?"

7. Chris Black, "Where's Bill? Fiddling With His Legacy—and His Party," *The American Prospect,* February 25, 2002.

8. *Meet the Press,* December 7, 2003, retrieved from http://www.msnbc.com/news/1002438.asp.

9. Much of the speculation that I make in this chapter assumes that George W. Bush will be reelected. If he is defeated, conservatives won't be the only ones who are crying. If a Democrat is elected, then Hillary Clinton will have to wait

eight years before attempting her run and the Clintons will no longer be the power base in the Democratic Party.

10. For a thorough compilation of the failures of the Clinton administration, see *Legacy: Paying the Price for the Clinton Years,* by Rich Lowry and *Losing bin Laden* by Richard Miniter (Washington, D.C.: Regnery, 1993).

11. Matt Pyeatt, "Clinton Paid 'Lip Service' to Terror Attacks, Expert Charges," CNSNews.com, December 5, 2001.

12. Miniter, *Losing Bin Laden.*

13. William J. Clinton, "Remarks and Question and Answer Session at the Adult Learning Center in New Bruswick, New Jersey," *Public Papers of the Presidents,* March 1, 1993.

14. Pyeatt, "Clinton Paid 'Lip Service' to Terror Attacks, Expert Charges."

15. Ibid.

16. Laurie Mylroie, "The World Trade Center Bomb: Who is Ramzi Yousef? And Why It Matters," *The National Interest,* Winter 1995/96.

17. Ibid.

18. Ibid.

19. Ibid.

20. Ibid.

21. "Massive Bomb Rocks U.S. Military Complex," CNN.com, June 26, 1996; Pyeatt, "Clinton Paid 'Lip Service' to Terror Attacks, Expert Charges."

22. "Suspect In USS *Cole* Bombing Kills Self in Yemen," CNN.com, February 14, 2002.

23. "Massive Bomb Rocks U.S. Military Complex," CNN.com.

24. Bill Clinton, "Clinton Statement On US Embassy Bombings In Africa," Unitied States Information Agency, August 7, 1998, retrieved from http://usinfo.state.gov/topical/pol/terror/98090703.htm.

25. Judy Aita, quoting Lewis Schiliro, "Bin Laden, Atef Indicted In U.S. Federal Court For African Bombings," United States Information Agency, November 4, 1998, retrieved from http://usinfo.stat.gov/topical/pol/terror/98110402.htm.

26. Make no mistake: I have the highest regard for the men and women who serve in our law enforcement divisions. Federal and state agencies like the FBI, ATF, and the NYPD play a vital role in protecting our nation and fighting the War on Terror. I merely question Clinton's judgment to treat the attacks in the 1990s as separate, criminal events, rather than acts of war.

27. Milton Bearden, "Graveyard of Empires: Afghanistan's Treacherous Peaks," in Gideon Rose, ed., *How Did This Happen? Terrorism and the New War* (New York: PublicAffairs, 2001), p. 93.

28. "Clinton's Secret War," *Sunday Times* (London), January 20, 2002.

29. Toby Harnden, "White House Invitation for Palestinian Prime Minister," *British Telegraph,* April 26, 2003.

30. Along with Shimon Peres and Yitzhak Rabin, Arafat was awarded the Nobel Peace Prize in 1994. The Official Web Site of the Nobel Foundation, 2003.

31. Mortimer B. Zuckerman, "Arafat Must Be Stopped," *U.S. News and World Report,* September 29, 2003.

32. Ariel Cohen, "Fighting to the Last Palestinian," *National Review* Online, April 10, 2002.

33. Bill Clinton in remarks to Pentagon personnel, February 17, 1998, retrieved from http://www.washingtonianinstitute.org

34. U.S. Department of State, Korea, Democratic People's Republic of, "Country Reports on Human Rights Practices—2002," released by the Bureau of Democracy, Human Rights and Labor, March 31, 2003.

35. Agreed Framework Between the United States of America and the Democratic People's Republic of Korea, October 21, 1994.

36. Charles Krauthammer, "The Clinton Paper Chase," *Washington Post,* October 25, 2002.

37. Editorial, "Toasting Kim Jong Il," *Washington Post,* October 27, 2000.

38. Doug Struck and Steven Mufson, "North Korea's Kim Sheds Image of 'Madman,' " *Washington Post,* October 26, 2000.

39. Doug Struck and Steven Mufson, "North Korea Mulls Curb of Missile Program; Kim Accepts 'Idea,' But Albright Leaves Without Agreement," *Washington Post,* October 25, 2000.

40. "Clinton: 'Rally Behind the President,' " Associated Press, September 11, 2001.

41. Jonathan Freedland, "Clinton's Coded Jibes at Bush Give Conference What It Wants to Hear," *The Guardian,* October 3, 2002.

42. Bill Clinton, "What Should the World Do About Saddam," transcript of Labour Party address, Salon.com, October 3, 2002.

43. David Von Drehle, "Clinton Splits With Bush on Iraq," *Washington Post,* March 13, 2003.

44. Robert Fife, "Bush Criticism 'Uncalled For,' Clinton Says: Former U.S. President Defends Chretien's Stance," *National Post,* November 27, 2003.

45. Madeleine Albright, "Bush's Foreign Policy 'Not Good for the World,' " Agence France Presse, October 16, 2003.

46. Warren Christopher, "Get Foreign Policy Back on Course," *Washington Post,* November 27, 2003.

47. John Aloysius Farrell, "McAuliffe Accused Bush of Making 'Absolutely Ludicrous and Insane Statements,' " *Denver Post,* September 11, 2003.

48. J. R. Ross, "DNC Head Campaigns in Wisconsin, Criticizes Bush," Associated Press, November 20, 2003.

49. Jennifer Harper, "Inside Politics," *Washington Times,* September 12, 2003.

50. Herb Keinon, Gil Hoffman, Janine Zacharia, and Melissa Radler, "Seven Days," *Jerusalem Post,* November 7, 2003.

51. Ibid.

52. Joseph Curl, "Bush Gets Flak For Visit to Iraq," *Washington Times,* November 29, 2003.

53. *Meet the Press,* December 7, 2003, retrieved from http://www.msnbc.com/news/1002438.asp.

54. Barbara Olson, *Hell To Pay: The Unfolding Story of Hillary Rodham Clinton* (Washington, D.C.: Regnery, 1999), p. 132.

55. David Bar-Illan, "The Press and Mrs. Clinton," *Jerusalem Post,* November 19, 1999.

56. Ibid.

57. Neil A. Lewis, "White House Pushed Clemency For Terrorists," *Chattanooga Times Free Press,* October 21, 1999.

58. Joel Siegel, "Hil's Still Opposed to Release," New York *Daily News,* September 9, 2003.

59. "Remarks of Senator Hillary Rodham Clinton on the Need for an Independent Commission to Examine Events Leading Up to 9/11," May 16, 2002, retrieved from http://clinton.senate.gov.

60. Hillary Clinton, "To Provide For the Common Defense," remarks at John Jay College of Criminal Justice, January 24, 2003, retrieved from http://clinton.senate.gov.

61. Erin Duggan, "Clinton Vows to Help Oust Bush," *Albany Times Union,* December 11, 2003.

62. Committee Jurisdiction, U.S. Senate Committee on Armed Services Committee, website, available at http://www.senate.gov/armed_services/about.htm.

63. Hillary Clinton, Press Release, November 27, 2003, retrieved from http://clinton.senate.gov.

64. Douglas Turner, "Clinton says, 'Stay the Course,' " *Buffalo News,* November 29, 2003.

65. Carl Limbacher, "Hillary to Troops: Support for War Fading," NewsMax.com, November 29, 2003.

66. *Meet the Press,* December 7, 2003, retrieved from http://www.msnbc.com/news/1002438.asp.

67. William Safire, "Hillary, Congenital Hawk," *New York Times,* December 8, 2003.

8. PLAYING POLITICS AT THE WATER'S EDGE

1. Farragher and Mishra, *Boston Globe,* September 15, 2003, p. A1.

2. Press Release, "Levin Statement on President Bush's Address to Con-

gress," September 20, 2001, retrieved from http://levin.senate.gov/releases/092001pr2.htm.

3. Press Release, "Official Statement By Senator Jay Rockefeller on the Terrorist Attack Against America," September 12, 2001, retrieved from http://rockefeller.senate.gov/news/2001/pr091201.html.

4. George W. Bush, State of the Union Address, January 28, 2003, retrieved from http://www.whitehouse.gov/news/releases/2003/01/print/20030128-19.html.

5. Colin L. Powell, *All Things Considered,* National Public Radio, June 27, 2003.

6. David E. Sanger and Thom Shanker, "For the Iraqis, a Missile Deal That Went Sour; Files Tell of Talks With North Korea," *New York Times,* December 1, 2003, p. A11.

7. U.S. Senate Select Committee On Intelligence Press Release, "Senate Select Committee On Intelligence Will Conduct A Review Of Intelligence On Iraqi Weapons of Mass Destruction," June 4, 2003, retrieved from http://intelligence.senate.gov/030604.htm.

8. U.S. Senate Select Committee On Intelligence Press Release, June 20, 2003, retrieved from http://intelligence.senate.gov/030620.htm.

9. Center for the Study of Intelligence, "How Intelligence-Sharing With Congress Has Evolved," retrieved from http://www.cia.gov/csi/monograph/lawmaker/1.htm.

10. Federal News Service, Prepared Statement of Vice Chairman Kerrey Before the Senate Committee On Intelligence, July 15, 1998.

11. Zell Miller statement, November 5, 2003.

12. Mary Orndorff, *Birmingham News,* June 7, 2001.

13. Speech, November 16, 2002, retrieved from http://globalsecurity.org/military/library/report/2002/021116-ww4.htm.

14. James G. Lakely, "Memo Infuriates Senators," *Washington Times,* November 6, 2003.

15. Statement Delivered on the Senate Floor by Vice Chairman John (Jay) D. Rockefeller IV on the Leak of a Draft Staff Memo, November 5, 2003.

16. Greg Miller, "Democrats' Iraq Inquiry Plan Is Leaked," *Los Angeles Times,* November 5, 2003, p. 26.

17. David Goldstein, "Memo On Inquiry Angers Roberts," *Kansas City Star,* November 5, 2003, p. A1.

18. Liza Porteus, "GOP Slams Dems for Politicizing Iraq Intel," November 5, 2003, retrieved from http://www.foxnews.com/story/0,2933,102265,00.html.

19. Lakely, "Memo Infuriates Senators."

20. "Sen. Roberts Must Take Charge," *Washington Times,* November 7, 2003.

21. Michelle Cottle, "Sugar and Spice," *New Republic,* January 1, 2001.

22. David Lightman, "Johnson, Others Don't Want the Presidency to Become a House Call," *Hartford Courant,* December 8, 2000, p. A1.

23. Allison Stevens, "Sen. Barbara Mikulski," *The Hill,* May 2, 2001.

24. Cottle, "Sugar and Spice."

25. Emily Pierce, "Rockefeller's Friendly Fire; Some Democrats Think Intel Ranking Member Isn't Team Player," *Roll Call,* July 23, 2003.

26. *Nightline,* November 6, 1990.

27. Mike Dorning and Ron Eckstein, "It's Open Season on Hyde, and Durbin Fires Away," *Chicago Tribune,* February 14, 1999, p. 2.

28. Ken Foskett, "Tracing the Money," *Atlanta Journal-Constitution,* July 6, 1997, p. 4A.

29. Julian Coman, "Democrats Open Second Front Against Bush in War Over Iraqi Secrets," London *Sunday Telegraph,* November 2, 2003.

30. Press Release, Senator Dick Durbin, "Durbin Condemns Gas Price Gouging; Pledges to Hold Gas Stations Accountable," September 12, 2001.

31. Pierce, "Rockefeller's Friendly Fire."

32. Coman, "Democrats Open Second Front."

33. Michael Beschloss, *The Conquerors* (New York: Simon & Schuster, 2002), p. 87.

34. Peggy Noonan, "The Anti-Ikes," *Wall Street Journal,* February 24, 2003.

35. David McCullough, *Truman* (New York: Simon & Schuster, 1992), p. 258.

36. Lawrence L. Knutson, "Eternal Waywardness: After Every Miscue, Congress Investigates," Associated Press, May 3, 1987.

37. "Hillary: 'I Am Sick and Tired' of Patriotic Critics," NewsMax.com, April 29, 2003.

38. Christopher Smith, "Hatch Says He's 'Shocked' At Hacking of Files; Hatch Decries Hacking By Staffer," *Salt Lake Tribune,* November 26, 2003, p. A1.

9. THE CANDIDATES

1. Charles Krauthammer, "The Delusional Dean," *Washington Post,* December 5, 2003.

2. Steve LeBlanc, "Kennedy Says Iraq War Case a 'Fraud,'" Associated Press Online, September 18, 2003.

3. Ibid.

4. "Graham's Criticism of Bush Misses the Count," Associated Press, July 14, 2003.

5. "Graham Says Bush Conduct Worthy of Impeachment," *The Bulletin's Frontrunner,* July 28, 2003 (quoting the *Financial Times*).

6. Bob Benenson, "On Iraq, Bush Has a Full Reservoir of Trust," *Congressional Quarterly Weekly,* June 27, 2003.

7. John Wagner, "Candidates bash Bush at forum," *News & Observer,* June 22, 2003.

8. Anne E. Kornblut and Glen Johnson, "Dean and Lieberman Tangle in Debate, Remarks on US Role in Mideast Draw Rebuke From Senator," *Boston Globe,* September 10, 2003.

9. David T. Cook, "Excerpts from a Monitor Breakfast on the 2004 Presidential Election," *Christian Science Monitor,* September 11, 2003.

10. "McAuliffe Accuses Bush of 'Ludicrous and Insane' Statements," *The Bulletin's Frontrunner,* September 11, 2003 (quoting the *Denver Post*).

11. William Kristol, "Less Safe and Less Secure?" *The Weekly Standard,* August 4 and 11, 2003.

12. Howard Dean, "Defending American Values—Protecting America's Interests," Foreign Policy Address, Drake University, February 17, 2003.

13. Howard Dean, "Restoring American Leadership: A New Direction for American Foreign Policy," speech delivered to the Council on Foreign Relations, Washington, D.C., June 25, 2003.

14. Howard Dean, "Security America at Home & Abroad," *Howard Dean for America,* 2003.

15. Ibid.

16. Ibid.

17. Howard Dean, "Fulfilling the Promise of America: Meeting the Security Challenges of the New Century," Speech to the Pacific Council, December 15, 2003.

18. Dean, "Restoring American Leadership."

19. Ibid.

20. Howard Dean, *Meet the Press,* June 22, 2003.

21. U.S. Department of State, "Iraq Country Reports on Human Rights Practices—2002," retrieved from http://www.state.gov/g/drl/rls/hrrpt/2002/18277.htm.

22. Bret Baier and Ian McCaleb, "Videotape Shows Saddam's Men Torturing Iraqis," FoxNews.com, October 31, 2003.

23. Howard Dean, quoted by Howard Kurtz, "Dean Assails Bush on Defense," *Washington Post,* December 1, 2003.

24. Howard Dean, "About Howard Dean," *Howard Dean for America,* 2003.

25. *Hardball with Chris Matthews,* December 1, 2003.

26. Rush Limbaugh, "Howard Dean Very Nearly Goes Mental," retrieved from www.rushlimbaugh.com, September 10, 2003.

27. Jill Lawrence, "As Dean Forges Ahead, His Temperament Gets Closer Look," *USA Today,* November 11, 2003.

28. Mark Z. Barabak and John M. Glionna, "Dean's Remarks on 9/11 Stir Furor," *Los Angeles Times,* December 9, 2003.

29. Chris Wallace, *Fox News Sunday,* December 7, 2003.

30. Robert Novak, "Dean Won't Let Go of 9/11 Urban Legend," *Chicago Sun-Times,* December 11, 2003.

31. Brit Hume, "Unnecessary Roughness," FoxNews.com, October 14, 2003.

32. Jane Hook and Nick Anderson, "Congress Backs War on Iraq," *Los Angeles Times,* October 11, 2003.

33. David M. Halbfinger, "Kerry Still Nagged by Questions on Vote to Authorize Iraq War," *New York Times,* October 23, 2003.

34. Hume, "Unnecessary Roughness."

35. Ibid.

36. Ibid.

37. Halbfinger, "Kerry Still Nagged by Questions on Vote to Authorize Iraq War."

38. Michael Crowler, "Hidden Prophet," *The New Republic,* September 23, 2002.

39. John Pike, "The Many Faces of Senator John Kerry," *The Nation,* September 29, 2003.

40. Ibid.

41. Dan Balz, "Kerry Angers GOP in Calling for 'Regime Change' in US," *Washington Post,* April 4, 2003.

42. Pike, "The Many Faces of Senator John Kerry."

43. Richard Gephardt, Democratic Presidential Debate in Detroit, October 26, 2003.

44. Bill Lambrecht and Deidre Shesgreen, "The Evolution of Gephardt," *St. Louis Post-Dispatch,* July 6, 2003.

45. Ibid.

46. Ibid.

47. Lois Romano, "Majority Speaker's Gavel Elude Gephardt," *Washington Post,* November 9, 2000.

48. Lambrecht and Shesgreen, "The Evolution of Gephardt," *St. Louis Post-Dispatch.*

49. Quoted in Lambrecht and Shesgreen, "Abortion Stance Shows Wider Shift On Social Issues," *St. Louis Post-Dispatch,* July 6, 2003.

50. "Gephardt attacks Reagan foreign policy," UPI, September 9, 1987.

51. Lambrecht and Shesgreen, "The Evolution of Gephardt."

52. Ryan Lizza, "Divide and Rule," *The New Republic,* June 23, 2003.

53. Gephardt, Democratic Presidential Debate in Detroit.

54. Ron Fournier, "Democrats Slam Bush in First Major Debate," Associated Press Online, September 4, 2003.

55. "Gephardt Gets Poor Reviews from Iowans," *The Bulletin's Frontrunner,* January 21, 2003.

56. Susan Page, "Debate's Flaw: No One's Watching," *USA Today,* October 24, 2003; Sara Fritz, "Cracks Appear in Bush's Armor," *St. Petersburg Times,* September 14, 2003.

57. Richard Gephardt, Democratic Presidential Debate Sponsored by the Congressional Black Caucus Institute and Fox News, Baltimore, Maryland, September 9, 2003.

58. "Quotes from Dem Presidential Debate," FoxNews.com, September 4, 2003.

59. Joseph Lieberman, *Fox News Sunday,* November 30, 2003.

60. Ibid.

61. Joe Lieberman, Speech at Council on Foreign Relations, February 26, 2003.

62. Joe Lieberman, Democrat Presidential Debate, September 4, 2003.

63. Howard Dean, Democrat Presidential Debate, September 4, 2003.

64. Richard Gephardt, Democrat Presidential Debate, September 4, 2003.

65. John Kerry, Democrat Presidential Debate, September 4, 2003.

66. Wesley Clark, *The News Hour with Jim Lehrer,* October 30, 2003.

67. Naomi Koppel, "Libya Opens U.N. Human Rights Meeting," Associated Press, March 17, 2003.

68. Stephen Schwartz, "U.N. Go Home," *The Weekly Standard,* April 14, 2003.

69. Ibid.

70. Clark for President Website, retrieved from http://clark04.com/about/.

71. Martin Fletcher, "Kosovo Clash of Allied Generals," *The Times* (London), May 23, 2001.

72. Ken Ringle, "The Haunting," *Washington Post,* June 15, 2002.

73. Ibid.

74. Wesley Clark, *60 Minutes II,* November 19, 2003, retrieved from www.cbsnews.com.

75. "Foothill College Celebrity Forum Audience at Flint Center," September 24, 2003.

76. Wesley Clark, *Meet the Press,* November 16, 2003.

77. Chris Cillizza, "Military Critiques of Clark Deemed OK," *Roll Call,* November, 19, 2003.

78. Peter J. Boyer, "General Clark's Battles; The Candidate's celebrated—and Controversial—Military Career," *The New Yorker,* November 17, 2003.

79. Ibid.

80. Ibid.

81. Ibid.

EPILOGUE

1. Center for Security Policy, "Back on the China Front," July 16, 2002.

2. U.S. Department of State, *Country Reports on Human Rights Practices, 2001—China,* released by the Bureau of Democracy, Human Rights and Labor, March 4, 2002.

3. Ibid.

4. Central Intelligence Agency World Fact Book, Taiwan, August 1, 2003.

5. "Taiwan Strait," GlobalSecurity.org, July 21, 1995–March 23, 1996.

6. Zhu Rongji, March 16, 2000, quoted on GlobalSecurity.org.

7. Edward Timperlake and William C. Triplett II, *Red Dragon Rising: Communist China's Military Threat to America* (Washington, D.C.: Regnery, 1999), captioned photos following p. 128.

8. Ibid., p. 13.

9. Richard D. Fisher, "China Accelerates Navy Building," *China Brief,* vol. 3, issue 15, July 29, 2003.

10. Richard D. Fisher, "To Take Taiwan, First Kill a Carrier," *China Brief,* vol. 2, issue 14, July 8, 2002.

11. "Taiwan Strait," GlobalSecurity.org.

12. Timperlake and Triplett, *Red Dragon Rising,* p. 133.

13. Ibid., p. 123.

14. Ibid., p. 125.

15. Ibid., p. 13.

16. Charles R. Smith, "China Is a Threat to America," NewsMax.com, March 14, 2002.

17. Christopher Cox, *Report of the Select Committee on U.S. National Security and Military/Commercial Concerns with the People's Republic of China* (Washington, D.C.: Regnery, 1999).

18. U.S. Department of State, *Country Reports on Human Rights Practices, 2001/Iran,* released by the Bureau of Democracy, Human Rights and Labor, March 4, 2002.

19. Ibid.

20. "George W. Bush, PM Berlusconi Discuss Iraq and War on Terrorism," White House official website, July 21, 2003.

21. U.S. Department of State, "Overview of State-Sponsored Terrorism, Patterns of Global Terrorism—2001," May 21, 2002.

22. Amir Taheri, "Recipe for Disaster," *National Review* Online, November 14, 2003.

23. Ibid.

24. Michael Ledeen, "The Future of Iran," *National Review* Online, July 9, 2003.

25. Michael Ledeen, "The Ayatollah's Bomb," *National Review* Online, September 17, 2003.

26. Sebastian Rotella, "Probe Links Syria, Terror Network; Italian Investigation Finds the Country Was a Hub for Shuttling Money and Recruits to Iraq," *Los Angeles Times,* April 16, 2003.

27. Robin Wright, "Pressure on Damascus Grows; Powell Urges Syria to Return Hussein Officials to 'Face Justice,' U.S. Stops Oil Flow from Iraq," *Los Angeles Times,* April 16, 2003.

28. Henri J. Barkey, quoted in Robin Wright, "Pressure on Damascus Grows," *Los Angeles Times.*

29. Editorial, "Syria and the New Axis of Evil," *Washington Times,* September 30, 2003.

30. Yedidya Atlas, "Syria's Partnership with Evil No Surprise to the Informed," *Insight on the News,* June 9, 2003.

31. Jed Babbin, "Regime Change, Again," *National Review* Online, November 12, 2003.

32. Ibid.

33. Editorial, "Syria and the New Axis of Evil," *Washington Times,* September 30, 2003.

34. Paul Richter, "Crisis; Two-War Strategy Faces Test; Battling North Korea amid Iraq Conflict Could Mean Longer Fighting and More Casualties," *Los Angeles Times,* February 13, 2003.

35. "Profile: Kim Jong-il," *BBC News,* July 31, 2003.

36. Paul Wiseman, "Steep Price Tag Expected for Victory in N. Korea," *USA Today,* February 28, 2003.

37. Yoshiharu Asano, "North Korea's Potential Nuclear Threat Worse than Ever," *The Daily Yomiuri,* February 2, 2003.

38. Ibid.

39. Philip Gourevitch, "Alone in the Dark, Kim Jong Il Plays a Canny Game with South Korea and the U.S.," *The New Yorker,* September 8, 2003.

40. "Desperate Straits," *The Economist,* May 3, 2003.

41. Ibid.

42. Lou Dobbs, "Nuclear Nightmare," *U.S. News & World Report,* May 5, 2003.

43. James S. Robbins, "Where's Bolton?" *National Review* Online, August 13, 2003.

44. Doug Struck, "Heroin Trail Leads to North Korea; Freighter Delivered Shipment of Drugs to Australian Coast," *Washington Post,* May 12, 2003.

45. "North Korea's Missile Programme," *BBC News,* March 13, 2003.

46. Struck, "Heroin Trail Leads to North Korea."

47. Ibid.

48. "Desperate Straits," *The Economist*.

49. John Hartley, "Tis the Season to Be on Alert," *Courier Mail* (Queensland, Australia), December 12, 2003.

50. "FBI Official: Al Qaeda Degraded, but Strong," CNN, November 1, 2003.

51. "Evidence Indicates Al Qaeda Helped Plan Suicide Bombings in Turkey, *The Bulletin's Frontrunner,* December 11, 2003.

52. Bill Gertz, "Al Qaeda Pursued a 'Dirty Bomb,' " *Washington Times,* October 17, 2003.

53. Bill Gertz, "CIA Says al Qaeda Ready to Use Nukes," *Washington Times,* June 3, 2003.

54. Jonathan S. Landay, "Al Qaeda Planning Attacks, CIA Says," *Miami Herald,* December 11, 2003.

55. "Interview: Dr. Saad Al-Fagih," PBS *Frontline.*

56. Douglas Farah and Peter Finn, "Terrorism Inc.; Al Qaeda Franchises Brand of Violence to Groups Across World," *Washington Post,* November 21, 2003.

57. Ibid.

58. Jerry Seper, "America's Open Border," *Washington Times,* December 10, 2003.

59. Lee Hockstader, " 'Unique Opportunity' Lost at Camp David; Arafat Unmoved by Jerusalem Concessions," *Washington Post,* July 30, 2000.

60. Julie Stahl, " 'Paradise Camps' Teach Palestinian Children to Be Suicide Bombers," CNSNews.com, July 23, 2001.

61. Richard W. Carlson, "Arafat's Fat Wallet," *The Weekly Standard,* August 25, 2003.

62. Ibid.

63. Martin Walker, "Walker's World: Yom Kippur 1973 Revisited," UPI, October 13, 2003.

ACKNOWLEDGMENTS

I have two loves in my professional life—television and radio. My two jobs, at Fox News and ABC Radio, make for a very hectic day. Add a writing project to that crazy mix, and you can imagine how I feel about the people in these pages, who have not only helped keep me sane, but pulled alongside me to help realize the original vision. It is great fun to work with people like this, and a great privilege.

David Limbaugh, author, syndicated columnist, and my attorney (don't ask me where he finds the time), has been a central blessing in my life ever since my days as a talk-show host in Atlanta. I was lucky to find him then, and am very lucky to know him now—and to benefit from his prodigious talents on all levels. From advising me on all manner of things to making this book possible, David is a true force.

The other force who, like David, also worked with me on *Let Freedom Ring* is my good friend, national columnist Mark Levin—an invaluable and tireless adviser and a great attorney as well. And yes, he's the one who gets me in trouble on the air with his frequent "Dr. Levin" calls. The Great One, as I call him, helps keep my professional life a continual challenge to make things better and get things right. I am very grateful for his contributions to this book.

Both David and Mark were incredible resources, especially in the time-consuming process of editing and re-editing this book. Their help was invaluable this time, as it was the last time.

Bob Just is an old friend and fellow talk-show host, who has been with me through thick and thin going back to my college radio days. Also a national columnist, Bob was invaluable in the research and development of this book, and I'm grateful not only for his friendship but for his significant effort in helping me fulfill the vision of this book. Thanks again, Bob. You're one of the good Democrats.

Judith Regan, Cal Morgan, Jennifer Suitor, and the team at ReganBooks were wonderful all over again. As they did last time, they pulled around me as a team, and guided me through the wild world of book publishing. I appreciate, more than I can say, their steadfast pursuit of excellence. Thanks to Jennifer Suitor for your extra effort planning and orchestrating the book tour, bringing it all together; to Cal Morgan, a special thanks for those intense weeks getting the editing just right—an especially difficult process with my unpredictable schedule; and to Judith Regan—thanks, Judith, for your confidence in me, and for your one thousand percent unfailing support!

To my Fox News family:

Needless to say, my friends and colleagues at Fox News are an important part of my life. It is an honor to be part of the Fox News adventure, made possible every day by the continual efforts and insights of Roger Ailes. Roger startled America with a basic truth, summed up by the words "fair and balanced." Everyone at Fox works toward that simple principle, which for too long was forgotten in this country. I am grateful to Roger both personally and professionally for giving me a shot at being part of this shining light in the news world.

Television talk-show hosts are not birthed whole; it is an intense learning process, and I am grateful to Kevin McGee and Chet Collier for their guidance. In this business, what people see on camera is usually the result of some wise counsel. I was especially lucky to get Kevin and Chet.

Bill Shine, one of my closest friends, was our first producer at *Hannity & Colmes,* sharing in those early days of the Fox News adventure. Now a Fox News vice president, Bill's also the best executive producer in television news. His good advice and aggressive support have always been a source of comfort and inspiration to me. Thanks, Bill.

Our outstanding *Hannity & Colmes* team just keeps improving the show. First and foremost, I am very grateful to my partner Alan Colmes for helping make that happen. Of course, our always-faithful and hard-working senior producer, Meade Cooper, is central to everything we do, as is our standout director Chet Lishawa. I would like to thank them and our dedicated staff, including: Maureen Murphy, John "Fin-Man" Finley, Tara Nicaj, Jack DeMarco, Erin McKenna, Christina Meyer Garfinkle, and Lauren Clabby.

And I also want to thank the behind-the-scenes production folks at Fox, from the hair and makeup staff to the set crew from camera to sound to teleprompter—they are all key to helping Alan and me get through the whole process.

My ABC Radio family:

First and foremost I want to thank our Program Director at WABC Radio, Phil Boyce, who urged me to take the show national and has been a true force in making *The Sean Hannity Show* the success it is today. He said it would all happen just the way it has, and here we are. Thanks, Phil.

I've said it before, but Mitch Dolan of ABC is simply the greatest radio executive in America today. He keeps me focused on results and not stressed about ratings and revenue. I never forget that my show depends on the loyal listeners who give me those three hours a day, but it's the people behind the scenes like Mitch who are the ones who make that possible from the start.

My special thanks goes to Traug Keller of ABC Radio Networks. As we've battled our way to prominence in national radio, it has been great to have Traug working alongside me, making everyday an adventure in network radio.

John McConnell—one of my favorite Hannitizing targets—always keeps us out front. Thanks, John for making those day-to-day problems disappear. And one of these days I'll beat you at tennis!

And to John Hare, who's been an enormous help and support throughout the whole syndication radio process, I'm grateful for everything.

Thanks also to Tim McCarthy, our general manager at our flagship station in New York City. As I always remind my audience, 77 WABC is "The Most Listened-To Talk Radio Station in America." It's true, and Tim is a big part of that stunning success. Tim, thanks for your help.

The award-winning *Sean Hannity Show* radio staff is simply the best:

First and foremost, to my senior executive producer James "Sweet Baby James" Grisham. Every day in radio is a new journey, and I always know James will keep the team doing great radio. James covers my back, and keeps the show on the cutting edge. He's one of my very closest friends, and as I said before, one of the hardest-working people I know. Thanks for the extra effort you always give, James.

Then, of course, there's Flipper—Jill Vitale, my associate producer and call screener—who keeps me on my toes with her zany humor and wildly liberal views. Flipper, congratulations on being a mom! Greg Ahlfeld, our engineer and production manager, is my go-to-guy for all those creative/technical things that make the show work. Thanks, Greg, for putting up with all those last-minute requests and making it all look easy. And thanks also to the rest of the team that keep things together every day, Rachel Yemini and Caroline Smith.

Bill Russell, John Rosso, and Darion Melito get special kudos as the affiliate relations gurus who have been a key reason why *The Sean Hannity Show* is being called the fastest-growing network show ever! Amazing! Thanks, guys. As I did last time, I want to acknowledge Bruce Anderson and Heather O'Rourke, two real professionals who keep me on my toes. It is a pleasure to work with you two.

This year was a great year of awards and professional acknowledgement. I want to thank all those who helped us win the Marconi Award at the *Sean Hannity Show*, especially including all the PDs and GMs across America who have become such a loyal part of the Hannity radio family. We couldn't have done it without your support.

No one makes it in this business or survives for long without a close set of advisors to lean on. Special thanks go to this inner circle of guys I know I can also depend on when the going gets tough: Eric Seidel, Greg Moceri, Eric Stanger, Dave Stone, Bill Dunnavant, and my old buddy John Gomez. Where would I be without you guys?

I feel greatly privileged to be able to make personal appearances around the country, getting to know America more directly—and meeting the people that make this a great country. I'm grateful to Duane Ward at www.premierespeakers.com, who makes it all possible. Thanks, Duane. I don't know what I'd do without you guys.

As before, I save the best for last. I am so grateful that God created the family, and that he blessed me so much with mine. The wonder of my wife, Jill, and my children, Patrick and Kelly, never ceases to amaze me. Every day I know I am a very lucky man to be able to share in their lives, and to have them in my life. Whenever things seem overwhelming out in the world, whenever the news is bad or work stresses seem too much, I think of them safe at home, and everything seems right. When I take on something extra like this book project, I know the precious extra time comes out of our personal life. My wife and children are the ones who make the sacrifice. I cannot say too much about what that means to me. I am blessed to love them and be loved by them.

I remember always how much I owe my parents, Hugh and Lillian Hannity. I think of how significant the commandment to honor your parents really is—and how much we need to value our time with them. The recent loss of my parents has been very difficult for me, as it is for most of us. Suddenly, you forget the silly differences and remember the warmth and unfailing support. I feel deeply the loss of their presence, their advice and their continued love. I was privileged to know them and to be part of the family they created, which blesses me still.

I cannot say enough about my very special extended family, who are a rock of support to me—my sister Therese Grisham, her husband, James, and Christopher and baby Sarah, and my sister Mary-Jo Kuchta, her husband, Dr. Steven Kuchta, and their three children, Cassandra, Brandon, and Michael. They, along with my immediate family, are the most precious people to me, the ones who bring me the most real and lasting joy. Their daily love and support made this book possible.

Thank you all.

INDEX

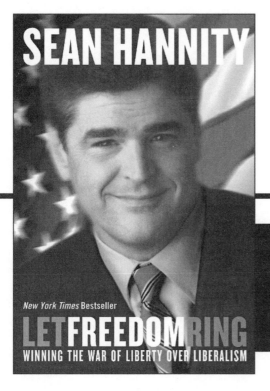